LISTENING
TO WHALES

LISTENING TO WHALES

What the Orcas Have Taught Us

ALEXANDRA MORTON

Ballantine Books • New York

A Ballantine Book
Published by The Ballantine Publishing Group

Copyright © 2002 by Alexandra Hubbard-Morton

All rights reserved under International and
Pan-American Copyright Conventions. Published in the
United States by The Ballantine Publishing Group, a division of
Random House, Inc., New York, and simultaneously in Canada
by Random House of Canada Limited, Toronto.

Ballantine and colophon are registered trademarks of Random House, Inc.

www.ballantinebooks.com

Library of Congress Cataloging-in-Publication Data is available
from the publisher upon request.

ISBN 0-345-43794-2

Text design by Holly Johnson

Manufactured in the United States of America

First Edition: May 2002

10   9   8   7   6   5   4   3   2

To my dear sister Woodleigh

In memory of John C. Lilly

Kingcome
Inlet

CHARLES
CR.

Belleisle Sd.

Watson
Cove

Iwats Pt.

Rainy
Pt.

Bond Sound

Ahta R.

Wahkana
Bay

Tribune

Channel

Thompson Sound

Viner Sd.

Loose L.

Gitford
Island

Glendale →

Inlet

ight

Minstrel
Island

channel

Clio

Bones Bay

Port
Neville

Chapter 1

$\mathcal{S}$ome nights I hear whales in my dreams. They start off distant like the sound of wind in the trees but gradually pick up to the point where they're all I can hear. Most times I can make out which pod is calling—the sisters, transients, G clan, or any of a dozen other orcas I've spent nearly a quarter of a century listening to. On a good night it's the exquisite dialect specific to the family of the fifty-four-year-old matriarch Tsitika, a series of rippling harmonics so perfect it imparts a deep sense of peace in me, like a shuddering sigh.

Some nights I wake from one of these dreams and find it hasn't been a dream at all.

I trundle downstairs in stocking feet, put my ear to the hydrophone speaker, and hear Tsitika calling to her children. I press the record button on my tape machine and note the time and date in the sound log. And so begins another day of work.

In the kelp bed floating outside my window, a hydrophone dangles down 15 feet into the water of Cramer Passage. A black cable snakes through the kelp, up the rocky beach, through the salal brush, around my kale garden, past the greenhouse and chicken coop, and up through the floorboards into my house, which is perched on a low bluff on the western coast of Canada.

I begin my mornings with a strong cup of coffee at my desk, writing, entering data, or sorting through black-and-white photos of dorsal fins. If there are no whales that day, the first sound I hear is often the crackle of shrimp coming alive with the lightening of the

1

sky. Sometimes I hear otters chirping or dolphins letting loose those high-pitched twitters that make them sound like monkeys on helium. The hydrophone doesn't discriminate. More often than not, I hear the scream of outboard motors. The community in which I live, Echo Bay, has no roads. Everyone gets around by boat.

To study a wild animal, you must adapt your life to its rhythm. It's the only way you'll increase your chances of encountering your subject, and perhaps more important, it's the only way you'll begin to understand how your subject encounters the world. We landlocked humans experience our surroundings primarily through our eyes: land and vision. A killer whale's aquatic world comes to it almost exclusively through its sense of hearing: water and sound. Living in Echo Bay has put me in a world as close as I can come to the killer whale's without actually living underwater.

I'm constantly listening and looking for whales. As I wake my six-year-old daughter, cook breakfast, brush my teeth, talk on the phone, my ear remains cocked to the speakers. My eyes constantly scan the water for the misty plume of a whale blow. I press my eyes against a pair of high-powered astronomical field glasses seventy times a day, panning slowly back and forth over the water, always hoping for the rise and fall of an orca's black fin. I've spotted whales while I've been gardening, baking bread, writing papers, braiding my daughter's hair. I've spotted orcas while I've been taking a shower. And when I spot one, I'm gone. Into my boat—*Blackfish Sound,* a 22-foot dory—and out on the water, following the whales wherever they take me. I note their breathing intervals, record the sounds they make, watch them interact with the world around them. I am their shadow.

I came here when I was twenty-two years old. I'm forty-four now. When I began watching killer whales, I thought I could sit by a marine park tank and, merely by listening, crack the code of language used by the performing orcas held within. Now I realize I have to understand far more about who they are and how they fit into their environment. There are so many other things to be learned from killer whales.

Not long before I first arrived here, people shot orcas for sport. They were considered predators, wolves of the deep. Small children were encouraged to throw rocks at them from shore. Marine parks paid fishermen to steal infant whales from their mothers, move them across the continent in trucks, and imprison them in concrete tanks. The government tried to cull their population with machine guns.

Things have changed. It's now a federal crime to harass a killer whale. Marine parks are no longer allowed to take killer whales from American and Canadian waters, although the horror of captivity continues. Our understanding of the killer whale's world has increased exponentially. We know now that orcas organize themselves into so-phisticated social groups and develop some of the strongest mother-child bonds possible. They hunt with amazing stealth and are capable of prodigious feats of learning. Their intelligence has yet to be ade-quately analyzed; indeed, their powers of cognition may be too complex for us to accurately quantify. In brainpower they may sur-pass us.

The killer whale, *Orcinus orca,* is found from the Beaufort Sea to the Weddell Sea and in every ocean in between, including the Mediter-ranean. Although they belong to the order Cetacea, which includes baleen whales like the gray whale and blue whale, orcas are more closely related to dolphins and porpoises, with whom they share the suborder Odontoceti (toothed whales). Killer whales are known as a "cosmopolitan species" because they've learned to survive in di-verse habitats around the globe. Off the New Zealand coast, they eat stingrays. In the Antarctic they eat whales and penguins. Off the coast of Norway, they eat herring; in Patagonia, sea lions; in the open Pacific, sharks; in Japan, squid; in the Antilles, sea turtles; in the Indian Ocean, tuna. Just as human hunter-gatherer societies differed from one another based on their geography, climate, and food source, so have the different conditions faced by various orca

Transient whales, male and female

populations given rise to differing orca "cultures." As Polynesians differ from Eskimos, so do Mediterranean orcas differ from the orcas plying the waters outside my cabin.

The killer whales of British Columbia are organized into four communities: northern residents, southern residents, transients, and offshore orcas. *Community* refers to a breeding population, whales that are known to swim together and peaceably share both calls and a feeding area. I work predominantly with the northern residents, who range from Pender Harbour, a few miles north of Vancouver, north to Prince Rupert, just south of Ketchikan, Alaska. Within that community exist sixteen pods, an orca's basic social unit, a group of five to twenty whales who travel together their entire lives.

In the twenty-five years I've spent with wild orcas, they have gotten to know me as well. They know where I live, the extent of my home range, and the fact that I scurry home when darkness falls. I don't mean that they demonstrate recognition. For the most part they ignore me, and I like it that way. I came to observe whales being whales, not whales responding to humans. But they are too intelligent an animal not to have learned a few things about the woman following them with the dangling hydrophone.

They must find us an exceedingly strange species. Only two generations ago the human attitude toward orcas was one of aggression and attack. Now we want to love them to death. In the 1970s there was no whale-watching industry to speak of. Now it's a multimillion-dollar business that threatens the waters of Johnstone Strait with gridlock every summer.

The whales are no longer harmed by our direct actions. But in the last ten years we have become more aware of the indirect actions that, in the long run, may pose just as big a threat to the whales' existence. Instead of killing them with harpoons and rifles, we are slowly poisoning their habitat and killing off their food supply. Industrial logging desecrates the watersheds that produce the salmon vital to this coast; development dumps more of the noise and chemicals of civilization into their backyard; mismanagement of the commercial catch and the proliferation of corporate salmon farms are combining to snuff out the great wild runs of salmon that sustain the orca pods of the Canadian and American coast.

Every day I continue to watch and listen for killer whales. I hope that I do not have to watch them die out. In the course of spending my adult life recording and describing their behaviors, I've seen firsthand that the orca, like any other species, does not exist alone. It requires an entire web of life to sustain its presence. In an age in which hundreds of species may go extinct every day, anyone who studies a wild animal faces the challenge of, in effect, making a case for its life on earth. I pray that mine is strong enough.

Chapter 2

Lakeville, Connecticut, was so small that it had just one stoplight, and it only went to yellow. The New England village, nestled in the foothills of the Berkshires in the upper left corner of Connecticut, had lost any semblance of wildness long before my family arrived in the 1950s. Fields of corn and tobacco etched the land into neat squares defined by knee-high stone walls, with stubborn patches of forest surviving in the spaces between the walls. Two centuries ago local ironworkers turned out cannons for George Washington's army here; today Lakeville may be best known as the home of the exclusive Hotchkiss prep school. Looking back, it's hard for me to imagine a more whaleless environment. But it was in this tamed land, in the tiny creeks meandering through the Housatonic Valley, on the banks of muddy ponds that collected here and there, in the abandoned apple orchards and winter fields where white-tailed deer browsed and red fox hunted field mice, that I developed a lifelong love affair with the animal world.

We moved to this quiet corner of Connecticut for the quality of light it had to offer. I come from a family of artists and writers, and my father said the canyons of New York City were just too dark to paint in. I loved New England, each season rich with a different kind of life.

As I grew, I found myself increasingly drawn more to the company of animals than to humans. My parents were very social, gathering

Portrait of Alexandra by her father, Earl Hubbard

eclectic groups of people into our house for conferences on the potential of humanity. I met nuns, musicians, businessmen, and hippies. Ed Sullivan, Wernher von Braun, Timothy Leary, and many others were guests. Conversation was never mundane around our dinner table, but I let most of it slip by unnoticed. What caught my attention was the way a deer sets her ears when a twig snaps, the screams of an owl after it makes a kill, the sounds the crows make when mobbing a hawk. Everything looked clear and uncomplicated in the animal world. When they spoke, there was understanding among them. I suppose I also appreciated existing outside their social pecking order. Among my own kind I was not exactly fitting in. I was lost at the bottom of the social order of my peers.

What set me apart was my fascination for all things slippery, furry, scaled, and feathery. Especially slippery. The fields and forests behind our house were filled with animals. White-tailed deer nibbled tender shoots of grass; raccoons left their tracks in the clean white snow; opossums could be glimpsed in the thick sugar maple canopy; brilliant red eft salamanders and myriad species of turtles made their living in the creeks and ponds near our property.

What fascinated me the most were reptiles and amphibians. New England is home to a wondrous array of these species, a world unto itself for me to explore. One day I brought a beautiful red, white, and black banded milk snake to show my class. When I discovered the wee Houdini had escaped from my locker, I cried, "Where's my snake!?!"

Instantly twenty-five half-dressed girls jumped up on benches screaming an unholy noise. So I came by my reputation for being odd honestly.

Another day in the middle of class I looked out the window to see a stray dog pawing and snapping at something on the ground. When the dog lifted his head with a snake hanging off his nose, I dashed, unexcused, out of the room to shoo the dog away, leaving my teacher furious and earning myself an hour of detention. I became known as the girl who loved snakes—not the most direct road to grade-school popularity.

Every day after school I'd return home, throw down my books, and flee into the woods with my younger brother and faithful companion, Wade. We dammed tiny creeks and played in the pools, built forts we were too timid ever to sleep in overnight, and once excavated a skeleton we were sure was a dinosaur. (We spent the better part of a week digging out our exciting find, until we unearthed the head. It was only a cow.) Our greatest passion was the frog pond, a gently flowing pool full of infinite possibility. To get to the frog pond, Wade and I had to dash through the neighbor's pasture, which held new and unfamiliar horses every week. We never knew how they'd react to our slipping through the fence and walking among them. They often came after us, heads down, sometimes curious, sometimes menacing, and we fended them off with our long-handled dip nets.

With the stealth of puppies, Wade and I crossed through the

marsh at the pond's tail end, stepping over the black masses of tad-
poles swarming among the reeds. The long marsh grass raised welts
and cuts on our legs, and the mosquitoes drilled into our skin, but
we thought the frog pond was heaven. Our every step released rotting earthy scents. As the ground firmed up under our feet, we scru-
tinized each foamy green island of algae for frogs. Frogs are hard
to catch. They lay on the surface, their hind feet kicked out under
the water weeds, with only their marvelously spherical eyes showing
above the surface. The pronounced curve of those gold-speckled
eyes allows frogs to detect a predator's approach from any direction.
With hearts thumping, Wade and I crept closer until the little peri-
scopes vanished with a *bloop*. Then we'd rush in and swing our nets
over the mats of freshwater vegetation. We named each frog we
caught and took them into our modified catch-and-release program.
That is, we would catch them, take them home for a few days, and
then return them to their place on the banks of the pond. Over
the years we discovered that each frog had a distinct territory. We
learned to distinguish the different kinds of frogs by their calls. Some
of the sounds they made seemed impossibly huge for such small
creatures. Wade learned to imitate these calls with uncanny precision. In the most proper of situations, my angelic-looking little
brother delighted in approximating the gut-rumbling calls of the
king of the pond. I know our poor mother sometimes regretted that
we moved to Connecticut.

The frog pond teemed with murky, mysterious life. We never knew
what would appear in our nets. We caught green frogs with yellow
throats, tan frogs with black racing stripes, and spectacular spotted
leopard frogs. Sometimes giant black water beetles scuttled angrily
against the net, or we'd bring up salamanders or, best of all, turtles—
eastern painted turtles with beautifully red-edged shells, dome-shelled
mud turtles, or the ferocious snapping turtles. Once, at a pond in
town, Wade and I caught an enormous snapping turtle. His shell was
20 inches across. It was a terrific struggle requiring both nets and a

Frog

mad scrambling and grabbing at roots to get him up the mud bank. When we had landed him, we tied him to a tree and called home for a lift. This turtle was far too big for the bike basket.

Townspeople gathered around us and our turtle. Wade and I were heroes: we'd caught the terrible killer of Lakeville's beloved mallard ducklings. The newspaper came out and took our picture. Then the chef at the White Hart Inn appeared and asked if we'd sell him the monster to make soup with. Wade and I, horrified, glanced at the ancient reptile powering through the turf with mighty claws, still tied fast to the willow sapling. I remember how in that instant he changed. The mighty adversary became a poor, pathetic victim. When help came from home, we heaved him into the back of the Buick and took that snapper to a little pond far in the hills. Later I realized we probably destroyed the fragile balance of that pond by introducing such a voracious predator. I learned early that laying claim to any wild animal brings difficult decisions.

———

The greatest mystery of "our" pond was a creature that lived at the very farthest end, where the water was deepest and no cattails or shrubbery veiled our approach: the giant blue bullfrog.

I can still remember the first time we spotted Bluey. Wade, a few feet ahead of me at the water's edge, whispered so loud it was almost a scream, "Alex, a bluuuuuuuuuuue frog! Look right there."

I crept alongside and glimpsed the biggest frog we'd ever seen, and he *was* blue, the most amazing shade of light Caribbean blue. At least as brilliant as his body was Bluey's throat, which was painted a yellow bright as the stoplight in the middle of town.

When our excited report tumbled out back at the house, most of the adults wouldn't believe Bluey was real. A blue frog? Please. This drove us to stalk that frog relentlessly. Wade and I tried to move more slowly than even a frog's eyes could detect. We tried waiting for him to reappear, our nets in position, to no avail. Bluey had the best seat in the pond. He was invincible. There was no getting near him. Though we rushed in as he submerged, he dove too deep for our nets. Once disturbed, he remained out of sight the rest of the day. We never caught him. We never even came close. Finally, after years of trying, we lost to nature itself. When the next spring arrived, Bluey never came out of hibernation. Our chance was lost.

Years later, reading a science magazine, I learned that two pigments, yellow and blue, mix to create the frog's green skin. On rare occasions a frog may lack one of the two pigments, and if it lacks yellow, the frog will appear blue. Bluey had an explanation—he was real! Years after our failed hunt, I called Wade with the news.

"Wade, guess what? I just found out what makes blue frogs blue. There really are blue frogs!"

"Come on, Alex," Wade roared with laughter, "you didn't let *adults* talk you out of believing what you saw . . . did you? We already knew blue frogs exist."

———

I realized I had done just that. Wade was right, and that day I learned a lesson that I've recalled many times since: the inability to explain is no reason to forget, modify, or deny the extraordinary information that sometimes comes through our ordinary senses. The unbelievable is sacred knowledge that must be kept.

My family was very close. There were five children. My mother created books from her conversations with my father. Sometimes they talked all day, papers spreading around their breakfast dishes like petals of a blossoming flower. My brothers and sisters and I pushed two beds together every Christmas Eve to sleep in one happy heap on that special night. After dinner, in winter, we'd sit by the fire while my dad read us *Treasure Island* and *The Swiss Family Robinson* in a spellbinding warm voice I can still hear in my thoughts.

In summer our family often went for walks in the evening, and it was on one of these walks that my fascination with snakes was born. One evening we came across a snake crossing a narrow pathway. It was a harmless garter, but Dad, who had spent part of his childhood in the copperhead and water moccasin territory of Florida, didn't take any chances with his children's safety. He grabbed an ax and cut it in two with a single stroke. As I watched, stunned, Dad was transformed from a highly civilized man into a dominant male primate protecting his family. That moment froze in my memory like a fly in amber. I was thrilled and deeply impressed. In the domesticated hills of New England, no one I knew had ever needed to be protected from anything. My dad's act of a moment compelled me to learn everything I could about snakes.

It's odd that children seem drawn to the very things from which their parents try to shield them. As a specieswide survival strategy, it seems deeply flawed, but it explains why we have spread ourselves across the globe. Tell a child not to venture beyond the known, and that is precisely where she will go. Shield her and she steps around you.

I went to the reference section of the library in the nearby town of Salisbury. When I climbed the winding iron stairs that led to the massive volumes, I found an enormous book dedicated entirely to snakes. The librarians at first refused to let me check the book out, but I spent so many hours poring over it on the library's cold glass floor that one of them finally took pity on me and put it on my card. I dropped the book into my bicycle basket, confident that I would soon know everything there was to know about snakes. What exhilaration—to be in possession of so much knowledge! I rode home, took it to my room, shut the door, and entered the herpetological world. I read how some snake poisons affect our nerves and others our blood. That snakes can unhook their lower jaws to swallow large prey and have a cluster of nerve endings in the roof of their mouths, which they place their tongues against to interpret the world by taste. I was shocked and fascinated to learn that their penises were as forked as their tongues.

No species can quite match the snake for pure satisfaction with life. Their expressionless eyes calmly survey the world; no squinting or rounding eyelids give away their thoughts. Their darting tongues sample the molecules afloat, and they move only when a decision has been reached. If they want to bite, they strike like lightning, no hesitation; if they aren't hungry, they might let the mouse chew on them. They were so perfect, so streamlined, so different from the floundering, questioning mammal that I was. Snakes embodied the ease and perfection that attracted me to the animal world. Animals always knew what to do and where they belonged. There was no awkwardness about them. What a remarkable state of being! When I watched crows gather in the arching boughs of the elm trees near our house, I saw a social system that worked; everybody was part of the gang. Sometimes, when I was alone in the woods, I would stop, listen, be still like a deer, and let the tangle of words and human thoughts drain away, to be replaced by the language of sweet living scents and sounds of the forest.

I didn't necessarily want to become part of the animal world; I just wanted to observe it and revel in its unconscious perfection. My idea of a perfect day was to crouch by my glass aquarium to watch a tadpole get its fourth leg. The tiny young frog accepted the miracle of its new limb with complete aplomb. As soon as the arm broke free of its membrane, the little fellow tucked his chubby, brand-new appendage under his body and moved forward with life.

Shortly after I turned twelve, I realized that I had reached an age at which I was expected to abandon my frog-watching habits and start behaving like a normal teenage girl. In my neighborhood only children spent time playing with animals—children much younger than I. As I grew, I felt the crushing pressure to be "normal," as any young member of a species as social as *Homo sapiens* must. If I had been a young chicken, I'd surely have been pecked to death, but despite natural xenophobic tendencies, we do, begrudgingly, tolerate considerable latitude in our definition of "normal."

For a short time I tried to curtail my animal obsession. I put away my snake books and checked out volumes on another, more respectable, field of science, astronomy. I memorized the sequence of the planets and the names of stars. But as soon as I stepped outside, my interest in the heavens evaporated. Every rustle in the grass was a magnet. Every decaying piece of wood called out, "Look underneath me." I was impossibly drawn to life on earth.

———

At the Indian Mountain School, our playing field lay directly beneath the migration route of the monarch butterfly. On those breathtaking October days when the hills went ablaze with the red, yellow, and luscious orange leaves of the sugar maple and birch trees, I was annually bewitched by those brilliant insects fluttering overhead. They weaved along looking so helpless in any breeze, I wondered how they could possibly maintain their course. Unfortunately there was usually a field hockey game going on at the time, and I was supposed to be playing it.

"Alex! The ball, *the ball,* look at the ball! What are you doing!?"

"Sorry!" I'd offer, determined to keep my eye on the game.

The monarch butterflies had just departed their summer grounds and were embarked on an epic journey headed for Florida, Mexico, and South America. They always appeared from the far northeastern corner of the field and flew a diagonal path headed for the small valley between the mountains behind the school. As I stood there counting them, hockey stick in hand, I wondered how they all knew to migrate, how many would survive, how such an impossibly small creature could beat its wings enough times to travel thousands of miles in a reasonably straight line, and what was guiding them. My reverie was all too often interrupted by a stampede of red-bloomered girls thundering toward me.

Two women came to my rescue. Nowadays women scientists are taken for granted, but in the sixties, the only female scientist I'd ever heard of was Marie Curie. In our science books Curie appeared in blurry black-and-white pictures, standing stout and severe in her lab coat, her hair close-cropped and her world confined to rooms full of test tubes. Frankly she frightened me.

It was my subscription to *National Geographic* that threw me the first lifeline. On the cover of one issue was a scientist like none I'd ever seen. Standing tall and feminine, her hair in a ponytail, Jane Goodall was everything I wanted to be—a confident, graceful woman researching animals in the wild.

Goodall freed my heart. She embodied unimaginable adventure and beauty; she was a goddess. I pored over every word in that *Geographic* story, trying to glean the details of her life. I couldn't believe that this young woman had dared to go into the jungle to study wild chimpanzees in their natural habitat. She'd been the first human witness to chimp tool using and war, two activities previously considered solely within the human domain. Jane Goodall became a beacon for a girl lost without a role model. Now I knew where I was going. I knew it was possible to have a life in the wilderness studying animals.

It never occurred to me that there might be obstacles to actually achieving that life. With Goodall to look to, the lack of peers, my unenviable social status, and my tame Connecticut surroundings—all became part of the past.

While my mother and father were writing and painting, my siblings and I were looked after by a no-nonsense Frenchwoman, Jacqueline Baldet. While very strict, Baldet read children as clearly as road signs. She knew what we needed before we did, and she knew I needed peers and provided me with my second lifeline. After a little investigation she discovered a local group of amateur and professional reptile and amphibian scientists—herpetologists—who met every month in various community centers around the state. The Connecticut Herpetological Society had many members, but none who enjoyed the hours of snake talk more than I did. At the time local naturalists were concerned that the area's rattlesnakes were being driven extinct as the development of houses, roads, and shopping malls destroyed their dens. This gave my forest wanderings a focus: Wade and I became scouts, combing the hills for shed skins and other clues that might reveal the existence of a rattlesnake denning cave.

My dear dad once even allowed a contained rattlesnake briefly into our dining room. Mike Walker, an enthusiastic scientist from the meetings, went with Wade and me to confirm one of the dens we'd found. There he collected a snake. That night I carried the cotton cloth bag into the circle of light of an Oriental lamp. The primal warning buzz from the snake mingled with Chopin as my dad peered in and thoughtfully commended his daughter's actions to protect the same creature he had been raised to destroy.

The alumni rolls of the Milton Academy, a two-hundred-year-old institution located near the edge of Boston, read like a who's who of American arts, sciences, and politics: T. S. Eliot, Buckminster Fuller, Robert and Edward Kennedy. I couldn't have cared less. I wanted to know one thing: did it have a strong science program?

Entering Milton Academy was exciting to me. I loved the very smell of the place—the long, dark polished hallways, the imposing stone buildings, the wet autumn air. I don't even remember who drove me the four hours up to school. I was only looking forward. "Here I am," I thought, "launched at last. I am going to be a scientist!"

I earned top grades, but Milton's curriculum had too little hard science for my taste. Since I was bound and determined to follow the career path of Jane Goodall and Dian Fossey, I wanted to jump right in and get some real research going—now. But prep school was not what I'd hoped it would be. I felt it was more about being shoe-horned into the upper crust of society, and the goal—to become a debutante—was not for me. If the school authorities wouldn't let me further explore the field of animal behavior, I told my mother, I'd drop out altogether. My parents were wasting their money here.

During my second year at Milton, the school did allow me to set up a little lab in the science building. I designed an experiment in perception with mice, offering them a choice between two doors: one with horizontal lines, one with vertical lines. If they chose the vertical door, they were rewarded with food. If you started slanting the lines, I wanted to find out at what point the mice could no longer distinguish between vertical and horizontal. I detailed the trials and produced a report.

That Christmas, when report cards came out, the only reference to my research was that I spent "too much time down at the lab playing with mice."

I couldn't believe my eyes. "That's it!" I thought. "I've had it— I'm not going back." I made plans to head out west on a bus. While I was thrilled at the prospect of striking out on my own, the plan seems so half-baked today that I don't know what I was thinking. My mother has maternal antennae that won't quit, and at this point she began calling me.

"Alexandra, are you all right?" she'd ask on the way to and from meetings. (Mom was always on the move.)

"Sure, Mom. I'm fine." But she didn't believe me and kept calling.

Finally, at the prompting of my dearest childhood pal, Jenny Swing, I said, "Mom, they're taking my edges off. I feel like a cube being forced down a tube. I can't stay here."

Now, if I were my mother, I'd have panicked. But she didn't miss a beat. She knew exactly what I was talking about. She had gone through exactly the same thing as a teenager and had it even tougher than I did. At least I had a love of science and the Goodalls and Fosseys of the world breaking ground before me. Mom had had to search for her role in life as a social architect with no inkling of what it might be. And so the mother of the headstrong seventeen-year-old delivered an answer I never expected.

"You can leave school," she told me. "But you have to do something with your life."

I remember stomping on the mental brakes: "What now?"

Chapter 3

I knew John Lilly only from his books—*Man and Dolphin, The Dolphin in History,* and *The Mind of the Dolphin*—which I had checked out from the Salisbury library and read with great interest as a young girl. In my own pantheon of scientific heroes, he didn't approach the status of Jane Goodall and Dian Fossey, but Lilly remained a mythical figure in my imagination: the man who tried to talk with dolphins.

By the time I encountered him in the mid-1970s, Lilly had established himself as one of the twentieth century's boldest and most controversial thinkers. For a man so associated with unconventional ideas and risk-taking research, though, Lilly's scientific training had been surprisingly conventional. As a neurological researcher in the 1950s at the University of Pennsylvania medical school and the National Institutes of Health, the Ivy League–educated physician pioneered devices that stimulated and recorded the brain's electrical activity. Then, in 1955, he joined a group of neurophysiological researchers on a trip to Marineland, an aquatic theme park in St. Augustine, Florida, to conduct tests on the large mammalian brains of dolphins. What began as a simple field trip quickly developed into a lifelong calling. After watching the complex interactions between the dolphins and their human handlers, Lilly began to suspect that the creatures possessed immense intelligence. At the time dolphins were assumed to be about as smart as your average dog.

The more Lilly investigated, though, the more he became convinced that the conventional wisdom was wrong. Not only was a dolphin's brain larger than a human's; its cerebral hemispheres were deeply crevassed, a trait that scientists considered necessary for sophisticated cognitive ability. The more deeply wrinkled the outer surface of the brain, the more complex the thought process. While the human brain was more furrowed than the brains of other primates, the dolphin's brain exceeded even our own. This was disturbing to a man whose research included the placement of electrodes into living animals. Rather than deny that he may have hurt a sentient being, Lilly had the integrity to change his methods. "A large, complex brain," Lilly argued, "implies large, complex capabilities and great mental sensitivities."

The dolphin brain beckoned for exploration, and Lilly set out to map the territory, but in a way that wouldn't harm the creature. Abandoning his established career, he set up his own dolphin laboratory in the Virgin Islands and conducted a series of experiments that would fracture a number of long-held beliefs about the sanctity of human intelligence. Lilly believed we would never truly fathom the intelligence of dolphins until we could speak with them, so he experimented with different ways of teaching them to speak English. His young assistants spent hours repeating the phonetic elements of language to Cheechee, Elvar, Sissy, and Peter, four bottle-nosed dolphins who lived in specially constructed tanks at Lilly's Communication Research Institute in St. Thomas.

Lilly was encouraged by the dolphin's ability to "lock in." Unlike a parrot with the ability to mimic, the dolphin listened to the sounds being taught and, waiting politely for his turn to respond, would reproduce the same number of sounds with 92 percent accuracy. "No other animal (with the one exception of unusual humans) can match this performance," Lilly wrote in *The Mind of the Dolphin*. There are only three types of mammals that can even attempt to learn new sounds—humans, dolphins, and bats.

Lilly and others found that the acoustic portion of the dolphin brain was ten times the size of the same area in the human brain. Dolphins' phenomenal ability to remember the sequencing of sounds wasn't entirely surprising, but what caught Lilly's imagination was the enthusiasm with which dolphins entered into the mimicry experiments. It spurred him on to a lifelong search for a language that humans and dolphins could share.

Lilly's most successful experiment involved a young woman named Margaret Howe, who agreed to live with Peter, a five-year-old bottle-nosed dolphin, for ten weeks during the summer of 1965. The best way to get a dolphin to communicate with a human, Lilly thought, would be to create a situation in which the human was the only social contact available to the dolphin. He called it the *mother-child teaching-learning model*. Lilly removed all dolphin companionship from young Peter and replaced it with Margaret Howe, giving the dolphin round-the-clock contact with the woman. Lilly knew that Margaret would also be compelled to interact with the dolphin out of loneliness. It was an uncomfortable circumstance for both the land and the sea mammals.

Howe had little training as a scientist. Lilly picked her because he wanted his human subject to enter into the experiment with a completely open mind, free of scholarly skepticism. If the human subject believed that the dolphin could be trained, then training would occur. But if the human believed that the dolphin could be her intellectual equal, then communication might take place.

These were the same criteria Louis B. Leakey had used when selecting another young woman, Jane Goodall, for wild chimpanzee research. While both men respected education, they saw how it defined a person's perception, causing them to discard possibilities before they had been tested. They also felt that women, with their supposedly heightened senses of empathy, endurance, and intuition, were better suited to the task of understanding animals.

Howe slept on a bed set on a raised platform in the tank and worked at a desk and chair set in shallow water. The two companions spent much of their time playing games and trying to establish a common English vocabulary. Peter would toss a ball at Howe until she joined in, and when she grew tired, he'd invent new games with different toys. Howe encouraged Peter to use words by responding with enthusiasm and affection, as well as food, to his every attempt to vocalize a word. As Lilly wrote in a 1961 *Science* article, the best results occurred when the dolphin was free to touch the researcher, come and go at will, and both initiate and terminate sessions.

After much struggle, Peter eventually learned an approximation of Howe's first name and a few other words. But dolphins and humans are equipped with radically different sound-making mechanisms, and English is a poor fit for a dolphin's vocal physiology. Dolphins simply lack vocal cords. Instead, they have a complex muscle called a "monkey muzzle," topped by a tree of air sacs that branch outward between their skull and the rounded bulge of their forehead. Peter was keen to communicate with Howe. He produced a few words spontaneously and appropriately but was hindered by the acoustic equipment mismatch. Howe grew depressed near the end of her ten weeks in the tank. Her clammy bed was constantly soaked with salt water, and her saturated skin was beginning to chap and peel. Lilly pronounced the experiment a beginning, believing that it showed that close interaction encouraged dolphins to learn from humans. He felt the experiment would have gone much further had it not been for the simple problem that dolphins can't produce the sounds that make up the English language. This physical difference, in the end, proved too difficult to overcome.

In the mid-1960s Lilly turned away from his dolphin research and focused on a more immediate subject: his own mind. Intrigued at the possibilities for opening up the unconscious mind, Lilly began years of experiments on himself, combining LSD with the isolation tanks he'd invented in the 1950s. "My consciousness expanded all over the universe," he later said, in recalling that first LSD tank experience. "I cried to be forced back into my body and its limited reality. Ever since, I've been trying to escape."

Lilly moved west, and joined the staff at Esalen, the mind/body retreat and alternative culture hothouse near Big Sur, California. Lilly's ideas about interspecies communication and the potential of the human mind fit right in at Esalen, where philosophers, psychologists, artists, and spiritual thinkers were bringing practices like Rolfing, tai chi, Gestalt therapy, yoga, meditation, and Zen Buddhism to American culture.

———

When I saw him lecture at a Los Angeles community college in 1976, John Lilly was returning to his first love. With the help of his new organization, the Human Dolphin Foundation, Lilly hoped to use computers to take a great leap forward in human-dolphin communication. Lilly said he was developing a system called JANUS (Joint Analog Numerical Understanding System) that would function as a sort of human-dolphin translator. He hoped to develop a language that the computer could output to the dolphins at their frequency and to the humans at our frequency. This, Lilly hoped, would overcome the problems he had encountered in the Virgin Islands. It would be, he told us, the equivalent of teaching sign language to chimps.

I left the auditorium that night on fire. I drove home in my little Corolla and immediately began sketching a pen-and-ink drawing of two heads, dolphin and human, superimposed over each other and sharing one eye in a merging of minds. (Yes, it looked strange.) The next day I sent the drawing to Lilly, along with a letter requesting a job at his new foundation.

I waited for him to call. And waited. After a week I couldn't bear it. I picked up the phone and dialed. As famous as Lilly was, his number was still listed in the book—"Lilly, John C." But before anyone could answer, I slammed the receiver down. Who was I kidding? What would I say to him? I dialed and hung up, dialed and hung up. Finally someone picked up before I had a chance to panic. It was Lilly himself. Yes, he'd gotten my package. We talked about dolphins a bit, and then I blurted out that I'd like to meet him.

"Okay," he said. "How about this afternoon?"

A few hours later I drove into the sagebrush hills above Malibu. My art portfolio sat beside me as the only thing I had to show for myself. Lilly and his wife, Toni, lived at the end of a dusty road that rose up steep switchbacks and wound through dry, crumbly hills. An avocado grove surrounded their elegant, low-lying house, which was built to make the most of the cool ocean breeze. Cascades of red and

Pacific white-sided dolphin

orange bougainvillea bushes shaded the porches, and everywhere there were sliding glass doors opening into cool tiled rooms. I was determined to not leave that house without a job.

John Lilly was an intimidating man. Tall and lean with a sharp nose and chin, at age sixty-two he looked like a farmer who'd been worked over by a lifetime of midwestern winters. He didn't talk much, and when he did, words escaped him in deep, monotonic cadences. Dressed in a sky-blue jumpsuit, Lilly met me in the kitchen and looked over my work at the bar. It wasn't much—a few pen-and-ink sketches of dolphins and whales, some graphics I'd done for television shows. We did not hit it off famously. He's got a quick, dry sense of humor, and I'm always three steps behind a joke. As we talked about dolphins and the potential for interspecies communication, I hoped Lilly would perhaps see another Margaret Howe in me. But he needed a painter, not a researcher.

"We've got this hallway we want decorated," he told me. "We were thinking about some kind of mural. I have to ask my wife, but could you come up with some sketches and bring them back?"

It wasn't what I'd hoped for, but at least I had my foot in the door.

I painted every Sunday. After sweltering in my Santa Monica apartment all week, I'd escape to Lilly's cool refuge in the clouds of coastal fog. I came up with a design reminiscent of my father's work, with the barest elements of a human face on one wall and a dolphin's on another, their minds meeting around a stained-glass lamp on the ceiling.

As I turned the blank hallway into a fresco of dolphin-human coexistence, I got to know the Lillys a bit. John's wife, Toni, a beautiful Armenian-American tigress, ran the household with a strong hand; she made sure John didn't have to do anything but breathe and think. Her husband will be the first to admit his fondness for beautiful women, and Toni was no fool. She loved John fiercely and made it clear that an admiring eighteen-year-old female follower was only marginally welcome in her home. To keep my own intentions clear, I always addressed her husband as "Dr. Lilly." I may have been young, but I wasn't completely oblivious to the dynamics of the house. I'd catch glimpses of Lilly here and there, wandering the house in his jumpsuit—I don't know if the man owned a shirt and pair of pants—lost in thought.

Serendipity played a big part in my experience with Lilly. The more time I spent at the house, the more I saw how seldom Lilly, or anyone, picked up the phone. Our initial conversation so many weeks ago must have been as rare as a lightning strike. So, too, was my introduction to his world of dolphins.

As I set up my paints one Sunday, I felt a cool draft across my face. It came from a door at the end of the hall, which someone had left cracked open. I meant to close it but couldn't resist a peek. All the curtains were pulled closed in the chilly, dark room. I flicked on the lights and saw packing crates—dozens of them stacked up to the ceiling. In each crate were shelves, on each shelf were reel-to-reel tapes, and on each tape was a label: Cheechee. Elvar. Jobe. Peter. My God—these were tapes of the Virgin Island dolphins! I had stumbled into Lilly's mother lode. Here was the data behind his dolphin books. Once again I felt in awe of a gathering of science comparable to the reptile tome I had put in my bike basket so many years before.

Perhaps a Rosetta stone of interspecies communication was buried here, one that might lead us out of the isolation of our human existence. Maybe I could find it where others had failed. Those 1,280 tapes called to me like the sirens to Odysseus.

It was all I could do not to cue them up right there. I shut the door and returned to my painting, barely able to contain my excitement. That evening, as I prepared to leave, I worked up the courage to ask Lilly about the storeroom.

"By the way," I said, "the door to the back room was open, and I noticed a lot of tapes in there. It looked like your work in the Virgin Islands. Could I listen to them?"

Lilly looked alarmed. "No," he said.

My face must have betrayed my disappointment, because he immediately reconsidered. "Well . . . we do need somebody to catalog them."

My heart leaped, and I pressed my advantage. "Could I listen while I catalog?"

He went for that, figuring that I'd do a better job if I knew what was actually on each tape. I drove home that night ecstatic. As far as I was concerned, it was the beginning of my life, the first concrete step toward a career of studying nonhuman intelligence. When I dropped out of Milton Academy, school officials had told me I'd never amount to anything. Now those words floated away as I rolled down the switchbacks of the Malibu hills.

Listening to the dolphins was like entering another world. First of all, it was cold. To preserve the fragile tapes, Lilly kept the storage room so frigid that I had to bundle up in sweaters I hadn't used since leaving New England. I'd clamp the headphones over my ears and step into a tantalizing world of clicks, chirps, and whistles. I heard for myself the tapes of Margaret Howe's work, an experiment I dreamed of repeating. I listened to Peter the dolphin trying to communicate. When Margaret entered the room, he swam up to her with a great swishing-of-water noise and would cry "Hiiii" in a Donald Duck–ish accent. Peter also knew to call his favorite toy a "baaaalllll." I felt certain that, if Peter had been physically better equipped to speak English, he would have learned a much broader vocabulary.

In other experiments researcher Scott McVay spoke long strings of nonsense syllables, "ra, tee, cha, fa, che . . . ," to dolphins trained to repeat the sounds. While the dolphins were incapable of producing accurate reproductions, their responses were close enough that I could follow the sequences. I had to write down the syllables to keep track of them, but the dolphins reproduced the long sound sequences with unerring, remarkable accuracy. Whereas my brain had ten times the visual processing ability of the dolphins' brains, it was clear that the dolphins far outstripped my acoustic abilities.

The tapes represented one of the first scientific attempts to end our interspecies silence. Similar experiments were also being undertaken with primates by researchers like Allen and Beatrix Gardner, the renowned experimental psychologists at the University of Nevada at Reno. At first young chimpanzees were raised like human children to test their ability to acquire human language. But as with Lilly's dolphins, a flaw soon became apparent. Any cross-species talk would be more complicated than teaching an animal English. Dolphins could not reproduce the frequencies and sounds required by our language; chimps lacked brain structures required for spoken language and so needed a language based on gestures. The Gardners, and later their protégé Roger Fouts, went on to communicate with chimps through sign language. Lilly had not achieved a similar breakthrough, but with his JANUS project he hoped to cross that bridge.

The sounds of dolphins attempting English were interesting, but I was most drawn to the recordings of dolphins communicating with dolphins. Dolphin communication consists of rapid, light, wispy whistles at the upper edge of our hearing range and beyond. They don't speak through their mouths; dolphins project sound into the water through the melon, the rounded, bulbous part of their heads, and receive sound through the oil-filled sacs in their lower jaws. I heard the dolphins examine objects with penetrating echo-location buzzes, individual clicks produced so rapidly that they ran together in a sound like the opening of a creaky door. While dolphins use echolocation to "see," they use whistles, quacks, and chirps for social communication.

I still hadn't seen a real, live dolphin, but I felt sometimes as if I were actually inside the magnificent animal's head. Lilly put suction-cup microphones right on the head of a dolphin named Jobe. In those recordings Jobe's whistles streaked back and forth between my right and left ears and swirled in my brain in between. Once, Lilly had given Jobe LSD to see what might happen. On the tape of that session, Jobe vocalized continuously but never used the "distress whistle." If only we knew what he had said!

As I listened to the tapes over months of Sundays, it became clear that I would not work with Lilly. I was more interested in the dolphins speaking to dolphins than in the attempts to teach them our language. The painfully clumsy "words" Peter learned were nothing compared to the quicksilver whistles darting back and forth between dolphins speaking "delphinese," as Lilly called it.

I often wished for a flash of intuition while listening to dolphin-to-dolphin conversations. "This is the sound of two highly developed brains communicating," I thought. "And I'm listening with another highly developed brain. We should be able to bridge the gap."

Was the information carried in their sounds? Was it in the whistles themselves, in their velocity, in the silences between the whistles, in something I couldn't hear, or in something I simply hadn't thought of yet? The only thing I knew for certain was that it was imperative to keep an open mind so as not to ignore any clues that might be offered. Lilly instilled this in me. As I completed university, he warned me, "Be careful how you educate yourself. It will affect how you see the world."

———

Working with Lilly was a never-ending series of encounters with the unexpected. One day he asked me to interview him through a strange mirror setup in which I could see my face superimposed over Lilly's face. A camera recorded our dialogue. Staring into Lilly's unblinking stare and my own face at the same time was simply awful. I've always avoided mirrors, so I found the exercise impossibly inhibiting. I couldn't think of a single question to ask the man.

Another time Lilly walked up to me with a pair of rubber ears. "Here," he said, "put these on." It was always as if I was supposed to understand the point of these projects. And Lilly was not one for explaining. In this case he had cast replicas of his ears out of rubber, then mounted tiny microphones in them. He was curious to see if I could orient myself with someone else's ears. I could, but it was like wearing someone's glasses. I had trouble finding where sounds were coming from. Lilly told me that human ears are oriented toward the space directly in front of our feet. This, he said, is the most important zone of influence for a terrestrial mammal—the space you're about to step into. Dolphins, he reasoned, have been released from this need and have evolved a much broader, multidimensional scope. He said this will likely cause dolphins' awareness to be profoundly different from our own. Our cultures are so far apart that only the most open mind will be able to cross the interspecies void.

In addition to his dolphin work, Lilly was also returning to his isolation tanks around this time. He had constructed two of them at his Malibu house, and he required everybody who visited to undergo a session and write up their thoughts, which were later collected in his book *The Deep Self*. Lilly located his tanks away from the house in a cinder-block bunker to keep any sound from penetrating. Each 8-foot-long, 4-foot-wide tank contained about 10 inches of water so saturated with Epsom salts that it sloshed with the consistency of syrup. Bathing suits were optional and rarely worn; this was California in the seventies, after all. In the tank, Lilly once explained, "all the muscles that you have been working to hold you up against gravity can now let go" in what he called "a surcease from total activity." Total inactivity, he believed, would free up masses of neurons from their body-maintenance chores and allow the floater to reach new depths of mindspace.

Even hallway painters and audio archivists like myself were required to hit the tanks, and my first attempt may have been one of Lilly's worst on record. My boyfriend at the time was a freelance stage manager. As a member of the Directors Guild, he voted on the Academy Awards every year and was given free passes to all the nominated movies. For the 1976 awards, the nominees included *Jaws* and *Dog Day Afternoon*. For some reason a local theater was still playing *The Exorcist*. We saw all three in one week. A few days later I went into the tank.

In the tank the salty water is so buoyant that your body bobs like a cork. The temperature is set at a perfect 93 degrees. (You'd think it would be set at body temperature, 98.6 degrees Fahrenheit, but the body itself produces heat, which must dissipate. Water at 93 degrees absorbs that heat without cooling or warming the body.) The air smells humid, briny, and your first reaction is to stretch out in complete relaxation. The human mind, however, abhors a vacuum. It wants some stimulation and begins casting about for something to do. My mind wandered back to the most stimulating images it had seen that week, which unfortunately included a killer shark rising to bite a swimming woman, satanic possession, and a crazed Al Pacino. The last vision I remember before thrashing my way out of the tank was of a gigantic green eyeball descending to engulf me.

Despite my initial fright, I found myself drawn back to the tanks. Lilly believed that floating in the tanks came as close as an adult could get to being in the womb, and I have to admit that I found something to that. During subsequent sessions I felt such a sense of familiarity and comfort that I lost all track of time. Sometimes I'd go in for five minutes, other times for forty. I could never tell the difference. During the week between visits, I often longed to return to the comfort of that saline cocoon. I wanted to pipe dolphin sounds into the tank, thinking I might better concentrate on the sounds in an environment devoid of terrestrial pressures. Lilly refused, however. The tanks were for sensory deprivation only, and there would be no modifying of his experiment.

The hushed quiet of the Malibu house was broken only by ethereal music, the soft tinkle of wind chimes, and the tremendous laugh of Burgess Meredith. When he dropped by the house, the actor filled the halls with the most wonderful gaiety I'd ever heard. I wasn't invited to join these gatherings, so I never had to worry about not getting the joke. I could just enjoy the mirth as it filled the house. Meredith was always a good antidote to the quiet seriousness of Lilly, and I could understand why the Lillys enjoyed his friendship. Meredith may have been the most gregarious and cheerful visitor (and not without reason; *Rocky* had just been released and was drawing huge crowds), but he was by no means the only member of the Hollywood glitterati to visit the retreat. Jeff Bridges showed up for dips in the isolation tank; John Denver once joined us for lunch at a Buckminster Fuller seminar. Lilly fascinated the Hollywood crowd; he seemed to be at the center of so many mind-expanding movements, he had the imprimatur of a scientific genius, and this was the beginning of the public's love affair with dolphins. Already one movie had been inspired by his work—the George C. Scott thriller *Day of the Dolphin*—and two others, *Altered States* and *Brainstorm,* would go into production in later years.

Lilly enjoyed the attention, but he was no starstruck fan. His courtship of the rich and famous was born of necessity. When he stepped out on his own in the sixties, the scientific establishment had increasingly ostracized him. His ideas had always been contentious to begin with. Once he examined the dolphin brain, he began theorizing that dolphins used their brain for sophisticated communication that held together a complex society. He wasn't content with suggesting that they might be intelligent; he recklessly asserted that they were more intelligent than humans. His peers in the scientific world found Lilly's ideas outlandish and unproven.

Science is built on one carefully proven step after the next, but John Lilly was taking great unsubstantiated leaps into the unknown. Scientists can be a ruthless group; they must protect the purity of science, which is based on irrefutable proof. While his opponents berated Lilly for anthropomorphizing (projecting human qualities on animals), Lilly warned them not to "zoologize." In addition to having no proof, Lilly was treading on dangerous theoretical ground. No one is going to easily convince a scientist that he or she is less intelligent than an animal.

His drug experiments didn't help. After being confronted by the dolphin's potential for intelligence, Lilly increasingly used his own body as his main experimental tool. When he began exploring psychedelic drugs like LSD and ketamine, which he called vitamin K, he gave up his claim to serious scientific standing. For Lilly these experiments were always voyages of discovery. He wanted to understand intelligence and the organ that housed it, the brain, and he wasn't about to allow the stigma of illegal drugs to hamper his exploration. The drug work, the isolation tanks, and the dolphin research were merely different attempts to solve the same riddle. Lilly wanted to look from both the inside out and the outside in.

The scientific world's shunning hurt Lilly deeply. During the time I worked for him, Lilly spent months writing a grant proposal to the National Science Foundation, hoping to secure the financial backing that would get the project up and running. The NSF's rejection came as a crushing blow. Because of his drug history, the foundations wouldn't touch him. Ambitious projects like JANUS would cost hundreds of thousands of dollars; the only thing keeping his dream of interspecies communication alive was Hollywood money.

Lilly managed to touch quite a number of prominent actors, musicians, and producers for desperately needed cash. Olivia Newton-John (remember her swimming-with-the-dolphins phase?), Robin Williams, Lee Majors, songwriters Paul Williams and John

Sebastian, est founder Werner Erhard, science fiction author Frank Herbert, and dozens of others kept the Human Dolphin Foundation afloat. Toward the end of my tenure with Lilly, I turned into a fund-raiser myself and convinced others to donate money to the cause.

Ironically my success as a fund-raiser proved to be my downfall. When I'd first come aboard as a mural painter, Toni Lilly had expected me to lose interest and fall away like so many of her husband's other young acolytes. But the more money I brought in, the more secure I felt at the foundation. I began to represent Lilly's organization at environmental fairs and on radio talk shows. I was becoming integral to the operation, and as long as Toni ran the show, that would be a dangerous place for a young woman to be. Sensing the growing tension, one day I asked Toni if everything was okay. No, she said. Everything was not. She lit into me like a wildcat. In a torrent of words, Toni expelled me from the nest.

I'll always remember her parting words: "You have such laser-beam intensity, Alexandra," Toni said, as if casting a furious spell. "One day you will be watching whales while your husband drowns beside you."

Chapter 4

After I'd spent two years listening to dolphin sounds in Lilly's refrigerated room, it was time to meet the real thing. I often saw wild dolphins in the waves when I went to Black's Beach in La Jolla, black torpedo shapes surfing with enviable power and ease. But without a boat they were beyond my reach. The closest dolphins I could find were at Marineland, an oceanarium on the Palos Verdes Peninsula south of Los Angeles. I drove down, bought a ticket, and was swept into the lush, tropical park with a river of excited children. Marineland smelled of fish and suntan lotion. The exhalations of dolphins, whales, seals, sea lions, and walruses mixed with the sound of gurgling water. I showed up early for the 10:00 A.M. dolphin show. I wanted to get a good seat.

From the stadium high above the tank, I could see four dolphins swimming figure eights in the water. When the music began, they took turns leaping high into the air. Dolphins are mesmerizing creatures—clean, muscular, their skin the color of a handful of pearls. They seemed always to be smiling. I was spellbound. As the dolphins waved to the crowd, took fish from a trainer's teeth, and jumped through hoops, it never occurred to me that these dolphins might be better off in the wild. It looked as if they were having fun.

After the show I made my way through the tourists to find a quiet dolphin tank at the seaward edge of the park. I stood next to the water and watched eight of them circle gracefully around their small enclosure. They flicked their eyes up at me as they passed. They were enormous, much bigger than I'd imagined. Some were light gray; others were black. One was so scratched that every inch of his skin was crosshatched with scars. I stood there, bewitched by their movement, breathing in the sea air. I fell in love with the place.

That night I sketched out a proposal to study the sounds of the eight dolphins in the auxiliary tank. After talking my way into an appointment with Marineland curator Tom Otten, I pitched my idea to Otten and Brad Andrews, his second in command. Otten's office was hidden away in the staff area, where water ran over concrete floors and carried the smell of vitamins and disinfectant. Both Otten and Andrews wore shorts, which were common workday attire at the park, and both men were astonishingly tall. When they rose to shake my hand, I felt I had entered a land of giants.

In the world of oceanariums my experience with John Lilly did not count in my favor. Scientists were skeptical of his work, and the marine park folks were doubly wary. Although he himself had conducted experiments on captive dolphins, in later years Lilly spoke out against keeping the animals in tanks. He felt that such an intelligent animal deserved freedom. I was lucky Tom Otten and Brad Andrews even bothered to meet with me. Perhaps they were curious about Lilly. I found that people wanted to either argue his principles with me or try to get me to introduce them to him. Timothy Leary once invited me to lunch to learn more about him. No one was indifferent to Lilly.

While I told them about my work with Lilly, I made it clear that I planned to study the dolphins, not teach them English. My plan was simple. Using an underwater microphone called a hydrophone, I would record the dolphins' sounds while taking copious written notes on their behavior. Later the sounds and notes would be entered into a computer to find out which sound went with which behavior.

Otten and Andrews took a tremendous chance with me. I was clearly wet behind the ears, but the field of marine mammal research was itself so young that they saw some value in allowing a "scientist," no matter how inexperienced, to study their animals. They gave me permission to enter the park anytime, day or night, as long as I called ahead. I could set up an acoustic monitoring station with hydrophones, although they wanted a trainer to accompany me at first so the dolphins wouldn't get tangled in the cord. I was so happy, I could barely contain myself from hugging them both. I turned to leave.

"Oh, and Alex, there's one more thing," Otten said. "The park was recently bought by Hanna-Barbera, and we're going to close for a year for renovations."

He explained that the dolphins I'd be working with were nonperformers—the very young, the very old, and the burnouts— who lived in a tank away from the show dolphins. Otten was concerned that they would become bored and restless without a steady supply of tourists hanging over their tanks.

"The trainers and staff don't have enough time for them," he said, "so I wonder if you'd swim with the dolphins every once in a while?"

I couldn't believe my ears. "Sure," I said.

I walked out of Otten's office on cloud nine. Now all I had to do was find myself a tape recorder, a pair of hydrophones, and a computer.

In theory I knew what a hydrophone did. But I had never actually seen one. I neglected to tell Tom Otten this, of course. I didn't have equipment, but I knew where to turn for help: John Gale.

John was one of the original technohippies. He had dropped by John Lilly's house now and then, drawn by Lilly's work in interspecies communication. John and his business partner, Dan Slater, both in their early twenties, had formed a company called Magicam, which created special effects for television shows like *Wonder Woman*, *The Greatest American Hero*, and Carl Sagan's *Cosmos*. The Magicam slave system, conceived by special effects visionary

Douglas Trumbull (whose work you can see in *2001: A Space Odyssey*, *Close Encounters of the Third Kind*, and *Blade Runner*), could thread a person through the eye of a needle or place someone aboard a miniature model of a spacecraft, complete with his or her shadows. During the summer of 1976, John and Dan had made some of the earliest recordings of wild orca calls, using a homemade hydrophone system dropped from a boat in British Columbia's Robson Bight.

"John, they're going to let me study the dolphins at Marineland," I told him over the phone. "I'm not sure what exactly, but I need some equipment."

"Can I come, too?" he said.

"Come where?"

"Hear the dolphins."

"I don't see why not."

"I'll be right over."

An incorrigible gear junkie, John wore heavy spectacles and lace-up sneakers. He kept airplane engines lying around his office just for the fun of disassembling them. If the equipment you needed existed somewhere within greater Los Angeles, John knew where to find it. The first thing he taught me was how to shop on a budget. Hydrophones were produced mostly by the navy to listen for submarines, and a new set could easily cost thousands of dollars. John took me downtown to the army surplus stores that sold electronic equipment by the pound. He sorted through mounds of black rubber–clad cable, odd circuit panels, and old switch boxes to find my first hydrophones. They cost $1.50. I felt as if we were stealing.

I still didn't have a recorder, but here again John came to my rescue. He was a technological Robin Hood. If someone he liked needed a piece of sound equipment, John just donated it. For me he found a professional-quality Nakamichi tape recorder and delivered it free of charge—a loaner I still have more than twenty-five years later.

On our first day of recording, John, I, and a third member of our team, Renée Prince, arrived at Marineland with boxes of equipment, wires hanging out everywhere. Renée and I had met while I was representing the Human Dolphin Foundation at a whale celebration. Renée's background in statistics would be essential for us to glean any kind of conclusions from our data. She was a cognitive psychologist who had worked with a dolphin named Julio but was currently laboring in a windowless lab testing pigeons. Renée had white blond hair, a great sense of humor, and a pigeon named Speedo, which she'd rescued from the lab. She was eager to join our unpaid team and work with dolphins again.

Tom Otten was protective of his dolphin charges. Neither John nor Renée nor I was a day over twenty-two, so Tom had a trainer tag along to make sure we didn't fry ourselves or the dolphins. We set the tape recorder in a little booth beside the tank, dropped the hydrophone into the water, and watched the cable snake into the tank. And snake. And snake. The dolphins were plenty game; from the moment we dropped the mike in the water, they were ready to run with it.

We tied the hydrophone to the booth. That worked until the dolphins began trying to tug the end right off. Then I rigged up a boom, running the cable down a tube that kept the hydrophone stable in the water and away from the wall. The dolphins bent several booms into pretzels, but finally I found a clamp from the local hardware store that held up to the dolphins' investigations.

For the first time I could hear and see the dolphins at the same time. The dolphins were much faster and more interactive than I was prepared for. My ears had been tuned by years of listening to Lilly's tapes, but this was like having the lights turned on: I was bedazzled.

The cacophony of whistles and buzzes was familiar and easily recorded. Taking notes on the dolphins' behavior proved more difficult. No human can write as fast as eight dolphins can move. They dashed past me nipping, rolling, and touching one another. It was like trying to document the strokes of a hummingbird's wing.

I glimpsed the enormity of the task ahead. John Lilly had recorded only two or three dolphins at a time. Compared to those tapes, the frenetic sounds coming out of this group of eight sounded like crosstown traffic. John Gale reassured me. "Don't worry, Alex," he said. "I'll slow it down for you later."

The common belief that dolphins are really gentle is only partially true. Dolphins are 350-pound torpedoes equipped with interlocking conical-shaped teeth and a baseball bat for a nose. When you confine eight of them to a tank the size of a medium swimming pool, their social dynamics go awry. When a human entered the tank, the first thing he or she encountered was the enormous wall of flesh known as Old Girl, a Pacific bottle-nosed dolphin. Old Girl was the dominant female, but she deferred to Lindy and White Pec, two alpha males who weren't afraid of using violence to keep the other dolphins in line. They were especially tough on Zippy, an ancient dolphin who looked as if he'd lost a fight with a cheese grater. Every once in a while, Lindy or White Pec would swim up to Zippy and slash him with his teeth or bodycheck him into the wall. If the dolphins had been swimming at sea, Zippy would have got the hint and moved out on his own, perhaps finding a few friends to associate with. But in the confines of the tank, all he could do was try to stay out of the dominant boys' way. I felt sorry for him.

The first time I slipped into the tank, the cold water took my breath away. I wore a short wet suit, flippers, and a mask. Lilly had advised me to wear a mask with clear sides to keep track of dolphins coming up behind. I couldn't see clearly out the sides, but I could detect movement. Once I got my face in the water, all I could see was Old Girl's eye hovering next to me, big and brown, checking me out. Her sleek daughter Angel, a hybrid Pacific/Atlantic bottle-nosed dolphin, slid between us. I began to swim, undulating as they did, and they moved precisely alongside.

As I gained confidence, I began to dive and twist about. Then the fun began. Pepe, the youngest of the group, snagged my armpit with his dorsal fin and began towing me. When he felt me grab his fin, he dragged me hard through the water, which frothed against my mask. All I could see was bubbles—and then my face smashed into the wall.

"Ow! That hurt."

Pepe reappeared at my side, his eye wide with glee. The next time he nudged my armpit, I held his fin with one hand and kept the other straight out. Although it didn't feel much better when I hit the wall, at least I knew it was coming. Swimming with the dolphins was the opposite of Lilly's sensory deprivation tank, but my reaction was curiously similar. After each session I couldn't wait to get back in. Eventually I learned to hold both Pepe's dorsal fin and his pectoral fin, so that when he tucked into a dive, I went with him, avoiding smashing into the tank wall. I'd passed his first test. Next he towed me to the bottom and eyed me, watching to see how long I could hold my breath. I never impressed the young dolphin here.

Its sheer physical strength isn't a dolphin's only means of aggression and defense. One morning several months into the study, the dolphins managed to pull the entire hydrophone cable into the tank. I put on a wet suit and went in after it. Tim Desmond, one of the dolphin trainers, kept an eye on me as I dove. The instant I entered the water, the dolphins clustered so thickly beneath me that I couldn't see the bottom of the tank. I cursed my stupidity. The tank was 30 feet deep with a dark bottom, and the cable was black.

After spotting the cable in a big coil over the central tank drain, I inhaled and exhaled several times, filled my lungs, and kicked hard for the bottom. Just as I neared the cable, two of the dolphins began buzzing at my head. They were dive-bombing me; they were actually sending out a painfully loud sound aimed directly at me. Having no intention of doing this twice, I kicked hard, grabbed a loop of cable, and made for the sky.

The dolphins parted as I stroked to the surface. Tim grabbed the cable and helped me out of the tank. *"What was that?!"* I asked. Tim was familiar with the buzzing. He figured the dolphins wanted to discourage me from retrieving the hydrophone, which they saw as their new toy and bait for attracting divers into their tank. Years later this chance encounter with the sonic power of cetaceans would lend me great insight into the ways in which killer whales catch up to their prey.

The modern oceanarium was born in 1938 as an afterthought to a failed film studio. The creators of Marine Studios in St. Augustine, Florida—where John Lilly first encountered the dolphin brain in the 1950s—envisioned a bustling movie studio filled with directors, actors, and aquatic stuntmen. The idea was to make money renting live sharks and dolphins out as the stars of animal features and documentaries; if a few tourists stopped in and paid a couple of bucks to see the place, so much the better. The movie idea never got off the ground, but on opening day twenty thousand paying customers mobbed the park. Dolphins originally were just one of many species to be displayed, but the owners quickly realized that trained cetaceans could hold their own as star attractions.

During the postwar boom of the early 1950s, the owners of Marine Studios built Marineland of the Pacific, south of Los Angeles, to entertain newly prosperous and mobile baby boom families. When it opened in 1954, one year before Disneyland and ten years before San Diego's SeaWorld, Marineland of the Pacific was one of the first modern theme parks in Southern California. Tourists came to gape at the fish in the park's four-story, half-million-gallon tank, to cheer on the performing dolphins, and to get up close and personal with Bubbles, the pilot whale.

By the time I came to Marineland, its original owners were long gone, replaced by a broadcasting company that also owned the rights to the Hanna-Barbera cartoon characters, like Yogi Bear and the Flintstones. The new owners hoped to create some synergy between their cartoons and Marineland, so after the yearlong makeover, the park reopened with costumed Yogi Bears wandering around the dolphin tank.

41

John, Renée, and I collected data on weekends, and during the week I tried to make ends meet by working a diversity of art jobs. We were getting plenty of material, but I wasn't sure of the next step. The problem with recording eight dolphins in one tank was not being able to tell which one was vocalizing. I could never be sure which sound went with which behavior. I lay awake nights trying to figure out how to organize our growing stock of data. If I had come from another planet and wanted to figure out human speech, how would I do it? Perhaps I would follow my subjects around, writing down every behavior that accompanied every sound and gradually tease out meaningful patterns. When a mother bent to kiss her child, I might record "Good night; sweet dreams" more often than any other phrase. Exchanges of food might be accompanied by "Thank-you" and hand-to-mouth gestures. Eventually a relationship between certain sounds and actions might emerge.

Putting these ideas into action, I abandoned pen and paper and picked up a microphone. Spoken notes were much faster. Luckily the Nakamichi had two tracks. I plugged the hydrophone into one and a microphone into the other, and began taking voice notes like an announcer calling a horse race: "Old Girl doing tail slaps in center of tank, deep pass by Zip, half breach by Lindy and White Pec, Spray and Merlin pushing the ball, Angel and Pepe reverse direction, White Pec hits Zip with his tail, fast pass by Spray, Zip chuffing on surface, Old Girl dives . . ."

Over the following months I visited the Marineland dolphins every weekend. When I had a few tapes recorded, I went to John Gale's office at Magicam, which was located on the Paramount Pictures lot and was always filled with technicians working all hours of the night on model spaceships for science fiction movies. John slowed the tapes to half speed, at which point I could hear the difference between a whistle rising and falling twice or three times, a distinction completely lost at normal speed. Using a large electronic pad, I drew boxes that contained the shape of each whistle as it rose and fell in frequency. When I played back a whistle, all I had to do was touch the stylus to enter it into the computer.

The work was maddeningly slow. A busy two-minute section of tape took all night to analyze. Each new sound had to be identified and checked against the ones already described. The dolphins constantly talked over one another, and each dolphin had the ability to make two sounds at once. The tape had to be replayed at half speed over and over while I tried to enter each sound. I then translated my voice notes into a code that could be entered into the computer. It didn't help that my typing skill was strictly hunt-and-peck.

Eventually John and I designed a behavioral template for the touch pad as well, which let me tap a stylus to the place on a dolphin shape where an action had occurred, then to a little box with the behavior code, then to which dolphin had received and performed the action. We developed a syntax that made sense of the entries: "Merlin nudges Spray with his rostrum [beak] on her flank." This let me work ten times faster. But I soon ran into a more fundamental problem: the eight dolphins were almost never doing the same thing at any given moment. Since I had no way of knowing which dolphin made which sound, I couldn't say for certain which behavior corresponded to a specific sound. One dolphin might have been eating while another chased his tank mate and another nursed: one sound, five dolphins, three different actions.

After a few months of this, I found my despair growing as high as my pile of tapes. The dolphins continued to move faster than I could talk, vocalized quicker than I could hear (even at half speed), and communicated in a frequency range that extended well above the capacity of my ears. After a day with the dolphins, I returned home to my apartment with a throbbing head, a weary body, and an exhausted spirit.

I never paid much attention to Marineland's two killer whales, Corky and Orky. They were kept in a tank on the other side of the park, and every time I walked by, they seemed to be motionless, lying side by side on the surface.

"They look boring," I once said to a friend. "They never do anything."

My friend smiled and said, "Don't always think you know everything, Alex. They might not be as boring as you think."

At the time—early 1978—a killer whale had given birth in captivity only twice before. In the early 1970s a baby conceived in the wild had been stillborn at Marine World Africa USA near San Francisco. Around that same time Marineland's Corky had given birth to a baby that had died just a few weeks later.

After the loss of Corky's first baby, Marineland began testing her blood monthly for changes in progesterone levels. With the help of these tests, in 1977 the park's veterinarian discovered that Corky was pregnant again. I was working with the park's dolphins at the time, and it occurred to me that a sound recording of a killer whale birth might be a useful contribution to the scientific record. I begged the staff to call me if it looked as if Corky was going into labor. On September 3, 1978, I got the call and sped to the park.

The killer whale stadium loomed high above the rest of the park. Corky and Orky's tank was smaller than the dolphin performance tank and entirely aboveground, with three stories of underwater windows. A crescent of blue bleachers rose above the tank. I set up my gear in a little ersatz fishing shanty that the whale trainers worked out of. I slid the hydrophone behind a ladder attached to the wall to keep the whales from tangling in the cable. The dolphins had immediately assaulted the device, but the whales' reaction was different. Orky, the big 28-foot male, drifted over to the hydrophone, brought his left eyeball to within inches of the cable, and just stared at it for twenty minutes. I was impressed by his thoughtfulness and patience. The hydrophone was nothing more than a black cord with a slight bulge at the end. That a whale could spend so much time gazing at so basic a shape was my first hint of the vast differences between the two species of cetaceans.

Whales, dolphins, and porpoises branched out from the group of animals called ungulates during the Paleocene period (about

57–67 million years ago) and returned to the aquatic environment 50 million years ago. Our best guess is that they went back into the water to access rich food resources and to escape fierce competition on land. Once back in the oceans, their bodies adapted to their surroundings. Their nostrils migrated to the top of their heads so they could roll smoothly and breathe at the surface without needing to lift their heads. Their hands—which still exist, with every bone we have in our arms and fingers—became encased in a paddlelike structure that we now call the pectoral fin. Their legs atrophied completely.

Cetaceans quickly split into two types: Mysticeti (baleen whales) and Odontoceti (toothed whales). The latter suborder includes sperm whales, beaked whales, all the dolphins, and the diminutive porpoise. The main biological difference between a porpoise and a dolphin is the shape of its teeth. A porpoise has spade-shaped, flattened teeth, whereas a dolphin has conical-shaped interlocking teeth. The easiest way to tell them apart is by the porpoise's smaller size and blunt face. Most dolphins have a more pronounced rostrum.

Cetacean names can be terribly confusing. The "right-whale dolphin" isn't a whale at all; it's a dolphin. The pygmy sperm whale is not a sperm whale. And the killer whale is actually the largest member of the dolphin family.

Although killer whales are dolphins, they occupy a quite different place in the food chain. Orcas are the only dolphin relatives known to eat dolphins, whales, and porpoises. They sit at the very pinnacle of the aquatic food chain: an orca will eat a shark. This lofty perch on the hierarchy seems to make orcas much more confident and far less skittish than their smaller cousins. I have often wondered if orcas even experience fear.

Corky was having contractions several hours apart. As each one arrived, the whale drifted to the surface, her body violently arched into a C. Her quivering sides sent lines of water rippling across the tank. I stayed in the park for five days, my sleeping bag stashed in a corner of the trainer's hut. Tom Otten seemed glad to have some-one volunteering to spend nights watching the whale. On the fifth morning the contractions came stronger and faster, now less than an hour apart. I phoned Otten at 4:30 A.M. and he arrived in time to see Corky fall asleep. The contractions stopped. It had been some kind of false labor. I was crestfallen.

I packed up my gear. I couldn't spend my whole life peering into a tank of whales. Before leaving, however, I wrote my phone num-ber everywhere and asked staff members to call again if birth seemed imminent.

The second call came a few weeks later, on Halloween night. By the time I got to the park, breathless and loaded with gear, the birth was over. Corky's daughter swam by her mother's side, her tiny dorsal fin still wilted to one side, her movements floppy and uncoor-dinated. Corky constantly nosed the infant off the wall. The small tank forced the whales to swim in tight circles, something beyond the ability of the newborn, so I watched Corky shove the baby away from the concrete confines of their world. I overheard Tom, Brad, and park veterinarian Jay Sweeny talking.

"This is where the problem begins," murmured Tom. "Every time the calf gets near the damn wall there's Corky's face in front of her."

"I see that," said Jay, "but we shouldn't get in there right now. Let's give them a chance to work it out on their own."

"You're right," said Tom. "We'll give her two days." He didn't sound hopeful.

I found Tish, one of the trainers, and asked what the prob-lem was.

"See how Corky's keeping the baby off the wall by putting her white eye patch in the calf's face?" Tish asked. "We're starting to think that's what prevents the calf from finding the right place to nurse."

Quietly I dropped the hydrophone into the whale tank and donned the headphones. The whales were talking. Their calls were so melodic and profoundly beautiful, it was hard to sense that anything was wrong. My head filled with long, lazy, sweeping notes punctuated with metallic crescendos. Even with the sudden appearance of a new infant, the whales' voices were calm, never overlapping. I realized that if I were working with killer whales instead of dolphins, I wouldn't need to slow their voices down. I checked that the tape was rolling and stepped out along the tank again.

"Corky was just a baby when she was captured," one of the trainers was saying. "Maybe she was taken too young from her mother to have learned how to nurse a baby."

I hadn't thought of this. The intelligence of the whale mind was working against this mother and daughter. Smaller-brained mammals rely much more on instinct. A mother shrew would not have found herself in this predicament of not knowing how to nurse her own young.

"Should we rub black shoe polish on Corky's eye patch?" someone suggested.

"No," said Tom Otten. "It's too late and too invasive."

In the background excited public relations staffers tried out names for the little whale born on Halloween night. "Spooky," suggested one. "How about Goblin or Devil?"

Two days later Jay Sweeny decided to tube-feed the infant before it starved to death. Tom, Brad, and head trainer Tim Desmond lowered themselves into the tank with ropes tied around their waists. Other trainers held the lines, ready to yank them out at a moment's notice. Even with the ropes, the three men were engaged in a potentially life-threatening act. Approaching any animal with a newborn is a risky proposition; the slightest hint that you mean its baby harm can incite a ferocious attack. We've all heard the warning about not coming between a mother bear and her cubs. The three men were, for all intents and purposes, about to come between a powerful cetacean grizzly and her starving cub. Corky could pulverize one of the men, even unintentionally, as she swirled about positioning herself as close as possible to her baby. No one would have a chance to yank on the safety rope in time. Though Corky and Orky were well trained, they were not house pets. Up until a few months before the birth, the whale trainers had ridden Corky and Orky in their twice-daily show. Then, during a training session, Orky grew cantankerous and refused to carry a trainer named Jill Straton, who happened to be Tom Otten's fiancée. As the session deteriorated, Orky sank and set his passenger afloat. Not content with this misdemeanor, the whale surfaced beside Jill, tucked her under his chin, and carried the woman underwater. With nothing to grab, Jill couldn't get out from under the whale's smooth throat. Tom reached the tank just as Jill lost consciousness. Unmindful of the fact that he was jumping into a tank of whales in the process of killing a human, Tom dove in and pulled Jill to the surface. Astonishingly Orky dove and rose just enough to give Tom a platform to stand on as he struggled with the inert body of his beloved fiancée. That shortened Jill's time in the water and helped save her life. CPR revived Jill a few seconds later, and she returned to consciousness with few ill effects. Around the park it was widely believed that the whale hadn't intended to kill Jill but simply had no idea that a human couldn't hold its breath like a whale. Nevertheless, that was the end of whale riding at Marineland.

The force-feeding of Corky's baby was the first time since then that humans had got into the water with the whales. Miraculously both orcas accepted the men's help. Orky drifted beneath the men and provided a platform for them to stand on, just as he had for Tom Otten. Corky floated beside her baby as the men restrained it, slid a soft plastic tube down its throat, and administered a mixture of milk, ground fish, and vitamins. No one knew how to mix whale formula, but they made a guess based on what had been given to other marine mammal infants in other parks.

On November 7 I got a call from Marineland. "We're going to take the baby out," a staff member told me. They wanted to put the infant in another tank where they could more easily tube-feed the baby. The calf was looking thin.

I arrived in time to document the transfer, after sundown, when the park was closed. This event was not open to the public. A crane reached out over the tank, carrying the baby whale in a sling. Its small, blunt face peeked out one end, its fluke tips out the other.

The little infant cried in a raspy, cawing voice. Corky circled anxiously. As her baby's voice left the water and entered the air, the mother threw her enormous body against the tank walls, again and again, causing the entire stadium to shake. I burst into tears. Corky slammed her body for about an hour. While this appeared to be an expression of rage, she never rose to strike any of the people working near the edge of the tank.

The baby was put in a shallow tank with the dolphin Old Girl. Old Girl kept her distance, frightened by the enormous bleating baby. The entire staff at Marineland, from the curator to the secretaries, took turns "walking" the calf around the shallow water twenty-four hours a day. As long as it was in physical contact with someone, it stopped crying.

When everyone left the killer whale stadium and the floodlights shut down, I unfurled my sleeping bag, put the headphones on, and settled down cross-legged. I had to see this thing through. The mother whale began calling.

I had learned a few orca calls while recording Corky's false labor, but the sound that Corky repeated the night she lost her baby was new to me. This wasn't a sweet rising and falling riff. This was strident, guttural, and urgent, like a dog yelping at the end of a chain. After each breath Corky returned to the bottom of the tank. As her delicately curved face grazed the cement bottom, she resumed her lament. Every fiber of her being begged for the nuzzling of her newborn baby. Orky circled slowly above her, his moonlit shadow darkening the wailing mother. He responded to her occasionally with the staccato retort of bullet shots in an old Western. The whale stadium remained closed. I stayed with the orcas and listened to their vigil of grief stretch on for three days and nights. Corky's calls grew hoarse as the hours continued, and I began feeling the grief as if it were my own.

As the third night crossed into day, the California sky lightened with pastel streaks of pink. Orky's short, sharp call rang out once again, but this time Corky fell silent. With a powerful downstroke, she lifted herself off the tank floor to fill her lungs, then answered her mate with the same resounding *pituuuuuuuu*. Orky swirled to her side and answered her in kind. The two whales moved together in perfect unison. Their blowholes opened at the same instant, their dorsal fins broke the surface simultaneously, and their calls rang out one after the other through the dawn. When the trainers arrived, Corky accepted the first food since losing her baby. After three days and nights of mourning the dead, Corky had been wooed back to life.

I walked down the stadium steps, intoxicated with exhaustion and changed forever. I wanted to ask someone, "Did I just witness grief, mourning, and healing between two whales?" My heart knew the answer. Unknowingly I had observed the founding principle of orca society—the familial bond. Nothing, not even life itself, rates higher for these mammals. I even knew what one sound meant to a whale—grief. My time with dolphins had come to an end. It was time to enter the world of the orcas.

Later that week I approached Tom about shifting my research from dolphins to killer whales. He was delighted with the idea. Tom, Brad, and Jay thought Corky would become pregnant again, and they saw my research as an opportunity to lay down a solid base of adult orca sounds. The next time a baby arrived, we'd be able to differentiate the infant's calls from those of its parents. I thought it might also be fascinating to study a baby whale in the process of learning its own language.

A lot of sharks and dolphins died in the early years of Florida's original Marine Studios because no one had even an inkling of their natural history. The curators there at one point captured a live manta ray, which eats mainly plankton. They tried feeding the ray mullet, and it starved to death. Just as the science on marine animals was in its infancy, so was the husbandry required to keep them alive. The keeping of whales in captivity far outpaced any understanding of what they needed to survive. Sadly, our knowledge of how to keep these creatures alive has been built on a heavy death toll.

In the aftermath of her second baby's death, Corky had taken to lying by the window to the room where the gift shop merchandise was stored. For hours on end, Corky sat next to tiny stuffed orcas stacked against the window. We were never certain whether the fuzzy toys reminded her of her baby or whether she thought one *was* her stolen baby.

The Marineland staff picked up on her interest and tried to use it to keep the next baby alive. When Corky became pregnant again a few months later, the trainers cast a model of her dead baby and began teaching Corky to roll on her side and present her mammaries to the nose of the little whale. Whale nursing isn't as instinctual as you might think. When a primate mother picks up her infant, she naturally hugs the baby close to the milk in her breasts. Even with an inexperienced mother, the baby has a good chance of smelling the milk and rooting around to locate nourishment. Whale newborns have to find their mothers' mammaries while both are swimming, and their location, inside two creases near the genital slit, can be difficult to find. In the week the Halloween infant was with Corky, we had seen her fixate on a particular white spot on her mother's face behind her eye. This led us to believe that baby orcas are led by instinct toward a white spot, much as a seagull chick pecks at the red spot on its mother's beak. Because Corky constantly had to use her head to push the baby away from the circular tank edge, however, the baby had fixated on the wrong white spot—the one behind her eye instead of the one beneath her tail, which marked the mammaries. I remembered watching the baby nuzzle her mother's white eye patch and then, finding the corner of Corky's mouth, try to nurse there. That was why they had considered putting shoe polish on Corky's eye patch.

Part of the problem lay in the extraordinary hydrodynamics of a killer whale's body. The surface of an orca exhibits something called laminar flow, which means it passes through water while barely raising a ripple. Water actually flows through the outermost layer of whale skin. As the whale swims—which it does almost continuously every moment of its life—it sheds this layer, leaving a skim of outer cells in its wake. The skin of an orca is as smooth as a beach ball, with a few gritty spots here and there. This gritty material is the buildup of sloughed skin cells. Whales love a vigorous rub to have it removed. To prevent water from snagging on any part of their body, whales have evolved into a ruthless sleekness. The fewer protrusions on a whale's skin, the less energy it takes for a cetacean to propel itself through water. Over millennia of evolution, the whale's outer ears, hair, and fingers vanished, along with anything else that caused water to ripple and back eddy. A female whale's nipples are naturally tucked into pockets to maximize hydrodynamic flow. To nurse, she has to bring them out and present them to her baby, who, without the benefit of movable lips, must latch on by curling its tongue. It's quite a complex operation.

No amount of training could get Corky to expose her nipples, but the staff prepared her as much as they could. They knew Corky wouldn't look away from her infant to receive a human hand signal, so they trained her to present her mammaries to the model baby with a unique underwater sound cue.

We now know that killer whales have a long sixteen-month gestation period. In the late 1970s, though, we had no idea how long it would be before Corky gave birth. Jay Sweeney had only just recently, with Corky's first calf, figured out how to read an orca's blood test for signs of pregnancy. Since a whale has no pelvic structure, a growing fetus isn't confined between the lungs and pelvis, as it is in primates and ungulates. There's no obvious bulge.

To collect baseline data on the adult whales before the next birth, I began observing Orky and Corky once a month for twelve continuous hours, alternating between 6:00 A.M.–to–6:00 P.M. and 6:00 P.M.–to–6:00 A.M. watches. Renée Prince and John Gale often joined me for these all-nighters, our foam pads and sleeping bags pushed up to the side of the whale tank.

The nighttime sessions revealed events so bizarre that I was sure no one would believe they had occurred. It was like trying to prove that that blue frog was real. This time, however, I came better equipped. As the sun set, the whales settled down to a long night of floating side by side. Floating is a captive-learned behavior. Wild whales rarely float; they travel even as they sleep, entering a rhythmic breathing pattern of four to five short (less than thirty-second) dives and then a long three- to five-minute dive. Marineland's tank was too small to navigate while asleep, so the whales had to learn to float using minute sculling motions. The hypnotic sound of flowing water and whale sighs often sent me drifting to sleep with my headphones on. As the sky lightened with the first hint of dawn, the whales jolted me awake with their calls. Killer whales are among the loudest creatures in the sea; I had to be careful to set the volume low to protect my ears.

Since the whale stadium had been built with a spectacular western ocean view, the grandstands acted as an enormous shade wall every morning when the sun rose. It could take upwards of an hour for the dawning sun to finally burst over the top of the stadium. During that time the whales diligently squirted water at a particular spot on the tank wall, right at water level. They licked that spot with their thick pink tongues and spyhopped next to it. As the sun finally peeked over the stadium rim, the first rays of light crept down the tank side and touched the water at the *exact* spot the whales had marked.

No one, I thought, was going to believe me. Was this some sort of ritual?

Through the months the spot moved in response to the earth's rotation, but the whales always knew just where the first shaft of light would hit their water. Once the sun touched the water, Corky exploded into action. Orky was less of a morning whale. As he tried to catch a few last moments of sleep, Corky ran the tip of her pectoral fin from the tip of his jaw, down his belly, and over his genital slit. If this didn't cause an immediate bulge in the smooth pocket that housed his penis, Corky escalated her tactics. She swam beneath him and pushed him into the air like a forklift picking up a rolled carpet. If this didn't succeed in waking her mate, she crossed the tank, then streaked toward him, ramming him with her head. His body shuddered on impact. There was no hope for more sleep.

What Corky wanted was sex, and whale sex is a turbulent affair. Water boiled out of the tank as the two entwined, spiraled, and made contact the entire length of their bodies. The actual act of mating was only a quick belly-to-belly moment, but foreplay took quite some time. Corky's genital area flushed with rosy excitement. I never saw Orky initiate sex, but when he was inspired, it was impossible to miss his arousal. His 3-foot, brilliant pink penis would pop out of its pocket seeking the warmth of Corky's body. The very strange thing was, once Corky became pregnant, Orky would do everything but actually mate with her, seeking instead the enormous water jets at the tank bottom. Did he know she was pregnant, by echolocating on her body or through the trace taste of hormones in the water they shared? I don't know. But it drove Corky wild.

Orky and Corky loved to invent complicated synchronized routines. One involved backing into the tank wall, humping up like a couple of greyhounds, and pushing off together with their tails in a motionless glide. Another had them lying side by side, spooning, with their flukes resting on the training platform and their right pectoral fins raised straight up in the air. They worked on perfecting this Esther Williams routine for months. One whale might end up facing the wrong way, or the other might move its tail too close to the edge and slip off. They were obviously communicating with each other about what they were doing. But how? Who came up with the ideas? Did they communicate vocally or by example?

When I first reported the synchronization and the dawn wall squirting, the whale trainers were skeptical. I was young, impressionable, and was surely embellishing. In the trainers' minds, these morning performances outmatched the complexity of any behaviors they were able to get the whales to do. It must have been a little irksome to hear that the whales were saving their best stuff for themselves.

This time I was determined to combat the blue frog syndrome

with proof. I began taking pictures from every possible angle. There they were, two whales lying side by side in their strange dyadic salute. There was Corky licking the spot, and a few minutes later there was the streak of light. I'd learned my lesson: document, document, document.

The orcas weren't content to execute one routine over and over. Once they perfected it, they quit and soon began work on a new production. The routines themselves were almost beside the point; the joy, it seemed, came from creating and perfecting the actions together. Watching animals is a little like mining. When you first witness a behavior, there's no way of knowing whether it will vanish or grow into a mother lode. As it turned out, the act of synchrony was a mother lode—another founding principle of orca society. For these whales the behavior itself seemed secondary; what mattered was doing it at exactly the same time with someone.

During my time at Marineland, I experienced a growing unease with the confinement of dolphins and whales. I'd listened to John Lilly's arguments against the practice but wondered if we should really apply the Golden Rule to an animal. Lilly once said that places of confinement providing free food and medical care "are called prisons." While his comment nagged at my conscience, Lilly's pronouncements struck me as a bit disingenuous. It was easy for him to condemn the practice years after he'd got the data he needed from his own captive mammals.

I could see the effects of confinement firsthand, and I knew I had become complicit in (and a beneficiary of) the practice. I couldn't help but feel sorry for the dolphins, condemned to swim round and round a cemented world, just a few hundred yards from their wide Pacific home. Corky the killer whale especially needed space. She was a traveler and spent hours relentlessly circling the whale stadium pool. As her flukes pumped up and down, she created a swell and rode her own wave. As I watched her, circling for hours on end, I wondered if her body craved the great distances that the rest of her family swam. Both Corky and Orky had been captured in British Columbia in the late 1960s; how much, I wondered, did they remember of those home waters? Would Corky's babies have lived if her own mother had been at her side? There was no reason to believe otherwise.

Oceanarium defenders often pointed to education as one of the strongest arguments for marine mammal captivity. "Look at what we can teach the children," they'd say. As one who saw the children taught, I had to disagree. Once in a while Corky or Orky would single a child out and follow him or her around the tank; these kids were delighted to play along with the enormous cetacean's curious game. More often, though, I'd see a different kind of interaction. Some kids taunted the whales and pitched popcorn at their blowholes. When the orcas failed to heed their commands to jump, the kids called them stupid. They argued over whether the whales were real. "They're like rubber, man. Look at 'em: just like the dinosaurs at Disneyland. They're stupid, fat, dead, fake . . ."

What exactly were these children learning? Before the advent of marine parks, killer whales had all too often been considered the wolves of the ocean, nomadic man-eaters, good for nothing but catching a bullet. But thanks to parks like Marineland and SeaWorld—especially SeaWorld, which made Shamu as cuddly as Mickey Mouse—public opinion had swung to the opposite extreme. By the late 1970s orcas had become Disney-fied. They were considered obedient, cute, tongue-wagging performers, tame enough for petting, and the children I observed were learning that it was a human right to enslave, harm, and ridicule another creature just for fun. In a single generation the human memory of orcas as dangerous predators had faded away—and with it the respect that predators command.

Chapter 5

During my time at Marineland, I met and fell in love with a young man named Jeff Norris. Jeff worked at the Hubbs-SeaWorld Research Institute, the scientific arm of the San Diego oceanarium that was Marineland's chief competitor, while he studied for a master's degree at the University of California at San Diego. Jeff shared my interest in whales and dolphins; he and I would often take camping trips to Mexico's Sea of Cortés and spend hours talking about the marine mammals we were researching. At the time Jeff's work involved studying the sounds of porpoises with an eye toward keeping them out of the gill nets of commercial fishermen. Through Jeff I was introduced to SeaWorld and the San Diego research community.

Over the years Marineland and SeaWorld had developed two distinct institutional cultures. Marineland had come out of the Marine Studios tradition of the aquatic theme park. Its founding curator, the renowned dolphin specialist Kenneth Norris, had an easygoing management style that translated directly into a casual atmosphere at the park. SeaWorld opened in 1964, eleven years after Marineland and nine years after Disneyland. The park was located in a navy town and had a self-important military-style hierarchy that would have appalled the Marineland staff. In Palos Verdes the dress code tended toward casual surfer wear; in San Diego the staff sported crew cuts.

SeaWorld had killer whales, too, of course—Shamu, the most

famous whale in the world before Willy came along. Or rather, the Shamus.

The San Diego oceanarium acquired one of the first captive killer whales in 1965 and quickly built the orca into one of the biggest names in theme park entertainment. Once it was determined that "Shamu," as that first whale was called, could be trained to do dolphin-style tricks, crowds packed the San Diego park. Dancing dolphins were one thing—but a trained killer whale! That was something people would line up to see. By the time Marineland obtained Corky and Orky a few years later, it was too late. SeaWorld surpassed Marineland in admissions and profits by 1970 and eventually opened new parks in Texas, Ohio, and Florida, each with its own "Shamu." Especially in those early years, keeping killer whales alive through capture and captivity turned out to be a tricky business that resulted in literally tons of dead whales. Captive killer whales had a habit of dying without warning on the cusp of maturity. SeaWorld got around this problem by calling all of its whales Shamu, although their trainers knew them by their individual names. Having a number of parks also disguised any potential whale problems. Since the water froze at the SeaWorld in Ohio every winter, all the marine mammals were shipped to other parks during the cold months, then returned to Ohio the following spring. All this moving around made it difficult to know when an animal had died or gone to Ohio. In fact, animals never died at SeaWorld; they just "went to Ohio." Sadly there's no happy ending to this story. In the mid-1980s SeaWorld purchased the financially troubled Marineland just to get Orky, who, as one of the few mature breeding males in captivity, was an extremely valuable commodity. By then the Pacific Coast had been closed to whale capture. With Orky SeaWorld could make more whales on its own instead of risking both public outrage and the high cost of importing whales from Iceland. Orky died soon after being transferred to San Diego in 1988, after fathering only a few babies.

Even with Jeff along, I was never allowed to interact with the whales at SeaWorld. In the eyes of the park managers, I was double

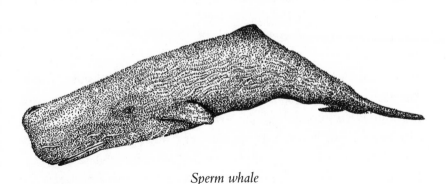

Sperm whale

trouble: not only did I associate with the competition, but my training had come at the knee of the extremist visionary John Lilly. Fortunately one of the senior scientists at Hubbs, Dr. Bill Evans, was kind enough to let me analyze Corky and Orky's calls on the institute's spectrograph. The spectrograph's visual depiction of sound allowed me to plot the more confusing orca vocalizations.

Whereas the dolphins constantly talked over one another, Corky and Orky maintained a polite protocol. They introduced conversations with one signal, vocalized, then signed off with that same signal. It reminded me of the way humans communicated on CB radios: "Roger that. Over and out"—very crisp and precise.

Previous researchers had focused on finding specific action calls—one sound for feeding, another for mating, another for signaling distress. That might work with chickens and small monkeys, but whales weren't so simple. They constructed whole sets of dialogue—and what sounds! Killer whale calls took my breath away. They beckoned, warned, and seduced in turn. Their calls were slow and discrete enough to let me code each one, which I'd do for hours on end, letting my heart slow and my mind settle into a meditative state. Once the whales got into my head, I couldn't shake them. After a long coding session, I'd see a human open her mouth and hear elements of killer whale language pour out. I'd hear Corky's cadence, timing, and inflection in a simple "How are you?" or "Uh-oh!" At night I'd dream of whales actually speaking to me, telling me where the information in their language lay.

In investigating whale communication, it would be foolish to assume that all the information is being delivered in discrete packets with each call. Even in our vocabulary-rich languages, we embellish words with our tone of voice, how fast we speak, and punctuation. Whales might choose whatever call best suited a noisy, quiet, or long-distance situation, then modify that call or the spaces between the calls to actually say something. It was imperative to investigate all possibilities, keeping an open mind.

Dr. Lou Herman, who founded the Dolphin Institute in Hawaii, taught two dolphins to recognize a specially adapted sign language and found that dolphins readily responded to concepts of syntax. They understood the difference between "Get the ring from John and give it to Susan" and "Get the ring from Susan and give it to John." Every clue was significant, and I took this to mean that the order of the whales' calls could be crucial to the context of their communication. Indeed, I had found evidence of this. While entering Orky and Corky's sounds into the computer, I learned to expect the call I'd named "A" immediately following the call type "D."

Another startling finding was dolphins' innate ability to recognize the concept of names. Many researchers felt that they had recorded "signature" whistles in bottle-nosed dolphins and that these appeared to belong solely to one individual. It might be his or her name. Diane Reiss, another researcher experimenting with dolphin language capabilities, found that when she taught a dolphin a sound that meant "ball," the dolphins began to use that sound to ask for the ball among themselves.

A controversial experiment conducted by Dr. J. Bastien suggested that dolphins could actually communicate detailed information using only sound. Two dolphins in separate tanks were given an underwater telephone and commanded to perform a task that required one dolphin to provide information to the other. They succeeded at this easily.

The sounds made by the entire dolphin family contain the universal acoustic communication features used by all life-forms on earth, including humans—a crisp start to their calls, fundamental wavelength use, and the "prosodic elements of rhythm and space"—but the devil lies in the details.

While I had managed to receive a bachelor of science from American University, I had no advanced degree. Despite this I was allowed to discuss ideas with some of the top cetacean researchers in the world. Dr. Sam Ridgeway, a scientist in charge of dolphin research at the Naval Ocean Systems Center in San Diego, invited me to an informal discussion group that he periodically hosted. Every few weeks ten to twenty researchers shared what they were learning. Most of the scientists dismissed Lilly's theories as ridiculous, but I found them not so different from Lilly in their passionate pursuit of knowledge about dolphins and whales. Over bottles of wine these brilliant men and women discussed the workings of a dolphin's inner ear, the proper diet of a leopard seal, the best way to keep porpoises out of fishing nets.

There's a strict hierarchy among the scientific community, and I was ignoring it at some peril. I don't know if it was the two years volunteering with John Lilly, my own eclectic education that jumped from mid-high school to university to graduate magna cum laude, or the unique pursuits of my parents, but during my time in San Diego, I was completely unfazed by the fact that I wasn't being paid for the research I was conducting. Around me I saw great scientists forced to study inner-ear parasites in porpoises or cetacean/fishery management problems—issues that paid the bills but were far removed from the questions they really wanted to study. I felt bad for them. I studied their work and pestered them day and night.

To my advantage, I was a rookie so far down the ladder that I didn't even register on their scale. Nobody was ever threatened by me. The Hubbs scientists knew I held them in awe, and their willingness to consider my questions led to one of the greatest learning experiences of my life. I was fortunate to fall under the guidance of Frank Awbrey, a marine biologist and acoustician whose two great passions were studying frogs and debating creationists. Awbrey gave me access to the recordings he'd made of killer whales in Antarctica and let me come along on his nighttime forays into the desert to record frogs. One summer Jeff and I joined him on an expedition to Alaska to record the sounds of Dall's porpoises. There Awbrey introduced me to the rigors of field science and the rule of field equipment redundancy. After we'd been dropped off on a remote Alaskan island, his primary tape recorder went on the fritz. If he hadn't thought to bring along a backup, our entire trip would have been wasted.

At Sam Ridgeway's informal meetings, the topics that invariably produced the most heated debate were intelligence and language. The scientists generally split into two camps. One held that dolphins were about as intelligent as pigs; the other thought they were more intelligent than dogs but perhaps not as intelligent as humans. Most of the San Diego researchers were firmly in the pig camp. Perhaps this was a backlash against Lilly's prediction of superintelligence in dolphins. In his groundbreaking work *Sociobiology*, biologist Edward O. Wilson captured the scientific community's attitude toward Lilly: "Lilly's books," he wrote, "are misleading to the point of irresponsibility." Perhaps it was just taboo for a scientist to suggest a level of intelligence on par with his own.

It was an exciting time to be a cetacean researcher. Recent studies on dolphins' echolocation abilities had shown that they could discern between two identically sized and shaped objects, buried in sand, made of different types of metal. A harbor porpoise could detect and avoid a wire only 0.5 millimeter wide. Scientists had made remarkable discoveries about the physiology of cetacean hearing. While a dolphin's ear contains only a few more of the same inner-ear hair cells that humans use to pick up sound vibrations, the cetacean has five times the number of nerve cells running between these hairs and the auditory portion of the brain. The sound-processing center of a dolphin's brain, in turn, is connected to the neocortex by a nerve similar to ours but capable of handling vast amounts of data. Compared to our bicycle path, the nerves connecting a dolphin's brain to its hearing center are a superhighway. They are twice the size of human nerves and much more numerous. This high-speed connection to the well-developed outer brain, which we know is associated with higher thought, makes it clear that dolphins may have information-processing capabilities beyond our wildest imagination. It also means that they have the hardware for self-awareness, but no one wanted to open that Pandora's box of possibilities.

The one unanimous point of agreement among the San Diego researchers was the chronic lack of funding. This tended to work against the very purpose of the meetings. Since the researcher with the most data usually got the money, few were willing to share their most important unpublished discoveries.

I also needed funding. Corky and Orky continued to command my weekends, but during the week I needed to make rent. Fortunately Sam Ridgeway needed a lab assistant, I had a newfound skill suited to the job, and I had recently moved to San Diego to share a room with Jeff.

Ridgeway's lab was at the Naval Ocean Systems Center in San Diego, a research facility located on a peninsula that offered a breathtaking view of the Pacific. Ridgeway had done remarkable investigations into the workings of the dolphin brain. During the early years of marine parks, dolphin sleep was something of a mystery. The first time an oceanarium vet had anesthetized a dolphin, it died. It was discovered that breathing isn't an involuntary response in cetaceans. Whales and dolphins must consciously draw every breath. An unconscious whale would sink and drown. In the mid-1970s Ridgeway discovered that dolphins slept half a brain at a time, which explained how they could "sleep" while traveling.

When I joined his lab, Ridgeway was trying to find out if you could predict a dolphin's ovulation by her vocalizations. My job was to sit between two dolphin tanks and mark "whistle" or "click" on a seismic graph machine that responded to a hydrophone in each tank. Two bottle-nosed dolphins occupied the right tank, and two common dolphins (a smaller striped species) lived in the left. Once a week I monitored the graph for twelve hours straight, alternating between day and night shifts. This was my kind of job; I had plenty of experience listening to whales on twelve-hour shifts. The rest of the week I graphed data and did other tedious tasks. The dolphins themselves, I never touched. They were cared for by two young women who loved their charges. One of them approached me as I watched the dolphins after a twelve-hour shift.

"If you're thinking about swimming with them," she said, "you should know Slan's trained to kill."

Ouch. "Thanks for the warning," I said. I stayed out of that tank.

At the Naval Ocean Systems Center, Ridgeway and other scientists tried to pick apart the dolphins' sensory skills. If they could figure out the cetacean's complex sonar system, they might be able to apply their findings to the nation's naval defenses. The dolphins' proposed ability to stun with sound was very intriguing. Experiments were also done to explore the extent to which dolphins depended on sound for navigation and food gathering. When latex suction cups were put over the dolphins' eyes, the mammals were unperturbed and swam through an obstacle course flawlessly. But when acoustic dampers were laid over the area of the hollow, oil-filled lower jaw, the dolphins first protested, shaking their heads, in an attempt to prevent the application, and then collided with objects in their darkened pool. Their lower jaw was an essential antenna. The U.S. Navy saw a living missile, guided by sound. This was a biological technology it yearned to duplicate. The U.S. Navy had a long-standing interest in dolphins; in John Lilly's early years, in fact, the navy had partially funded his work.

Ridgeway explored the dolphin mind by inserting electrodes into dolphins' living brains. When I confessed to Ridgeway that I found this deeply disturbing, he laughed in a kind paternal way but made it clear that a twenty-one-year-old lab assistant wasn't going to change his mind or his methods.

Sam Ridgeway's studies forced me to confront my own research methods. Was I any better? Two infant orcas had died in the captive environment upon which my research depended. I also had doubts about the assumptions behind my studies. If Orky and Corky had been captured before they had a chance to learn how to rear their young, what did that say about their language capability? Had it been stunted, too? Was any of their behavior representative of an orca in its natural habitat? I wondered whether I was studying whales in an environment so unnatural and restrictive that the poor creatures were insane.

The question wasn't wholly far-fetched. A few months earlier I'd drawn a pen-and-ink portrait of a Marineland dolphin named Dudley. Using a needle-fine pen, I replicated Dudley's every last detail. When I showed it to a senior researcher at Hubbs, though, he reacted with surprise.

"What's this?" he said. "Common dolphins don't look like this."

It turned out that Dudley had a terribly deformed lower jaw, which curled up over the tip of his upper jaw. I hadn't known any better: he'd looked fine to me. What if I was making the same mistake with Orky and Corky? I realized that I had no idea what "normal" was.

It was about this time that I heard about some fascinating research being done in British Columbia by a fellow named Mike Bigg.

By the mid-1970s killer whales had become such a popular and lucrative tourist attraction that some Pacific Northwest fishermen began specializing in live whale capture. In 1965 a fisherman who accidentally captured a full-grown male orca in his gill net north of British Columbia's Queen Charlotte Sound sold the whale to the Seattle Aquarium for $8,000—the cost of the net. Fifteen years later a live killer whale could fetch anywhere from $150,000 to $300,000.

Until the late 1970s, when the whale capture trade relocated to Iceland, most of the world's captive orcas came from the Pacific Northwest. Between 1962 and 1973, 263 killer whales were captured off the coasts of British Columbia and Washington State. Of those 263, 50 were ultimately sent to aquariums or marine parks. Whale captures were brutal affairs; 12 whales were killed during the course of their capture, usually by drowning in the nets. Marine parks targeted weaned juveniles on the theory that they'd adapt more readily to tank life.

Killer whales were such huge crowd pleasers that every aquarium and theme park with a tank wanted one, but few were equipped to care for them even as well as Marineland and SeaWorld were. Of the fifty orcas that were sent to marine parks and aquariums, sixteen failed to survive their first year in captivity. Demand for replacement whales further spurred on the orca market. Passage of the Marine Mammal Protection Act in 1972 made it difficult to take orcas in American waters, so buyers moved north to Canada. The Canadian Department of Fisheries and Oceans (DFO), which manages and protects the country's sea resources, decided it had better assess the population of killer whales in order to set a sustainable harvest level.

Nobody had any idea how many orcas lived off the coast of British Columbia. Estimates ran into the thousands. On some days residents on the northeastern coast of Vancouver Island reported seeing hundreds of whales in Johnstone Strait. Commercial salmon fishermen said the orcas were so thick at times, you could walk across their backs in Blackfish Sound, on the northeast coast of Vancouver Island. Since the whales weren't visible all the time, it was assumed that they lived part of their lives in the open sea, like salmon. And because killer whales had been reported throughout the Pacific basin, from the Arctic to the Antarctic, Japan to California, the killer whales seen on the British Columbia coast were considered part of a population that potentially covered the entire Pacific Ocean.

In 1971 the Canadian Department of Fisheries and Oceans hired Mike Bigg, a brilliant thirty-one-year-old marine mammologist fresh out of the University of British Columbia. Bigg had done his graduate work on the physiology of harbor seals, and the DFO needed someone to help assess the pelagic fur seal population near the Pribilof Islands, in the Bering Sea off the coast of southwestern Alaska. At the time this kind of research involved capturing and killing seals in order to examine them. Applying his trademark ability to view research questions in radically new ways, Bigg showed how the same research could be done without killing seals while still increasing our knowledge of the life cycle of the fur seal. When the DFO was assigned the task of counting the killer whale population off Canada's western coast, the agency naturally turned to Bigg.

Counting whales represented an enormous cultural shift for a fisheries department that only a decade before had attempted to cull killer whales with machine guns, depth charges, fragmentation bombs, dynamite, and mortars. Mike Bigg brought with him an assistant named Graeme Ellis, a former whale handler for various oceanariums in Canada. For three straight years, Bigg and Ellis circulated more than sixteen thousand questionnaires to fishermen, tugboat operators, seaside property owners, lighthouse keepers—anyone who might be on or near the water—asking them to count all the whales they saw on a specific summer day. He asked his census takers to note the number of orcas, the time of day, and the direction they were traveling.

By the end of August 1973, Bigg and Ellis had an estimate of how many whales there were in British Columbia waters: between 200 and 250. If Mike Bigg's figures were accurate, it is possible that one-fifth of the entire population in the Northwest had been taken or killed in captures. No species could survive that kind of brutal attention.

In the first year of the census, Bigg and Ellis took a few snapshots of whales. When they had the pictures developed, they noticed a female whale with a highly distinctive torn fin. When they came across the same whale the next summer and realized how easily recognizable she was, the two researchers wondered how many other whales could be identified by the shape of their fins. In the summer of 1974, Bigg and Ellis began taking pictures in earnest, using long lenses and high-speed black-and-white film.

Keen observers, the pair discovered that each whale had unique markings. At first they only recognized whales with damaged dorsal fins. But when they looked closer, they realized they could tell all the whales apart. Each had a uniquely shaped dorsal fin and gray patch, called the saddle, behind and beneath the dorsal fin. Some of the whales were so similar, they had to make the identification by viewing a picture negative through a microscope.

Using seven thousand pictures taken from 1972 to 1975, Bigg and Ellis compiled a catalog of nearly every killer whale living in the waters around Vancouver Island. In 1976 they revised their earlier estimate into the first-ever accurate orca count: 210.

In response to Bigg's surprisingly low population figure, the British Columbia government amended its wildlife act in October 1975 to require a permit to capture a whale. On Bigg's recommendation oceanariums were allowed only to replace whales that died.

Included in Bigg's report was his groundbreaking discovery that not all the whales associated together. There seemed to be a territorial boundary halfway up eastern Vancouver Island, where the tides split at Campbell River. Few whales ever crossed the line, which raised the possibility that breeding populations were even smaller than 210 individuals.

While some bureaucrats within the federal fisheries department continued to see the orca as a threat to salmon, public pressure mounted against the barbaric whale captures in British Columbia. Vancouver, the birthplace of the original "Save the Whales" group, Greenpeace, became a hotbed of anticapture activism. When orca carcasses washed up on beaches, their bodies wrapped in chains and their bellies slit, the public went ballistic.

The British Columbia government has not allowed killer whale captures since 1975; the American government passed similar orca protection laws in 1976. Through his dogged research and political follow-up, Mike Bigg prevented the extinction of several populations of whales along the northern and southern British Columbia and Washington State coasts.

Bigg and Ellis discovered something else, too. In the wild, killer whales usually live in families made up of about six to twenty whales. Over the years the researchers noticed that young whales never left their mother's group. Bigg called these units "pods" and defined them as matrilineal because pod members generally included several generations of female orca kin. They had no idea who the fathers were, but grannies, mothers, aunts, and their male and female offspring stayed together year after year. Bigg found that the huge males that traveled with the pods were sons, uncles, and brothers, a discovery that challenged the prevailing assumption that killer whales lived in male-dominated harems.

About this same time University of British Columbia biologist John Ford discovered that each pod used different sounds. Within the common language of larger communities of whales, each pod had a few calls unique to its own dialect. Northern resident whales share calls, but there is no shared dialect between the northerns and southerns, nor between residents and transients.

As I thought about moving my research into the wild, I worried about having to start all over again, as I had when I'd switched from dolphins to orcas. I thought I might not have to reinvent the wheel and learn a new dialect if I could find the wild whales that employed the same dialect as Orky and Corky.

Records at Marineland revealed that Corky and Orky had been captured from separate pods in 1968 and 1969 in Pender Harbour, British Columbia, about 40 miles north of the U.S.-Canadian border. It was rumored that by looking at photos of the whale captures, Mike Bigg had identified the families of some captive orcas. This caused a sensation in San Diego. The whales in captivity belonged to oceanariums, and the suggestion that they could be traced back to their families shattered the fairy-tale images of "happy" Shamu in his cozy little home.

The California scientific community viewed Mike Bigg's ability to photoidentify individual killer whales with great skepticism. At the same time some researchers at Hubbs were experimenting with branding dolphins by freezing identifying numbers on their fins. It seemed impossible that the young Canadian had discovered a method that allowed more animals to be recognized at lower cost without harming the whales. But I saw Bigg as the key to my future with wild whales.

Given the guarded atmosphere of the San Diego research community, I hardly expected Bigg to draw me a map to Orky and Corky's home territory. But I found his phone number and called anyway. When Bigg answered, I told him I was a researcher interested in studying acoustics in the killer whale pods from which the Marineland whales had been taken. Without hesitation Bigg told me I could find them in the waters off Alert Bay, British Columbia, in August.

"If you'll give me your address," he said, "I'll send you pictures of Corky's surviving family."

Orky, he told me, had been one of seven whales netted for the oceanarium trade. Six were sent to captive tanks; the surviving wild male had never been seen again. From what we know now, the loss of an entire family would have been enough to kill him.

I hung up the phone and danced a jig. I couldn't believe Bigg's generosity. With that tiny bit of information, he'd supplied me with a compass bearing to the rest of my life. Over the next two months, I arranged for a leave of absence with Sam Ridgeway, traded my Corolla for a small pickup, bought a 12-foot Zodiac inflatable boat, learned how to run an outboard engine, bought a map of British Columbia, and talked Jeff, Renée, and John Gale into joining me in a Canadian adventure. We were going north.

Chapter 6

To reach Alert Bay, you catch a ferry from the city of Vancouver, British Columbia, across the Strait of Georgia to Vancouver Island, then drive north for seven hours through small towns and remote coastal mountains forested with centuries-old cedar and Douglas fir. When you reach the logging town of Port McNeill, you drive onto a tiny ferry that will brave the swirling tides of Broughton Strait to deposit you on Cormorant Island, three miles long and shaped like a comma. In Alert Bay, the fishing hamlet tucked into the crease of the comma, you'll immediately notice the totem poles carved by artists of Kwakwaka'wakw descent, members of the Musgamagw, Tsawataineuk, and other tribes—formally called Kwakiutl—whose potlatch ceremonies were documented by the early-twentieth-century anthropologist Franz Boas.

When I drove off the ferry in the late summer of 1979, the first thing I saw, staring at me with unblinking eyes, was a totem pole crowned by the king of the coastal food chain: the killer whale. The strangeness of this art, its bold lines not unlike those in my father's paintings, spoke to me of ancient lineages. This wasn't a theme park billboard. This was a union of the human and the animal world, the mark of a family proud to say, "We are *Max'inux*"—sea wolf, the orca.

For anyone interested in wild orca research, Alert Bay was the center of the universe in the late 1970s. Native fishermen knew the whales well; they fished among them, and their ancestors had spoken

71

with them, been killed by them, and named their clans after them. They recalled great schools of whales congregating where the wide Queen Charlotte Strait funnels into the chute of Johnstone Strait. In 1970 a pioneering whale researcher and conservationist named Paul Spong had driven off the Alert Bay ferry looking for a place to study wild orcas. What he found up there in the Canadian wilderness would lure the world's orca researchers for the next thirty years. I rolled off the ferry nearly a decade after Spong, and never really left.

Spong, a New Zealand–born psychologist, was hired in 1967 by the University of British Columbia to study the sensory systems of a female orca named Skana, which had been captured and taken to the Vancouver Aquarium. Like John Lilly, Paul Spong came to cetacean research because of his curiosity about brain function. "A lot of my interest [in Skana]," he later said, "was that this animal had the second-largest brain on earth." (An orca's brain is four times the size of a human's; only the sperm whale's is larger.) To test her vision, Spong trained Skana to "read" two separate cards lowered into her tank. One card had a single line drawn on it, while the second had two lines. By steadily reducing the distance between the two lines and asking Skana which card had two lines on it, Spong was able to measure the whale's visual acuity. She successfully chose the card with the two lines until the lines were a mere one thirty-second of an inch apart, at which point Skana's responses became somewhat random, indicating she could no longer tell whether there were two lines or one.

The experiment was going according to plan: Skana's eyes were keen as a cat's. Research on dolphin eyesight had found that their vision was much better than previously assumed. They could see best at ranges greater than 3 feet in air and less than 3 feet underwater, where dim conditions obscured anything much beyond that distance anyway. Another adaptation perfect to their life-style equipped them to be most sensitive to the shades of blue found in their watery world. Their eyes are better at detecting motion than form and have an abundance of "mirror cells," which bounce light back to the receptor cells within the eye to maximize their ability to see in low light levels. In both humans and dolphins, the optical nerve crosses from the left eye to the right brain and vice versa on the opposite side, but curiously, while we humans also have a few optic nerves running straight back to the same side of the brain, dolphins don't. The left eye communicates exclusively with the right brain hemisphere, and the right with the left.

After twenty-four hundred tests, however, Skana suddenly began giving the wrong answers. Not just randomly wrong—*exactly* wrong, as if Skana knew the correct answer but had decided to give its opposite. Like a typical whale, she'd gone along with Spong's experiment only as long as it took her to master the operation. Then she demanded something new. Skana turned the tables on Spong. Instead of the subject responding to the scientist, Spong found himself responding to Skana. What did she want? What was she trying to tell him?

What she craved, he realized, was simply more interaction. The socially starved orca enjoyed learning the rules of Spong's experiment, but rote performance bored her.

Intrigued, Spong decided to see what would happen if he gave Skana what she wanted. He spent hours beside the tank playing his flute to her, stroking her with a feather, even letting her carry him around the tank. Skana cautiously guided Spong into a trusting relationship. She took his foot in her mouth and, with sharp, conical teeth big as a man's thumb, bit down hard enough to let him know her power but gently enough not to pierce his skin. She never hurt him, and he learned to trust her.

As his friendship with Skana developed, so did Spong's reservations about her confinement. If this friendly, inquisitive creature was as social and intelligent as Spong suspected, she had to be suffering terribly in her tiny concrete tank.

Eventually Spong made his views known to Skana's keepers at the aquarium, and then to the public. The public was fascinated, but the aquarium did not take his criticisms well. In quick succession Spong lost access to Skana, then was asked to spend time in a psychiatric ward. "You can check in voluntarily or not," his boss told him.

Spong didn't care if his findings were controversial. He knew what he knew. One of Spong's greatest characteristics is his willingness to take action. Spurred on by his experience with Skana, Spong and his colleague Robert Hunter began working with Greenpeace, the fledgling antinuclear group. Until Spong and Hunter came along, Greenpeace had focused primarily on stopping the spread of nuclear power plants. The two whale advocates started their own program within Greenpeace and soon led antiwhaling campaigns on the open seas with the full backing of the international organization. By the end of the decade, they had helped bring about the world moratorium on most whaling under the International Whaling Commission. Before "Save the Whales" became a cliché of the 1970s, Paul Spong actually did it.

When he wasn't placing himself between harpoons and their intended targets, Spong could be found on an island near the northern tip of Vancouver Island, where he'd first encountered the wild orcas in 1970. Equipped with little more than the flute he'd played to Skana, Spong pushed his kayak into the riverine tides of Johnstone Strait to float among the orcas. The locals thought he was reckless. Alert Bay and the nearby Vancouver Island village of Port Hardy supported generations of salmon fishermen who considered the killer whale dangerous. Most purse seiners—commercial fishing boats that caught salmon with a net that closed like a coin purse—had a rifle aboard, loaded and ready for firing at the first orca or sea lion that came near their gear. The Canadian Department of Fisheries and Oceans, looking to protect the province's salmon stocks, went so far as to mount a machine gun on a bluff overlooking Seymour Narrows, a bottleneck in the waterway dividing Vancouver Island from the mainland. They say the machine gun was never fired, but the holes and scars in still-living orcas testify to the number of rifles that did find their target.

The fishermen weren't imagining things. Orcas feed on the same fish the purse seiners, gill netters, and trollers landed, although their salmon take was sustainable compared to the destruction caused by European fishing methods, logging clear-cuts, and (years later) salmon aquaculture. With their own eyes, the fishermen had seen killer whales flay seals, sea lions, porpoises, and even other whales with their fearsome teeth. They had seen blood in the water, and many fully expected that one day it would belong to Paul Spong.

Spong followed the whales to a small bay on the eastern edge of Hanson Island, an uninhabited spot ten miles east of Alert Bay. There he built a tree house and stayed for weeks at a time. As the years passed, whale researchers and documentary filmmakers made pilgrimages to Spong's place, and eventually he decided to make the camp his permanent home. To do that, though, he needed a special land-use permit from the provincial lands office. The government insisted that Spong prove that the remote station was being used for bona fide research, so in the late 1970s Spong broadcast an open invitation for whale researchers to come up to British Columbia and use the place he called OrcaLab.

All of which is to explain how I came to pile everything I thought necessary to study wild orcas into the back of a pickup truck and drive from San Diego to a remote outpost in the Canadian hinterlands. John Gale, who had done some technical work for Spong a few years earlier, suggested that I take Spong up on the invitation. According to Mike Bigg's information, Spong's camp was in exactly the area where I might find Corky's pod.

First, though, I would have to find Paul Spong. Along with me that first summer were Renée Prince; a San Diego friend, Cindy Grey; and Cindy's boyfriend, Rob, whom I'd recruited as a voluntary field crew. Spong had promised to meet us in Alert Bay, but there was no sign of him when we arrived. The four of us dragged the Zodiac down to the pebbly beach, inflated it, and filled it with tents, sleeping bags, tape recorders, clothing, cameras, food, and tapes until the little boat resembled an overflowing laundry basket. Perched atop the load, I shoved off the beach and paddled over to the dock.

The commercial fishing fleet was in town that afternoon, their big seiners rafted together three and four deep down the dock. Their largely Native Canadian crews passed the time talking and laughing until the next fishing opening allowed them to set their nets in Johnstone Strait. A twenty-two-year-old California girl threading her little inflatable through their massive boats provided a welcome diversion. I ducked into the only free space left—cramped quarters directly beneath the ramp. Under the amused scrutiny of the fishermen, who knew the tide would eventually obliterate my parking spot, I tried desperately to look as if I knew what I was doing. I lowered the propeller of my brand-new Suzuki motor and expertly yanked the cord. Nothing happened. Another tug. I couldn't even pull out the cord.

Thoroughly embarrassed, I took off the engine cover and made repairlike motions. Before I'd got very far, a Canadian Department of Fisheries and Oceans boat named the *Chilco Post* pulled up. Two khaki-uniformed officers strode up the ramp above me while a third ducked down to say hello.

"You're not from around here," he said, his fingers loosening the nut on the flywheel.

"No," I said, taken aback. "I'm here to meet with Paul Spong and study whales." I bit my tongue to keep from protesting that I didn't need help; I could do this myself.

"Oh," he said with a sidelong smile. I wasn't telling him anything he didn't know. Every unusual-looking visitor to Alert Bay in 1979 was coming from or going to Spong's place.

He backed off the flywheel, applied a couple of drops of oil, replaced the lid, and pulled. The engine sputtered to life. The fishermen burst into applause. I waved back sheepishly. Welcome to Canada, greenhorn.

Spong still hadn't shown up, and it was getting late. I would later learn that this was standard operating procedure for the chronically tardy New Zealander. Renée, Cindy, and Rob, who'd gone into town to eat, joined me under the ramp for an impromptu picnic. The four of us sat on the pontoons of the Zodiac, savoring "Indian candy" (strips of honey-smoked sockeye salmon), and pondered our next move. We had no idea where Spong lived. We were dangerously ill equipped and ignorant. Apprehension knotted my stomach as I watched the northern wilderness succumb to the shadows of twilight.

Suddenly gunshots erupted over the water.

The four of us spun around.

"What the hell was that?" said Renée.

"Whales!" said Rob.

Across the bay I spotted silver plumes erupting from the water. Proud gloss-black fins cut through the reflection of the fading sun. Adrenaline rushed through my body. I felt for the first time a mixture of feelings that would mark my relationship with killer whales for the next quarter century: instinctive fear mingled with magnetic attraction. At first I just clung to the dock.

With our eyes riveted to the whales' flukeprints, the four of us timidly pushed away from the dock and motored the Zodiac toward the family. When I was as close as I dared, I shut off the motor. Renée lowered the hydrophone. I put on the headphones and pressed the record button. The familiarity of the calls made me suck in a shock of cold air. Echoing in the vastness of the deep, numbing water were the melancholy calls of Corky's family. These were exactly the whales I had traveled 2,000 miles to find—and they had found me.

As I had pressed the Nakamichi's record button, the scientist in me was trying to control the cheering little girl within. When I caught Renée's eye, both of us were laughing, trying not to let the tears spill over. I gave silent thanks to Mike Bigg. Darkness crept over the strait, and we bobbed in the swells set off by the plump youngsters nuzzling their mothers and squirming playfully on the surface. As their calls rolled on and on, echoing in the undersea canyon they filled, I couldn't dodge the thought that Corky should be here instead of me.

After a night camped out in a fisherman's front yard, we found ourselves back at the dock the next morning, part of a growing crowd of Spong-seekers. Apparently we weren't the only ones he'd stood up. A Japanese film crew, bristling with the latest technical gear, talked among themselves, packing and repacking their nylon bags. A wildly handsome fellow with leonine hair was there as well; he turned out to be Mickey Houlihan, a sound engineer for jazz musician Paul Winter.

"What are you doing here?" I asked.

"Waiting for Spong," Mickey said. "And I'll bet you are, too."

Here I was on the edge of the known world, and this guy looked as if he'd just stepped off Hollywood Boulevard. Mickey extended his hand and explained that he was here to record Paul Winter playing among the whales.

Finally a wiry, windblown figure puttered into the harbor at the helm of a drooping inflatable. He leaped onto the dock with the vigor of a fourteen-year-old boy.

Paul Spong greeted me with a bear hug. "Alex! Great to see you!" Without another word, he spoke Japanese to the man beside me, then clapped Mickey on the back. "Good to see you, too, mate."

Taking no notice of the crowd or his own tardiness, he sprinted up the ramp in bare feet. As was his custom, he wore only a pair of frayed shorts and a Greenpeace T-shirt. "Be back in an hour!" he said. The film crew, sound engineer, and we four San Diegans looked at one another in disbelief. In time we'd all adjust to Spong's hyperkinetic nature and learn to appreciate how much he could accomplish in a day. I remember glancing at Spong's feet, which were a welter of scabs and raw flesh. Clearly this guy was accustomed to covering rough terrain at high speed.

An hour later Spong reappeared with bags of groceries, beer, and hardware supplies and led us down the strait to Hanson Island. Orca-Lab's recently constructed laboratory and living quarters had been designed in classic seventies back-to-the-land fashion. The main glass-and-cedar house perched on a bluff above the jagged, rocky shore of Blackney Passage. An enormous glacial erratic formed one wall of the house, which was heated by a wood stove in the kitchen. Fresh water came in buckets from a trickling creek at the head of the bay; electricity came from solar panels and a tired generator hidden beneath a slab of plywood in the forest.

Living at OrcaLab was a multimedia experience. Speakers connected to a hydrophone broadcast live whale calls twenty-four hours a day inside and outside the house. Luxury came in the form of an iron claw-foot tub, which we filled with seawater and heated by building a fire under it. The old tub could be tricky, though. If the wooden plank slid out from under you and floated to the top, you got the butt scalding of your life.

Spong invited us to stay in the house, but we preferred a camping platform built on a little point on the opposite side of the bay. After helping set up our tents, I paddled the Zodiac out to a mooring buoy. The kayak I'd planned to return in had a pool of water in its hull, so I perched on the deck and began paddling to shore. Before I landed, though, the wake of a passing seiner hit the kayak and sent it bucking and rolling. I plopped into the seat to avoid capsizing and never quite got completely dry for the rest of the summer.

There was so much to learn, so many mistakes to be made. One afternoon I tied the Zodiac to a boulder onshore, only to return from dinner to find it dangling from its rope, the victim of a 15-foot tide. The Suzuki motor bedeviled me; every morning the little outboard thought up new and clever ways to fall apart. At one point a member of my crew simply quit talking to the rest of us. (Twenty years later I still rarely take on assistants.)

The Canadian summers could deal out their own brand of misery.

The no-see-ums were merciless, and we had no defense against the tiny bugs. Some mornings we'd wake with our eyelids swollen and our exposed faces and arms covered in welts. But the place was magic.

Our tents overlooked Blackney Pass, a major artery feeding the Pacific Ocean into Johnstone Strait. Blackney never rests. In full flood it roars south with the force of a river forced through a turbine; in slack it lies still and slick, then with the pull of the ebb, tiny ripples eddy and grow until it begins to throw itself about in another spectacular display of power. The orcas gathered here because of the salmon, which pour through Blackney in runs as thick as rain. Some days the sockeyes or pinks were so abundant you could smell them on the breeze.

The surrounding forest carried the aroma of ancient cedar and rich organic soil. The pungent fragrance of wood smoke mingled with barbecued salmon, the staple food of the Canadian rain coast. On clear nights I soaked in the saltwater tub and watched stars shoot over the burble and rush of the Blackney tide. The amplified sounds of deep whale calls blended with the *kwoof* of orca breaths tumbling across the water's surface, immersing me in a blissful sense of peace. By the end of my first week on Hanson Island, I knew I had at last found my place on the planet. This was my true habitat. I had come home.

The four of us had arrived with a stack of blank tapes, and we spent every daylight hour trying to fill them with whale conversations. Every morning we brewed a thermos of coffee, packed a lunch of bread and peanut butter, and motored into the mist of Blackney Passage in search of whales. Some mornings they appeared immediately offshore; other days we drifted for hours before picking up a faint call. Underwater orca calls have extraordinary range. Years later, at a spot north of Johnstone Strait, another researcher and I talked over the radio as we both listened to the same whale pod. After consulting our charts, we found that the same orca vocalizations reached both our hydrophones—10 nautical miles apart.

When we picked up the sweeping call of an orca, it might take us an hour or more to locate it. The shape of the human ear allows us to locate the source of a sound in air almost immediately. But my single hydrophone picked up sound with equal sensitivity in all directions, so I had no idea where the call was coming from. Renée scanned the horizon with binoculars, but if she couldn't pick up a blow, I pulled the hydrophone up and moved the boat behind a nearby island, which blocked all sound from one direction. If the whales were still audible, we knew they were on this side of the island and kept moving in that direction. If they weren't, we turned around knowing we would find the whales on the other side of the island.

Sitting knee-to-knee in the 12-foot Zodiac, the four of us functioned as a data-collection corps. Renée logged notes on whale respiration, and Rob took photographs, while I handled the sound gear, made voice notes, and tried to identify exactly which orca had surfaced. My tapes from that time have a tense, serious air about them, as we tried to record everything going on around the recorded calls: "A9 blew . . . simultaneous dive . . . male breach . . . tail slap . . . reverse direction . . . female breach . . . Dall's porpoise in the area . . ."

True to his word, Mike Bigg had sent me photocopied photographs of the Johnstone Strait pods, which made identification possible but not easy. The toughest part was simply getting a good look. By the time you spot a whale, her roll may be half over. I had only two or three seconds to memorize the tiny nicks on her fin and the shape of her saddle patch. After flipping through twenty-five plastic-sleeved photos of nearly identical whales, the details often slipped my mind. Was that scratch near the top of the saddle patch, or was it farther down? Did the notch in that fin slant up or down? When I looked up again, another whale had surfaced with another set of distinguishing marks. Over time I began to learn how to look at the whales, run my eyes down the fin, across the saddle patch, and recognize the well-marked orca. Eventually I trained my eyes to spot the minute differences that characterize each whale.

One thing that I learned from the start—and that still amazes me—is the orcas' ability to vanish on a moment's notice. At Marineland Corky and Orky were available to me twenty-four hours a day, above water and below. In British Columbia the whales set the schedule. Some days they'd play around the boat for ten hours at a stretch; other days they'd make a brief appearance, then dive to places unknown, unseen and unheard, leaving us wandering aimlessly around the strait. Naturally this frustrated my research, but it also heightened the mystery and power of the whales. They controlled our encounters; they chose to reveal clues about who they were—or not.

I liked knowing they could get away from me. Having wrestled with the troubling question of captive research, working with wild whales cleared my conscience and my heart: there was no guilt here. I was free to learn, and the whales were free to live their natural lives.

As Mike Bigg and Graeme Ellis sorted through their seven thousand orca photos, they developed a taxonomic system to keep all the whales straight. The first whale they could identify, a female with a piece of her dorsal fin missing, they labeled "A1." All the whales seen swimming with A1 were called "A" as well—A2, A3, A4, and so on. The next group of whales was labeled "B," until they came to "Z." Over the years Bigg and Ellis fine-tuned their system as more information about orca behavior became available. Not all the "A" whales swam together all the time, which led to the sometimes confusing formation of pods within pods within pods. The A1 pod, for instance, is made up of three subpods, the A12 subpod (named for the matriarch A12), the A36 subpod, and the A30 subpod. The A4 pod is divided into two subpods; A5 pod contains four subpods.

In the early years of whale research, popular names were based on a whale's appearance: Scimitar, Nicola, Hooker, Stripe, Saddle, Sharky. Our regimen is a little more strict now. When a new whale is identified, it is given an alphanumeric code based on who its mother is and a name—after a landmark near which it's been seen swimming. Because it can be years before we figure out whether a new baby is male or female, the names have to be unisex to avoid a large male ending up with a name like Betty, after Betty Cove, or Queen Charlotte.

In addition to learning Bigg's identification scheme, we had to train ourselves to spot whales. It's not as easy as you might think. The water is full of objects that look like dorsal fins—sailboats, kayakers, tree roots, deadheads. Black pelagic cormorants are the most deceptive. Bobbing gently on a log, their tall, tapered bodies look exactly like an orca fin coming at you. As a rule, if you have time to pull out the binoculars and get a good look, it's not an orca. We gradually figured out which black lines were whale fins more by their rhythm than by their shape. An orca fin rises and pauses for an instant before falling.

The human eye can't actually see much of anything when it's moving. Your eyes naturally want to jump from object to object, from island to tree to boat to mountain, without scrutinizing the empty space between. The trick with whale watching is to learn how to look at a blank, featureless space. Instead of sweeping across the horizon from log to island to boat, you must walk your vision across it. Move a tiny bit, then stop. Move again and stop. Stop and look at nothing often enough and a whale's fin will appear.

When killer whales swim together, they reveal their family tree with nearly every breath. In general juveniles surface closest to mom; adult males are the next farthest out; then come the adult daughters and their offspring. As the young whales mature, the females form satellite groupings with their own babies, but the adult males continue to flank their mother. Older mothers are the center of the pod, never abandoned or alone.

No other mammal constructs its society like this. Elephants come closest, but in proboscidean societies the male elephants emigrate and form all-male groups before eventually becoming solitary bulls. If a male killer whale loses his mother, he'll take up company with his sister. If he doesn't have a sister, he and his brothers wander among their closest relatives. If he has no siblings, his prospects for survival are poor.

For a long time researchers had no idea where the fathers were in orca society. The reigning hypothesis was that they must come from outside the pod to prevent inbreeding. Not until the 1990s, when researcher Lance Barrett-Lennard began studying the issue, did we learn that fathers do come from outside the immediate pod, but *never* from outside the larger community. Northern residents mated with northern residents, southerns with southerns, transients with transients.

Corky had come from the A5 pod.

In December 1969 twelve whales from A5 pod were corralled by a group of fishermen in Pender Harbour, north of Vancouver. (Marineland's first "Corky" had been captured there a year earlier but died shortly after reaching the marine park.) Six whales were kept from the 1969 capture; six were released. An entire generation of youngsters was taken from their family. Calypso, a yearling female, was shipped to France, where she died the following December. Nepo, a ten-year-old male, and Yaka, a fourteen-year-old female, both went to Marine World Africa USA, in Vallejo, California. Nepo died there in 1980; Yaka lived until 1997. Marineland bought the other three whales. Of those three, two died within three years; only Corky survived.

Ten years after her capture, Corky's pod had risen back to its original strength, twelve orcas, but the demographics had been grossly altered. There were old whales and baby whales; the entire generation of young adults was gone. Mike Bigg assumed that the whale Corky had been nestled against at the time of her abduction was Corky's mother. That whale was named A23, also known as Stripe, and she swam with the A5 pod.

In the summer of 1979, the A5 pod appeared frequently in the waters around Paul Spong's bay, and I slowly became familiar with Stripe and her extended family. The group was led by four mothers spanning two generations. Eve (A9), the forty-two-year-old grande dame of the family, slipped past me flanked by her two sons, Top Notch (A5) and Foster (A26). (The A5 pod should have been more properly named the A9 pod, after its leader, Eve. But in the early years of orca research, when it was assumed that the big males were the leaders, the pod was named after Top Notch.) Eve bore the scars of a firsthand encounter with a propeller many years ago. Two scoops were cut out of the matriarch's back, marks that went so deep, it seemed impossible that the propeller hadn't nicked her spine.

Eve's presumed daughter, twenty-six-year-old Licka (A8), traveled with her five-year-old daughter Havannah (A28). It was always easy to spot Saddle (A14), the fourth adult female of the A5 pod. Most northern resident killer whales have saddle patches that resemble big apostrophes, but Saddle's looked like a check mark. Saddle traveled with her daughter, eight-year-old Sharky (A25), named for her rugged, triangular fin, and an unnamed infant son, designated A15.

Sharky knew little fear of humans. As far as she was concerned, we existed purely for her amusement. She often circled my boat with her little brother in tow, stopping to watch when I held my fingers underwater. I could feel the tickle of her echolocation calls as she examined these alien appendages dangling into her world.

Orca reproduction is positively unhurried. Killer whales average one successful birth every ten years. Some whales may give birth more often, but calves often die during their first year for reasons that are still fairly unknown.

Orcas mature at a remarkably human rate. At five years a killer whale begins to venture away from mum to play with other youngsters. At fifteen, males sprout an adult-size dorsal fin. Prior to adolescence males and females are hard to tell apart; in our notes we called them "FIMs," or "female/immature males." A female orca's dorsal grows about 3 feet tall. The fins of late-teen orcas grow so quickly that we call them "sprouters." They're easy to spot; like a teenage boy growing into his gangly limbs, a sprouter swims with his new fin wobbling in the air. By the time a male orca has reached the age of twenty, his dorsal has thickened and become a massive, rigid 5-foot-tall blade.

To calculate a female orca's age, researchers count how many children swim next to a mother, factor in a sexual maturity age of twelve, and calculate a sixteen-month gestation period, loss of the firstborn, and several years of nursing between each birth, and voilà: whale age.

Males are more difficult to figure out. If they had fully grown fins when Bigg and Ellis began taking pictures in 1970, we know they were at least twenty at that time. If they have younger brothers or sisters, their placement in the family can be deduced by the maturity of their siblings. Most of the males that were counted as adults in 1970 are now dead; the oldest remaining ones were born in the 1950s. We don't know why, but there are many females still alive that were born in the 1940s or 1930s—even one from the 1920s. Female orcas live up to eighty years, much longer than males, which have a life span of about forty years.

Killer whales are one of the few whale species to exhibit sexual dimorphism, a physical difference between males and females. Male orcas grow a much taller dorsal fin and have larger pectoral fins. It remains a mystery why a species so dedicated to being streamlined would waste so much energy dragging huge fins through the water. While females are smaller and presumably less powerful, they don't have to work against the hindrance of those enormous dorsal fins. "They grow them because the girls like them," was Mike Bigg's short explanation. Called "runaway selection," the choice of mates by the females of a species is thought to have led to some extremes, such as the male peacock's tail, moose's antlers, and brilliant color schemes in fish, birds, and insects.

For me each whale became its fin, since I could only imagine the rest of its body. While we all have a fear of black fins slicing through cold water, I began to love the sight of some of those fins in Johnstone Strait—cheeky little Sharky, stately Top Notch, and lovely, deeply curved A1 pod matriarch Nicola.

After the trauma of watching Corky's calves starve to death, the sight of healthy young orcas in British Columbia brought me great joy. On drizzly mornings we watched infant whales ride the slipstream that formed behind the widest point of their mothers' bodies, just behind the dorsal fin. The little ones surfaced like shadows. *Kooof* blew the moms; *poof* went their babies (always in that order). The smaller whales wriggled over their mothers' heads, goosed seagulls from below, and pulled floating strands of kelp underwater. Corky's younger cousin Sharky proved to be the most playful of the pod. With her little brother tagging along, Sharky came right up to our boat and studied the hydrophone dangling over the side, her baby clicks pinging crisply through my headset. I watched her twist and turn, trying to gather as much information about one more bizarre, human object dangling down from my boat. Sharky had a disconcerting habit of chasing our Zodiac and sticking her delicately curved face inches from our propeller. With her dorsal fin slicing through the water, it looked as if we were being chased by the shark from *Jaws*.

The youngsters weren't the only whales cavorting in Johnstone Strait. Summertime in British Columbia brings the salmon home to spawn. Millions of chinook, chum, sockeye, coho, and pink salmon return to the coast with the richness of the open ocean stored in their flesh. The salmon of the mighty Fraser, Cowichan, Klinaklini, Homathko, Toba, and other rivers come home through Blackney Passage, right outside Paul Spong's OrcaLab, and where the salmon went, the killer whales were sure to follow. At their peak the salmon runs set the table for the summer gatherings that are essential to orca society.

Although whales swim in their mothers' pods for their entire lives, that doesn't mean they don't enjoy the company of others.

Contact with other pods is essential to orca reproduction, and those bonds depend on the presence of salmon. Orcas congregate where the salmon runs flourish, and when the runs collapse, the whales are forced to scatter.

Interpod encounters can be formal, with precise choreographed movements in which the two pods face off in parallel lines and then join in a boisterous knot. Other times they come together casually, reshuffling their order to mingle with one another. Grown males especially revel in these meetings. Often the boys from different pods go off together and put on a whale spectacle better than anything the trainers at Marineland and SeaWorld could imagine.

With their bellies stretched tight with salmon, these magnificent males explode out of the water in hot pursuit of one another. One afternoon in late August, when the sockeye ran thick through the passage, I watched a group of rowdy males flash white and black as they spun and rolled over one another above and beneath the water. It's nearly impossible to see the black of an orca from above, but their bellies flash brightly when they turn over. Every once in a while, I'd glimpse a streak of brilliant pink in these tangles of whales. The boys were sporting huge erections.

Curiously, my hydrophone didn't pick up a sound from the playful boys until I came in close enough to rock in their chop. I thought they had stopped communicating altogether until I detected a faint whistling as one male group streaked directly under my boat. They were engaged in a private conversation. Perhaps, I thought, guy talk wasn't meant to reach the ears of their sisters and mothers.

That type of whistling has since been found in other groups of playing orcas, not just in males, but they are indeed highly localized sounds that don't travel far. I found them difficult to catalog; they wandered all over the place, with trills and meandering rises and falls in frequency. This made me curious as to why some sounds were so precisely emitted, while these playtime whistles were so unstructured.

That first summer opened my ears to the possibilities of wild sound. I had loved listening to Corky and Orky, but their concrete-confined voices paled in comparison to the rich variety and subtle intonations of whale calls in the wild. In the early days of coding Corky and Orky's speech, I recorded eleven sound types with forty individual variations. More than twenty years later, that vocabulary runs to sixty-two distinct codes—and I've by no means reached the limits of their language. Wild whale voices can easily fill 100 square miles of water. Their voices are as loud as a trumpet played 3 feet from your ear.

A killer whale's call defines the very space around it. The calls are broadcast with enough energy to radiate for 10 miles, hit a rock wall, and travel back to the whale, letting her know where the sea ends and the coast begins. There are places near Johnstone Strait where I've heard whale calls produce five echoes, bouncing back and forth between channels, rocky islands, and bays. Sometimes the outgoing calls meet the returning echoes to produce a dreamy concerto of harmonies.

Many whale species are even greater masters of long-distance communication. Blue whales, the loudest animals on earth, can find an island in the middle of the ocean with sound. During the cold war, the U.S. Navy mounted hydrophones on the seafloor worldwide to listen for enemy submarines and ships. Through this array navy scientists picked up very low frequency 15-hertz rhythmic pulses. These sound waves were 300 feet across. As they tracked these sounds, sometimes for more than 900 miles over forty-three days, they discovered they were listening to migrating blue whales navigate. A blue whale in the North Atlantic can send out a call and fifteen minutes later hear an echo telling him which way to Bermuda.

While most species draw together at mating time, fin whales have the odd habit of spreading out over the vast South Pacific when they get the urge to procreate. In this case it was geologists with an ear cocked for the subsonic rumblings of earthquakes who picked up

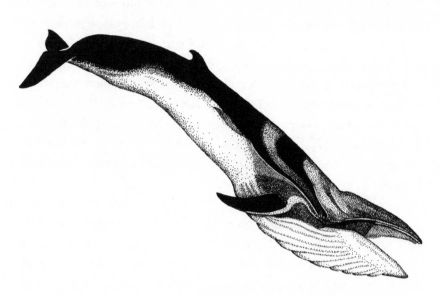

Fin whale

20-hertz pulses in a pattern too rhythmic to have been made by mother earth. These turned out to be fin whales 200 miles apart conversing. The whales' summons got a little scrambled at these ranges, with acoustic components arriving at different times, but the whales keep their calls simple and regular and apparently get their message across: "Helllooo. I'm way over here, but I'm worth the trip."

To us the undersea world is a dark, impenetrable place; to whales each sound might illuminate it in three-dimensional flashes of detail. Vision doesn't penetrate most surfaces, but sound does. Echolocation is like running your hands over your lover's face in the dark. Although you can't see the details, your sense of touch fills in the gaps. But with its remarkable echolocation, a whale can not only "see" in the dark ocean; she can actually see inside a number of objects, including other whales. Echolocation might even have its own code of socially acceptable use. John Lilly once suggested that, among whales and dolphins, echolocating on a friend might be considered rude.

Floating in a boat off the coast of Vancouver Island, you'd never know any of this was going on. Whale sounds usually don't make the transition from water to air. When the wind wasn't blowing, Johnstone Strait could be so quiet that I could hear raven calls miles away. Yet without my hydrophone, I would have been deaf to the symphony of oceanic sound beneath my feet.

Water itself began to sound different to me. In full flood Blackney Passage roared like an avalanche. Pebble beaches chattered; shrimp feeding in kelp beds crackled like frying bacon. Rock cod issued adorable low, serious grunts. Rain hissed. Herring burbled. Streams gurgled. I soon realized the vast amount of information a whale could pick up just by listening. I remember drifting past a channel opening into a large expanse of rough water and hearing the quiet stillness broken by thundering surf and clattering beach pebbles as I drifted past.

The most disturbing sounds came from passing tugs, freighters, and especially the floating hotels—cruise ships—that ply the Inside Passage all summer long. The whales always fell silent when the throbbing hum of humanity grew overwhelming. Whenever a ship of any size came near, I had to take off the headset to protect my ears. I wondered if a species that had taken millennia to evolve such a delicate and sophisticated sense of hearing could adapt to humanity's sonic onslaught. My notes from the time bear witness to the effect on my own primitive ears: "I have been listening to boats all day; my head is throbbing; the silence of my canvas tent feels good tonight—poor whales."

That summer I became aware for the first time of the fundamental difference between humans and whales. John Lilly had expounded upon the differences that freedom of movement through a third dimension might make to whales' intelligence, perception, and communication. I didn't understand what he was getting at until I began floating above this acoustic abyss, trapped between gravity and the density of water. To the whales my world was where they discarded spent air, staying only long enough to suck in a fresh lungful. I wondered if there was any hope of following a whale's train of thought as it dove into a world completely alien to my senses. Maybe enough sensory crossover exists to allow for some sort of interspecies communication—someday. But that first summer was such an onslaught of newness that I felt I was getting only the briefest glimpse of the whales' complex world.

Around the campfire each night, there were stories about whales, and one evening Michael Berry of Alert Bay joined us with an extraordinary tale, almost a fairy tale. Michael was a young biologist who had settled in Alert Bay to start his own biological consulting company, but on the way up from the south, he had engine troubles and found himself marooned at Paul Spong's. Taking a break from working on his boat, he and his wife, Maureen, a schoolteacher, went out whale watching for the afternoon with a visiting photographer, Peter Thomas. They left behind a large male German shepherd named Phoenix. Phoenix was a goofy dog, with very little sense but great loyalty toward his master. As they pulled away from Spong's, Michael's last words were "Phoenix, stay."

But Phoenix disobeyed, and when Michael and Maureen returned, their dog was gone. "We had to go looking for him," Michael told us. "He was too dumb to survive out on some island for long." So he headed out in Paul's old inflatable and checked every point of land from Johnstone Strait to Blackfish Sound, imagining the dog had entered the water to follow him and been swept away by the enormous tides. By eleven o'clock that night, Michael had given up. It was pitch-black, and hours of calling as he cruised every island had not produced so much as a whimper. Phoenix must have drowned, and Michael felt terrible: the dog's suffering had been his fault.

"I was sitting on a log down by the water crying to myself, when I heard the whales blow," Michael said quietly, "and I thought to them, Don't hurt my old dog; he's too stupid to know any better." The whale blows came closer until they were right beyond the beach. Michael could see the whales lighting up the water's phosphorescence as they passed, and then they were gone. "That's when I heard a soft splashing noise," Michael told us. "It was my dog." I glanced at Maureen, a no-nonsense woman in her early thirties, and her head was nodding. "Phoenix was throwing up salt water and could barely drag his wet body out of the water. It was days before he was right again." Then Michael's voice became defensive: "I don't care what people say. That's what happened. Those whales saved my dog. That's a fact."

Every once in a while, the humans of Hanson Island made their own acoustic offering to the orcas. Paul Winter, the jazz musician and leader of the Paul Winter Consort, had traveled to Paul Spong's that summer to record whale sounds and participate in the Japanese documentary film. (Spong had become quite famous in Japan for his efforts to stop whaling.) The year before, Winter had released his pioneering album *Common Ground,* a hauntingly beautiful work that featured the consort playing compositions along with the recorded calls of eagles, wolves, and humpback whales.

One morning Winter and Mickey Houlihan, the sound engineer we'd met in Alert Bay, asked if they could tag along with me in the Zodiac. Their own whale project was going well, they told me (Winter's next release, *Callings,* featured the sonic contributions of A5 pod), but they needed a break from the hubbub of the film crew.

Unlike other visiting musicians, Winter actually wanted to play to the whales, not just be filmed doing so. My overloaded little Zodiac barely made it up on a plane, but after some quick zigs and zags, we broke free of the water's suction and enjoyed the delicious salt and cedar wind of the strait in our hair.

The whales were nowhere to be found that morning, so we searched for interesting echoes instead. I'd never been echo hunting before, but Mickey proved to be an old hand. As we skimmed down the strait, he asked to stop off Robson Bight, a salmon estuary at the mouth of eastern Vancouver Island's last pristine river, the Tsitika. In later years the bay would become protected as an ecological reserve, but what caught Mickey's eye that day was the glint of a sheer cliff rising up several hundred feet. What an echo maker!

Paul Winter, a serious, gracious man, was quite protective of his saxophone. He tied the instrument to his waist with a twist of rope, then sat on the bow of the inflatable and began playing to the bay. His sweet notes floated over the water and ricocheted off the cliff, creating a rich melody of notes falling back on themselves. As we drifted to the music, we heard the faint blows of orcas to the south. A5 pod had arrived.

"Let's try something," said Mickey. He duct-taped a steel pipe to the edge of the Zodiac; the other end of the pipe ran into the water. Paul laid his sax against it and played. My headphones picked up the thin notes of the instrument as his music carried straight down the pipe and into the water.

Top Notch, the enormous son of Eve, swung wide from the pod and approached the boat. Paul attempted to imitate the calls of his family, but the whale seemed wholly unimpressed. Mickey suggested that Paul show the whale what sounds this human was capable of.

Paul thought for a moment, then began piping down a sweet melody from Johann Sebastian Bach. Top Notch stopped dead in the water. As Paul played against the pipe, the 8,000-pound whale gently sculled closer to the boat. He floated peacefully as Paul played. I held my breath. I don't know what the whale was thinking, but he did appear to be listening. It was a rare moment of contact, a peaceful act shared by whale and humans alike. When the song was over, Top Notch let loose a long sweeping call, exhaled, and vanished without a trace.

In addition to learning about whales, I was receiving basic training in a field researcher's most fundamental skill: roughing it. The Inside Passage can be pleasant in late summer, with temperatures in the sixties and seventies, but it's not called the rain coast for nothing. A damp, chilly fog often settled over the island in the early morning, and just about the time it burned off, the westerly wind arrived and blew till dark. Even when it's not raining, there's a perpetual moistness about the place. Most nights I tucked into my sleeping bag with a sweater or coat, or both, and resigned myself to living with damp fabric touching my skin. After suffering in the parched clime of Southern California, I found that I reveled in this relentless drench.

Despite her sun-loving nature, Renée made it cheerily through the whole summer. Near the end of our time there, we were joined by my boyfriend, Jeff, who proved to be an excellent campfire cook and a mechanical whiz with the blasted Suzuki.

Although Jeff was able to keep the outboard up and running, he couldn't perform miracles, which was what we needed when my brand-new Zodiac blew a seam big enough to flatten the boat in minutes. When your Zodiac won't hold air, you've got no boat. I was reminded of Frank Awbrey's rule of redundancy: When it comes to fieldwork equipment, always carry a spare. Since we had no backup boat, we had no choice but to fold our tents and return to California.

The day we loaded the lump of gray fabric that had been my boat onto a passing boat headed for Alert Bay, I felt physically ill. We had to return south—I'd enrolled at Mesa College in San Diego to pick up those missing chemistry, calculus, and biology credits, and Jeff had his graduate degree to complete—but every fiber in my body told me to stay.

As we drove south along the winding island highway, I looked out over Discovery Passage and recalled one of my final encounters with the wild orcas. It was nearing sunset, and the chilly bite of September already hung in the air. I huddled in my sweater and raincoat, listening to two males chase each other in the dark green water. The sun set through a curtain of moisture to the west, painting the sky a pinkish orange. As the heavens turned from fire to darkening blue, the whales stopped and began to mill in formation. Two males lay on their sides, the head of one against the fluke of the other. Slowly they raised their right pectoral fins together and froze. They held their salute for fifteen seconds, then rolled to dive in perfect synchrony. A thrill went up my spine. I'd often wondered whether Corky and Orky's sunrise routines were a by-product of a decade of captivity and show training or whether they sprang from some deeper source.

Driving south that day, I thought about the two whales and knew that I had glimpsed that deeper source. And I knew that I must return.

Chapter 7

B ack in California I saw Orky and Corky with new eyes. Now that I had watched their families roam the wide Canadian straits, the sight of a pair of orcas swimming in a tank only a few body lengths across looked as normal as two people living in a bathroom. I knew where whales belonged, and it wasn't in captivity.

While their families easily roamed 100 nautical miles a day, these whales had been parked for more than a decade. With their exquisite sensitivity to sound, all Orky and Corky could hear was the constant draining and recycling of their water. With their heritage of extraordinary kinship bonds, the only family Orky and Corky had was each other.

As I lowered my hydrophone into their tank, I felt the uncomfortable weight of understanding descend upon me. The smile on Corky's face was only the set of her jaw. In fact, there was no smile. I could barely bring myself to look her in the eye. Molecules of her mother's breath still clung to the frayed wool of my sweater. I had met her own brother, whom Corky would never know.

Orky and Corky probably recognized me as the human who had spent nights with them, but did they know where I'd been and what I'd seen? Thirty tapes of Corky's natal pod sat in my apartment, but I would never play them for her. Years earlier John Lilly had tried a similar experiment with dolphins. When the disembodied sounds of the dolphins' own voices were broadcast back to them in the tank, the captives bolted to the far side of the tank, quivering with fright.

John Ford, a marine mammal researcher at the Vancouver Aquarium, had an even more unsettling experience. When he played calls back to an orca pod, a young male streaked over to Ford's boat and tore the speaker off. It was an amazingly uncharacteristic act of violence for an orca. Ford seriously thought that the whale might kill him. Decades later a film crew at SeaWorld did play a recording of Corky's family back to her. While her Icelandic pen mates ignored the sounds, Corky's whole body began shuddering terribly. If she wasn't "crying," she was doing something painfully similar.

Despite my growing distaste for captivity, I was determined to learn as much as possible from Orky and Corky. As I watched them one day, I began to wonder what it took to communicate a human idea to a whale.

I asked whale trainer Tish Flynn how she taught Orky and Corky new behaviors.

"I'd be happy to show you, Alex, but they already know how to wave, dive, and jump," she said. "If you want to see them trained, you'll have to come up with a new behavior."

I thought for a moment and then suggested a dorsal slap. As I talked, I pictured the wild whales I'd seen slapping their dorsal fins on the surface of Johnstone Strait. In the years of watching Orky and Corky, I'd never seen them do it.

"I haven't seen it either," said Tish. "We'll try it next week."

Then something happened that has made me careful of my thoughts around whales ever since. As Tish walked out of the stadium, Corky rose to the surface and slapped her dorsal fin on the water's surface. After a moment's hesitation, she dove and surfaced to slap her fin again. As Corky continued, she gained momentum and rose higher the next time, sending a satisfying *smack* across the water. I stood in the grandstands watching, mouth agape.

"Tish! Tish, come quick. You've got to see this!"

Tish emerged from the stadium tunnel to see Corky flying around the tank, waves sloshing over the side. With each breath the exuberant whale rolled and smacked her fin on the water.

Had the whale read my mind, or was this just an enormous coincidence? Tish saw my expression of disbelief and smiled.

"That's whales for you," she said. "They can read your mind. We trainers see this kind of stuff all the time."

My last winter in San Diego passed quickly. I paid enough attention in class to pass my exams and spent every other available moment poring over the data I'd compiled on Orky, Corky, and their wild brethren. My research with Orky and Corky made it clear that their sounds weren't paired with precise behaviors. The whales didn't give a certain call before they jumped or swallowed a fish. In fact, they had long "conversations" while floating side by side.

My Canadian fieldwork had revealed that killer whales communicate in a manner that keeps all pod members in touch and traveling in the same direction in the murky green waters of British Columbia, where pod mates a few meters away disappeared in the gloom. Their constant calls appeared to inform the group about what was going on; whales made different sounds when foraging or at play. The long, sweeping *weeeooouuup* seemed to say, "I'm over here and doing fine." The dramatic call used during a change of direction was, surprisingly, the same sound Orky had used to rouse his grieving mate. Whistles usually correlated to play. Pulse trains, which sound like creaking doors, were associated with the pursuit of salmon.

Still, I had no explanation for why the whales produced so many different sounds or why some sounds seemed random and unconnected to any specific behavior. There was a great deal going on that I knew nothing about.

I was convinced that it wasn't the specific call that mattered so much as *how often* each call was made. The common *pituuuu* occurred throughout the day and night, but did it occur more often at certain times than others? Complex patterns can't be recognized through a peephole, though. I needed to keep looking until I could see the big picture.

When the whales were relaxedly circling their tank, they often sent out a long sweeping *weeeooouuup*: "I'm over here and doing fine." When Corky was distressed, *waawaawuuup* dominated their dialogue. When they were excited, their voices often rose straight up like the squeal of a firecracker right before it explodes. When this same call was made in the wild, it could attract pod mates, which led me to wonder whether it signified some general excitement or whether it meant, "Hey, there's a big school of fish over here!"

Sifting through what I knew of the sounds and behaviors of killer whales—changing direction, starting a conversation, attending a birth, the quicksilver shadows of babies at their mother's side, the simultaneous drawing of breath—it seemed that what mattered was synchronism. An orca spent its life acting in concert with its pod mates: breathing together, moving together, vocalizing together, staying together.

As the California winter dragged on, it became more difficult for me to study the captive whales. When Corky became pregnant for a third time, I stepped up my recording sessions, but I couldn't avoid wondering what the captive baby's life would be like. For starters, the tank was too small for three whales. One would have to go. Orcas are incredibly valuable (at the time marine parks were paying up to $200,000 for a killer whale). Marineland would probably have to sell the baby at some point, denying the infant its birthright, a life spent at its mother's side.

Then there was the unsavory prospect of watching another little whale starve to death. Having seen the rotund Johnstone Strait youngsters, I realized just how emaciated Corky's babies had been.

I've never been good at hiding my feelings. In order to keep my feelings about captivity from interfering with my research, I grew increasingly remote from the Marineland staff. They knew what was up; each one of them maintained his or her own willful ignorance about captivity issues. They did their best to make life better for the whales. No one wants to confront the fact that in a bad situation sometimes his or her best isn't good enough. Or that it's just plain wrong.

One morning that spring I parked my truck in a shady spot in the Marineland parking lot and noticed a stream of water pouring over the asphalt. I hurried through the gates and beheld a disaster. Rolls of toilet paper and paper towels were strewn everywhere in soggy clumps. Staff members used brooms and shovels to divert the flow and contain the debris. The water came from the whale tank.

Funny, I thought; I hadn't felt an earthquake the night before. As I entered the whale stadium, I saw that the orcas were swimming in unusually low water.

"She broke the window again," someone told me.

Corky's rostrum bore the scars of her own predawn attack. I could see deep creases in her face as she quietly floated in the far side of the tank, away from the shattered window. She'd chosen the window looking into a supply area where the little stuffed killer whales had been stacked along with the janitorial supplies. Chunks of ¾-inch-thick glass littered the room. Whales, as a rule, do not hit things. With their echolocation, they are endowed with exceptionally sensitive equipment for avoiding collisions. The thin bone layer over their lower jaw's acoustic fat pocket makes it somewhat fragile and easily broken by such a blow. Swimming full-bore into a plate-glass window is a very unorca activity. Was she acting out of rage, boredom, or blind need for a baby? Either way, something was wrong with the picture. I scooped up a piece of glass and tucked it in my pocket, a talisman for the freedom of whales.

The focus of my life was then and still is to understand what whales are saying. The glass in my hand meant "I want to get out." And yet I am ashamed to say I failed to stand by Corky. I left soon after her next baby arrived, stillborn and seven months premature, on April Fool's Day.

Rolling off the Alert Bay ferry with Jeff and Renée in the summer of 1980 felt like coming home. The orca totems were more welcoming than strange; even the clang of men working on their boats sounded familiar. During the previous winter I'd got through school by promising myself an entire year in Canada. I had arranged to sublet a tiny duplex apartment from Helena Symonds, Paul Spong's partner. Helena taught at the Alert Bay elementary school but had taken the year off to have a baby. I planned to spend the summer camping again, but at least I'd have a home base with a roof, a kitchen, and a hot shower come winter. The only drawback was the fact that Helena's next-door neighbor was the traveling dentist, which meant spending some days listening to the whimpers of children and the whine of his high-speed drill.

Jeff, Renée, and I loaded my new Zodiac—acquired under warranty—with recording equipment and an enormous canvas army tent. It didn't take us long to find the Hanson Island cove that Paul Spong had suggested as a field camp site. It had no name on the chart, but local fishermen called it Big Bay. It had a freshwater stream, a safe anchorage for the boat, and a flat camping spot on a point overlooking the strait, which gave us a spectacular view of the whales. We dubbed it Bigg Bay, in honor of Mike.

In midsummer first light reaches Johnstone Strait just after four in the morning. The chilly air, rich in fresh oxygen made the previous night by the forest surrounds, was so delicious, it felt more like drinking than breathing. If the sun didn't wake us, a nearby family of ravens acted as a *grawwwk*-ing alarm clock. As the Coleman stove boiled water for coffee, the three of us scanned the strait for orcas. We rolled our watch caps above our ears and cupped our hands to our heads, scanning to hear the whale blows that carried for miles over calm water.

I loved setting out in the morning, and still do. You never know what the day will hold. Skimming over the water in my new boat, which felt frisky as a filly out of the gate, I'd send pearls of salt water scattering over the surface of the strait.

Some days we'd sit in the company of whales from sunup to sundown; other times we'd hear nothing, see nothing, watch the marine life, and pass the time singing songs ("Dock of the Bay" was our

Minke whale

favorite). Dall's porpoises, chunky 400-pound dynamos, loved bow-riding, surfing back and forth on a boat's bow wave, trying to bump one another off the wave. Since the bow wave on a Zodiac is halfway back from the bow, we took turns standing up in the bow, holding the rope to watch them, and getting completely soaked. Minke whales, a diminutive member of the "great whale" family, also caught our attention. A minke is no longer than an orca but has baleen instead of teeth. Minkes often surged up through schools of herring with their mouths agape, water and fish cascading down their pleated throats. Often the whales took a whole school of herring, leaving a hungry flock of seagulls pecking irritably at one another.

Back at camp we relaxed under the gaze of a juvenile bald eagle whose mother's nest sat in a nearby fir tree snag. Like us, the youngster was still learning the ways of the rain-forest coast. One morning the young bird spotted a magnificent blue heron floating on a bed of kelp. The eagle, thinking this a pretty good perch, attempted to land on the kelp stipe. Eagles aren't made like herons, though; they're heavier, and their feet are designed to grab, not spread their weight over a large area. Again and again the eagle alighted and sank to his breast, flapping wildly to escape drowning. After trying all morning, he finally accepted the limits of his species and rejoined his mother on her solid wood perch.

It was hard to guess in those early years where the whales would be on any given day. The pod spreads across whatever body of water it occupies, females and young usually close to shore, males farther out in the middle. Foraging whales move forward, then swirl back and forth on the surface at high speed. When the males turn, their fins keel over like a sailboat broadside to the wind. Gulls often accompany feeding orcas, careening about competing for bits. On rare occasions a whale will surface with a silver and pink half-eaten salmon in her jaws.

In the early days of my research, I looked to the male orcas for an indication of where the whales were headed; they appeared the most purposeful in their movements, while the females and young-sters lagged behind to mill over good fishing spots. It soon became apparent, however, that while the males were foraging over a larger area, swinging wide on exploratory fish-finding missions, the eldest females were setting the course.

Not surprisingly the females duplicated the movements of the commercial fishing fleet: both found the fishing best close to shore. The fishermen usually set their seine nets at specific beach sites rather than out in open water, even if it meant going shoulder-to-shoulder with other boats. Their nets told the tale: those set just off-shore came up writhing with silver fish, while the deeper sets came up nearly empty. For some reason—we still don't know why—the male orcas kept to the less optimal deep water, leaving the best fishing holes to the females and babies.

Day by day the whales I'd painstakingly tried to identify the previous summer became familiar. Saddle and her children, the playful daughter Sharky and the young son known as A15, seemed to be thriving. Clearly Saddle was finding enough to eat, despite the possibility that she was still nursing two babies. Corky normally required 145 pounds of fish a day. During late pregnancy she ate up to 170 pounds a day. (That was a different species of fish, bonita, in warmer water, with less physical output, so these numbers are only a rough estimate of Saddle's consumption levels.) Figuring an average salmon weight at about 5 pounds, I estimated that Saddle would have to catch thirty-five to forty of the small pink or sockeye salmon a day. While Sharky was probably eating the abundant pinks as well, I suspected that she was taking a sip or two off Mom now and then. We're not sure how long orcas nurse, but researchers believe that young sperm whales and pilot whales may nurse for as long as ten years. Despite this high caloric demand, Saddle still had time to chase and romp with her children at the surface.

Saddle demonstrated a surprising lack of fear of my boat, often letting her little ones play with me. This struck me as curious given Saddle's history. Eleven years earlier she had been captured by fishermen in the same December gale as Stripe and her daughter Corky. In fact, Saddle had actually given birth in the terrifying clamor of nets and boats. The pod had likely been seeking sheltered water for the impending birth when it blundered into the trap. Saddle's five-year-old was taken, but the mother and her newborn were spared. Before she was released, however, Saddle had been trained to do tricks in the pen at Pender Harbour. It was hard to imagine that this wild whale could trust me near her last two surviving babies.

Eve, the forty-three-year-old matriarch of the A5 pod, continued to be wary of boats. She kept her distance from our Zodiac, often foraging far ahead of her sons Top Notch and Foster. This may have been due to the older whale's lesser tolerance for the hubbub of the younger members of the pod. Eve was in senescence. She hadn't had a baby in nine years, nor would she ever again. Her aloofness was understandable. She had grown up around humans buzzing her with lethal prop blades and shooting with murderous intent. Perhaps the most tragic aspect about Eve's A5 pod was the simple fact that there were no adolescents. All the whales born between 1960 and 1970, almost an entire generation, had been taken into captivity.

Given this history, it's remarkable that the older whales approached any boats at all. When Mike Bigg and Graeme Ellis began photographing the orcas in the early 1970s, the whales were difficult to approach. But by the end of the decade, when humans were bobbing about in all manner of craft, the whales had learned that the boats no longer meant them harm.

Watching the closeness of these families, the way they always seemed to be in touch with one another physically or acoustically, made me realize how scattered my own family was. The orcas' acceptance of pod mates made me homesick for the uncompromised sibling bonds of my youth. The acceptance, approval, and peace I saw within the whale clans was exactly what had lured me to study animals in the first place—the simple knowledge of where they belonged and what role they were to play in life. The synchronized breathing among family members signified a level of symbiosis greater than any I had experienced. As they passed beneath my boat, I watched them touch one another constantly. Their pectoral fins grazed lightly along the sides and fins of kin. Diving whales rolled toward one another, bringing their entire bodies in contact. These gentle touches spanned all ages and members. I could detect no outcasts in this society.

Whale watching is now a part of the economy around Alert Bay, but in 1980 the idea would have sounded absurd. Each one of the researchers and photographers working with the whales around Johnstone Strait had sacrificed careers, relationships, money, time, and the luxuries of civilization to be there. Although we all wanted the same thing—time with the whales—there were enough pods to go around, and the conditions we few humans endured were too rough to do anything but band together and look out for one another. Paul Spong and his volunteers were around, of course, but there were also photographers like Bob Talbot. Nowadays Bob's work can be found in framed posters around the world, but back then he worked with a few friends on a shoestring budget, camping out on Vancouver

Island's Blinkhorn Peninsula and roaming the straits in a leaky inflatable. A Victoria, British Columbia, film company called Aqua Cine operated two camps, one near Robson Bight and another across the strait in Boat Bay on West Cracroft Island, from which they filmed orcas with special underwater equipment. We could always spot Jeff Jacobsen, a graduate student from Northern California, from a mile away. He had a frightening habit of standing on the seat of his 13-foot Zodiac holding on to nothing and steering by shifting his balance. Jeff studied the social groupings of whales, and we always worried that he'd fall overboard and drown as he watched his boat motor away without him. The only whale-watching industry to speak of consisted of the *Gikumi,* an old coastal freighter run by Jim Borrowman and Bill MacKay, a couple of local guys who lived in Telegraph Cove, a sawmill settlement built on stilts just south of Port McNeill. The *Gikumi* was used mainly for hauling lumber, but Jim and Bill chartered her out to divers in winter and did a couple of whale-watching trips in summer.

We all lived within 20 miles of one another, and some nights we'd visit one another's campfires to drop off groceries, share dinner, and swap whale tales. Our most precious commodity was enthusiasm. Without it we'd have given up from the physical exertion of living and working in the Canadian wilderness.

The big talk that summer was about the latest fad rippling through the pods. Like Orky and Corky, wild whales enjoyed creating and learning new behaviors. Each year certain behaviors get started in one pod, move through the entire northern resident community, then disappear by the next summer. In 1980 it was headstands: the orcas treaded water vertically while waving their tails in the air. Some whales quickly became experts, rising straight up from the depths with their flukes aloft. Others wobbled and fell over on playmates.

It wasn't all fun and games. On cold, wet, wind-whipped, and whale-empty days, it could get mighty depressing on the rain coast of British Columbia. We looked out for one another and picked up our neighbors when the blues hit, reminding them that they weren't crazy for being out there. Bob Talbot once told me about dragging himself up the beach after a day of engine breakdown, camera failure, too much wind, and too few whales. "I sat down at the old wooden table we've got there"—he'd found an abandoned cabin to live in—"got myself a cup of coffee, and wondered if I was wasting my life chasing these whales. I got to looking at the tabletop, and I saw a little inscription left by the former resident. You know what it said? 'I HATE KILLER WHALES.'

"I laughed so hard," Bob said, "I nearly fell off my stool."

The commercial fishing fleet tolerated us with good humor. Renée and I operated a side business baking and trading campfire-cooked wild salal berry pie for fresh salmon, which did wonders to supplement the bland staples we imported from Alert Bay. Despite the plenitude of fish all around us, Renée, Jeff, and I remained hapless fishermen. On some days so many sockeye jumped around us that we'd hold a dip net out as we cruised for whales, hoping one would jump in and save us from another night of peanut butter and granola bars. None ever did.

One hungry evening Renée and I, determined to catch our own dinner, motored out to the tide rips of Weyton Pass, where we'd heard the fish were running fat and thick. All around us sport boats packed with seasoned fishermen landed salmon after salmon, some big 20-pounders that brought cheers from the decks. Renée and I dropped in our freshwater lures and waited for a bite. And waited. After a while we changed lures. We got nothing. Not a nibble. The other fishermen gave us their scrutiny and their condescending smiles, two women getting utterly skunked amid this abundance.

Finally my rod bent double. Fish on! I leaped up, ready to fight the mighty Pacific salmon. I realized almost immediately that I had snagged a ferocious, heart-pounding—strand of kelp. Fishermen on the other boats, drawn by my sudden action, nudged their buddies to check out the battle. I knew if I reeled in the kelp, I'd never live it down. I fought my prey valiantly, refusing to be humiliated by my ridiculous catch. After an appropriately long battle, I guided the lunker to the far side of the boat, where its exit from the water could be shielded by our bodies. Renée, playing along, made a believable netting motion and brought the fish aboard. I proceeded to club the life out of a 6-inch bulb of bull kelp. Without looking up, Renée and I sped off into the sunset, stomachs empty but pride intact.

After Renée returned to San Diego, Jeff and I moved camp to the mouth of the Tsitika River. (Jeff was keen to scale Mount Robson, which loomed above the river mouth.) After we'd set up our canvas tent at the edge of the virgin forest, I noted that the tide book called for one of the biggest tides of the year. This didn't alarm me, as our tent was in the grass, not on the beach, but to be safe, I set the alarm to ring half an hour before high tide.

The alarm never rang. In the middle of the night, I awoke to a rippling sensation. I sat up and saw the floor all around me quiver.

"Jeff," I said. "Wake up but don't move."

"What?" He stirred and—too late. As he put his weight on the canvas drop cloth that functioned as our floor, salt water flooded in.

Jeff and I pulled on our coats and boots and waded outside. Rain pounded our tent, and cold water seemed to be everywhere. Our camping spot sat shin-deep in brine. I couldn't see, but I could hear. *"Koooof, kooof, kooof."*

"Jeff!" I said. "The whales are in the meadow."

We couldn't see them, but after a summer with whales, we could tell how close those blows were. We stood drenched in the darkness, listening to the orcas circle low-lying shrubs and rub along the estuary grasses. I wondered if they explored the edges of the terrestrial world on every extreme tide. This was a dangerous place for the whales—linger too long and a falling tide could beach them and they would suffocate under the crushing weight of their own bodies. And yet still they were compelled to swim in on the high tide, explore this place that became available to them only a few times a year.

Fortunately the great flood occurred before my mother arrived.

Mom took time out from her busy life of bringing a positive future to mankind to surprise me with a visit to our remote campsite. In the middle of August, Mom, along with my younger brother Lloyd and his wife, Laura, met me in Alert Bay. My brother Wade and his partner, Gale, along with their four-year-old daughter, Jennifer, came along the next day, and I ferried them all down to Bigg Bay. The whole family was game for adventure. The only one who expressed any reservations about the accommodations was Jenny, who announced that she was *not* going to stay in my humble outpost. "Where," she asked, looking around incredulously, "are the buildings?"

Sitting in the tent, listening to Wade play guitar, my mother sipping hot coffee and rum, Jenny trampling Lloyd, Laura studying an eagle feather, I was reminded how strong the sense of tribe was within me. A deep sigh let the tensions of the summer drain away from me. We humans can build nests, burrow in caves, create heat, but as I'd seen with the whales, we crave no comfort greater than that of having our own family drawn in close.

My mother showed an entirely new side. An elegant, petite woman raised in New York City, she took to Bigg Bay immediately, peeing in the woods and scrubbing the dirty dishes with beach pebbles. Early one morning we sat listening to whales breathing in the fog. "You're a real pioneer, sweetheart," she said, giving my hand a squeeze. Mom always had a soft heart for pioneers.

"Not really, Mom," I said. "A lot of people found their way out here before me."

"That may be, but you found your way here from Milton in such a few short years. You know, I was afraid you'd thrown your life away."

I was stunned. "Mom, the only reason I'm here is because you had faith in me. I had no idea you were worried."

"I was, darling. I really was."

I made a mental note that I would remember to trust my own children the way she had trusted me.

While living in Los Angeles I'd learned firsthand how film crews can hijack your day-to-day life. They'd take over entire blocks, dispensing platoons of arrogant production assistants strutting like roosters, telling you where you could and couldn't go. I was irked to find that I couldn't escape them even in the northern wilderness. While visiting Paul Spong's place one day, a filmmaker asked Renée and me to act as token scientists in his documentary. What he wanted, it turned out, was to film our reaction as he read a poem—and I use the term loosely—attacking scientists as cold-blooded killers. I kept my mouth shut and my face blank and simply walked away.

I was doubly wary, therefore, when the Aqua Cine crew bumped their inflatable against mine and invited Jeff and me down to their beach to see some live underwater video. Michael O'Neill, an English teacher who had formed Aqua Cine with a photographer partner, told us he wanted to film a "scientist" reacting to the rare sight of whales underwater.

"It's really quite amazing what we can see with the cameras," he said. "I think you'll be interested."

"No thanks," I said. Then he made me an offer I couldn't refuse.

"How about I throw in ten gallons of gas?"

"Make it fifteen."

"You're on."

The next day Jeff and I met Michael O'Neill on West Cracroft Island. He shuttled us across the strait to his crew's encampment on a tiny beach near Robson Bight. Earlier in the summer Renée and I had recorded some mysterious goings-on at the same spot. Near the shore we could see killer whales exhaling violent explosions of air, and on the hydrophone we picked up what sounded like pebbles being raked.

As O'Neill set up his equipment, Jeff and I waited impatiently for his partner, a photographer named Robin Morton, who was apparently underwater inspecting the remote-controlled cameras. Frankly I was annoyed. I had a stack of blank tapes waiting to be filled with whale calls, and here I'd beached my boat on one of the last good-weather days of summer—and for what? To be an extra in a nature documentary.

And then my life changed.

From the icy water emerged a tall man in an orange wet suit. Robin Morton walked up the beach, set down his camera, and peeled off his neoprene skin. For a moment he stood stark naked: tall, slender, with a Kwakwaka'wakw killer whale tattooed on his right shoulder. I sneaked a peek; he caught me and gave me a big, broad smile and pulled on some sweatpants. I fell in love.

"Welcome to my underwater studio," he said. "I'm Robin."

"Quite the setup you have here," I said, trying my best to sound professional.

"I hope the whales show up today," he said, "because I think this is going to interest you. Did you know this is a whale massage parlor? Here, have a look."

Robin and Michael led Jeff and me through the thick salal to a television screen hooked up to a joystick.

"Robin noticed these furrows in the beach last year," said Michael.

"The rest of the rocks are covered with algae," explained Robin. "But in the furrows they're clean—furrows big enough for me to lie in. So I figured something was plowing the beach. The whales wouldn't hang around when I got in the water with them, so I built this remote-controlled camera last winter. Now I just sit here and wait for the whales to come to me."

Since Robin and Michael didn't have a hydrophone, Jeff and I gave ours to Robin, who propped it in the water near where he planned to film. After several hours we spotted several whale blows coming our way. As they approached, we retreated to the bushes, clearing the beach of all signs of humanity. As I stared at the black-and-white image of the underwater beach, a yellowtail bass flicked by. My heart skipped a beat.

Without warning an enormous shape rose out of the gloom. Like the space shuttle coming in for a landing, the whale swooped down and hit the pebbles with an audible *cuuuushhh*. Robin tilted the joystick and followed Top Notch's unmistakable fin. Cupping my face against the daylight, I saw the orca put the tip of his nose in the stones and twist.

With a view this good, it didn't take us long to figure out what was going on. Captive dolphins and whales love to be rubbed in their hard-to-reach areas where their constantly sloughing skin builds up. In the wild the pebbles of Robson Bight served the same function. When whales itch, this is how they scratch.

In the science of evolution, there's a theory known as punctuated equilibrium, which holds that species evolution happens in fits and starts with long periods of inactivity—equilibrium—punctuated by sudden change. I've found that my own life has evolved along similar lines. I'll slip into a rhythm that hums along for months or years at a time, then something will happen that forever alters the course of my life. Meeting Robin was one such defining moment. A few days later came a second.

Jeff and I had been following Saddle, Eve, Top Notch, and the others as they swam north into Queen Charlotte Strait with their distant H pod relatives. The whales confused and frustrated me that day. There was no consistent direction to their movements; the two pods spread themselves over 5 miles, socializing in private groups. I couldn't tell where they were going, and my recordings were too scattered and short to be of much use.

The sky had delivered a perfect late-summer day, but as evening approached, a fog bank rolled in from the west. I made a mental note to return south when Penfold Islet, in the Queen Charlotte Strait, disappeared into the white. But it's difficult to tell how far away a fog bank is; it's got no hard edges, and there's no size reference. It's just a soft white presence. Absorbed in my notebook, I looked up to find the wetness enveloping me. Jeff and I could have been in a glass of milk. The water, smooth as honey, had no wave pattern to read. The sun had disappeared entirely. And Jeff and I had no compass.

"Oh, Jesus," I said. "What do we do now?"

"Which way is our camp?" said Jeff.

Panic crept up my body. I knew exactly where we were: that was the problem. We were in the wide Queen Charlotte Strait, north of Hanson Island. Which meant that if we struck north, south, or east, we'd eventually find coastline. If we guessed wrong and headed west, I thought we wouldn't sight land until Japan.

Over the hydrophone I picked up the throb of a giant cruise ship. The suddenness of the sound meant that the ship had rounded the corner out of Blackney Passage, a major shipping lane, and was headed our way. We knew it came from the south. But where was south? The nondirectional hydrophone couldn't tell us. Our ears might eventually pick up the sound of the ship, but the fog was so thick, we might not hear it until just before its props churned us under. I imagined 100 feet of steel bow splitting the fog right in front of my face. I did a quick calculation of our gas supply, the gathering darkness, and our odds of picking the right direction. The answer did not ease my fear.

Then, out of nowhere, a smooth black fin appeared. And another. Here was the big male Top Notch, the familiar mother Saddle, the shy matriarch Eve, their fins spread like a hand of cards beside our boat. Stripe, Corky's mother, peeked at me just above the water's surface. Confidence washed the fear clean out of me. The presence of the whales wrapped me like a warm embrace. Instinctively I knew what to do. We would stay with the whales. Looking back, I don't understand the source of this confidence, as the whales had been heading out to sea all day.

I thought it would be tough to keep up with them, erratic as

Top Notch and family

they'd been all day. If they strayed even 10 yards from the Zodiac, we'd lose them in the fog. But I never worried. I trusted them with our lives.

For the next twenty minutes, Jeff and I followed the pod. They stayed tightly clumped around the boat, swimming shallow so we could see them underwater. Sharky and Saddle swam so close that I shifted the engine into neutral several times so the propeller wouldn't cut them. The entire family surfaced beside us in a fan of dorsal fins.

In time a tiny islet revealed itself as a faint pattern in the fog. I couldn't be sure it was real; once you lose your focus in heavy fog, your eyes can play tricks on you. As its outline took on substance, though, the whales disappeared. Jeff and I sped full-throttle toward the ancient cedars and rocky coastline. Just before we reached land, the fog bank cleared and we burst into a glorious rosy sunset. I recognized the island. The whales had taken us south toward Blackney Pass—they had taken us back home. I idled the boat at the edge of the fog bank and waited. I knew they were only a couple of hundred feet behind me. But they had vanished.

For more than twenty years, I have fought to keep the mythology of the orcas out of my work. When others would regale a group with stories of an orca's sense of humor or music appreciation, I'd hold my tongue. I was there to record their activity. I didn't have enough data to conclude that a killer whale told jokes or enjoyed music, and I resisted anthropomorphizing the motives and behavior of wild animals. Yet there are times when I am confronted with profound evidence of something beyond our ability to scientifically quantify. Call them amazing coincidences if you like; for me they keep adding up: the day Corky demonstrated the fin slap I'd visualized while describing it to Tish; the way Orky "held" my hand after three days of mourning. Here again I was confronted with evidence of . . . something. Fact: The whales had been widespread and traveling west all day. Fact: They had been difficult to follow, uncharacteristically wandering in their movements. Fact: They'd just spent the past twenty minutes clustered around my boat—even Eve, the aloof one—moving south as a tight pack. Fact: As soon as land became visible and my fear disappeared, they ceased moving south and turned back west or north. Fact: Nothing I'd ever measured in whale behavior had proved to be random.

Had Jeff and I just been rescued? Was that possible? I'd heard stories of dolphins pushing drowning people to shore—tales going back to the time of Aristotle—but until that day I had discounted them as wishful myths. Science wasn't the neat and tidy experience I had expected. There was more here than mere numbers could represent. I can't say that whales are telepathic—I can barely say the word—but I'm unwilling to ignore what I've seen with my own eyes. Did they somehow sense my terror? I have no explanation for that day's events. I have only gratitude and a deep sense of mystery that continues to grow to this day.

Chapter 8

When the late September rains arrived, I broke camp and moved into my cozy Alert Bay sublet. Jeff went out in the Zodiac for a few days without me. My apartment turned into a blizzard of paper. I wasn't merely anxious to write up the summer's field data. My research had been accepted for presentation at a killer whale conference at the University of Washington in October. The acceptance note had arrived in August, and since then I had been organizing the paper in my head. With the conference a few weeks away, I locked myself in the apartment and turned years of observation into tangible text.

The day before the conference, Jeff and I camped on the floor of a friend's house in Seattle. The next morning I dug out a wrinkled skirt and set out for campus. I was so nervous, I could hardly think. Until now, my scientific aspirations had existed entirely in my head. I'd done fieldwork from Alaska to the Mexican border, had studied under half a dozen renowned scientists, but I still operated without the imprimatur of any official institution. I had no way of knowing if my work made the grade.

I nervously shuffled my papers and stole a glance at the audience. For an instant it seemed like one of those nightmares in which everyone you've ever known crowds into an auditorium to watch you walk onstage in your underwear. Sam Ridgeway sat amid a group of the old San Diego cetacean crowd; Paul Spong stood in the back chatting with John Gale; Mike Bigg perused the conference calendar; Tom Otten and Brad Andrews from Marineland gave me a nod. My mother and sister Woodleigh beamed at me. A dozen other unfamiliar faces looked up at me, their name tags affiliating them with university this and institute that. After four years of research, the next twenty minutes would make or break me.

"The relationship between cetacean sounds and behavior has been a topic of interest, frustration, and confusion," I began. "The traditional approach attempted to correlate the occurrence of a sound with a specific behavior. In this study we looked at the percentage emission rather than the absolute occurrence of sounds . . ."—and away I went.

After analyzing 14,892 captive sounds from Orky and Corky and 12,582 wild sounds from the British Columbia pods, I and my co-authors, John Gale and Renée Prince, had come to the conclusion that orca sound use was highly flexible. Whales didn't match a single sound with a specific behavior. Using histograms (sound use represented as a bar graph of frequencies) and slides of dawn squirting, unison swimming, and other actions, I explained that what mattered wasn't the sound itself but rather the frequency of its use. *Pituuu* predominated when the orcas were most synchronized, as when the entire pod changed direction. *Wee-oo-uuo* was associated with tranquillity, as when the wild whales spread out to forage. It seemed to be a relaxed way of staying in touch.

By the end of the paper, I'd earned a degree of acceptance from the people I most respected. Brad Andrews and Tom Otten offered their congratulations. Sam Ridgeway told me it was the best presentation he'd seen at the conference. (Not true, of course, but I didn't mind basking in his praise.) I stayed with the lingering crowd until the janitor kicked us out, talking whales with scientists who now—finally!—embraced me as a colleague. I saw a dampness in my mother's eyes as we parted. She could cross me off the list of children to worry about.

On the way to my car, a familiar voice caught up to me.

"Terrific presentation, Alex," said Robin Morton. He and

Michael O'Neill had screened their orca footage for the conference earlier that day. "Tough crowd, eh?

"Listen," he said, "a lot of people at our screening were asking us for the names of the whales we shot. You know them a lot better than Michael and me. If you've got the time, why don't you stop by our place in Duncan on the way back up? We could show you some more footage, and maybe you could identify a few whales for us."

My heart leaped. "I'll see if I can fit it in," I told him.

Jeff and I said our good-byes at the conference. From Seattle he was continuing south to complete his degree; I was heading north to continue working in Canada. Although we parted as solid friends, we both knew our relationship had run its course. Jeff's life was in the academic world; mine was on the cold currents of Johnstone Strait. My heart filled with a mixture of separation, sorrow, acceptance, and the tingle of a new life and new love. As I closed the door of my pickup, I began a migration as powerful as the monarch journeys I'd admired as a girl on the playing fields of Connecticut. I had to go north.

Driving home from the conference, I made my way north from Victoria through an ancient forest on the slopes of the Malahat Mountain. There is a great beauty to the eastern coast of Vancouver Island. Jagged cliffs and mists alternate with pastoral landscapes. As I drove deep into thick stands of cedar and fir and looked in wonder at the translucent fingers of sunlight combing the outstretched evergreen arms, I entered a squawking white cloud. A snowstorm of seagulls wheeled and pecked as if auditioning for Alfred Hitchcock. I got out of the truck and discovered a stream beside the road writhing with spawning fish. Chum salmon filled the entire bed, bank to bank, some in water so shallow their backs were dry. In their libidinous death-throes color of striped brassy green, the males slashed at each other with fearsome canine teeth. Others pressed together, trembling, giving life as they lost their own.

The bank lay carpeted with hollow-eyed carcasses, fish with tattered skin and decayed flesh, giving the world one last defiant flop before melting into the gravelly bottom. Around me raged a rowdy bird banquet. Seagulls, ravens, crows, and bald eagles greedily ripped hunks out of dead and still-dying fish. Some waddled lazily on the bank, overfed to the point of stupor. Others dragged whole carcasses deep into the forest, where the salmons' uneaten remains would decompose and provide the nearby cedar trees with 30 percent of the precious nitrogen they require to grow. The bigger the salmon return, the wider the growth ring these trees would have.

I squatted on the damp bank and watched. A glimmer of recognition ran through me. These may have been the same fish that had flashed beneath my boat hundreds of miles to the north. These were the survivors of Top Notch's spectacular pursuits, continuing to contribute to the web of life. The air was thick with a pungent smell, but it occurred to me that the scent, so dense I could almost taste it, wasn't that of death. Salmon are a living artery keeping the entire coastline alive, connecting the Pacific gyre nutrients to the mountainous watersheds; they are the blood flowing through its body. What I sensed that day was the smell of life begetting life.

Robin and his Aqua Cine partner, Michael O'Neill, shared an unfinished house in Duncan, a large town north of Victoria. Michael and his family lived upstairs; Robin inhabited the downstairs space. That night the two of them regaled me with stories of their escapades in underwater filmmaking.

"It's another world down there," Michael told me. "Most people have no idea."

"And when you're filming, whatever can go wrong, will," said Robin. "Your batteries will fail. The whales won't surface in the right spot, and if they do, the boats will be out of position. You'll get water in the housing, bump the camera, catch too much glare, or not have enough light. Everything conspires against you."

We watched their footage of the previous summer's action on the rubbing beach, which had thrilled the researchers at the orca conference. Nothing like it had ever been seen before. I was surprised at how little final footage they'd obtained; just when the show warmed up, it was over. It took weeks and weeks and weeks of filming to get a few precious minutes of footage.

"Even the water's against us," said Michael. Earlier that year, he said, he'd dropped his 16-millimeter camera in the strait. "Fortunately the water was shallow enough for me to reach in and pull it out. But salt water corrodes the metal parts faster than you can believe." If rust formed on its delicate inner workings, the camera would be ruined. Every second counted. With no fresh water nearby to rinse the camera, Michael hit upon a desperate solution. "I stripped it down," he said, "and licked the salt off every last inch of that damned camera!"

Robin and I stayed up half the night working on a case of Kokanee beer, talking about whales, and swapping life stories. One of the stories Robin told me was astonishing, not because it was new but because I'd heard it before, only this time the man's name was Larry Martin and his dog was Karma. Larry was part of the crew of friends Robin and Michael O'Neill had enlisted to help them out on their killer whale filming expedition. Together they had built a tent and sheet-plastic outpost on West Cracroft Island at Boat Bay, and Larry kept the camp provisioned and the equipment running. Karma was a black, medium-sized, female lab/shepherd cross, and she was dedicated to Larry.

Robin explained that the dog had vanished when her owner was out kayaking. Thinking she had swum after him, Larry got back in the boat and paddled up and down the shoreline calling for Karma, but to no avail. When the whales passed their camp late that night, Larry was down on the beach feeling miserable, mourning the loss of his faithful companion. Robin didn't know Michael Berry of Alert Bay, and so when he told me the dog had appeared on the beach soaking wet and trembling to the point of collapse after the whales passed, I was dumbfounded. "I was there," Robin continued. "There's no doubt in my mind, those whales had pushed Karma ashore. Bizarre, eh?"

Robin grew up in Victoria, the high British provincial capital of British Columbia, and started diving as a teenager. He met Michael while working as a news cameraman for Victoria's CHEK-TV, and the two of them formed their company in the mid-1970s. They scraped by on family loans, odd jobs for marine manufacturers, and Robin's salary from CHEK.

I never understood how Robin could dive with the whales. As much as they fascinated me, the idea of hopping in with a pod of orcas completely unnerved me. Robin never gave the danger a second thought. Years later, in an article he wrote for *The Explorers Journal,* a magazine published by the famous Explorers Club, Robin explained what it was like:

It's an extraordinary feeling when you first go over the side. There you are, hanging, in the water. You may be surrounded by whales, but you can't see them and you don't know where they are. They see you initially with sound. They know your form density, and, using their sonar, your exact location. They know the volume of air in your lungs, and they can probably hear your heart, which is one way they could read your emotional state. Then, all of a sudden, from behind, a whale will glide by you, inches away, obviously looking at you. I'm telling you, there is nothing more real. They could easily break you in two. We've often wondered why they don't attack. It's one of the questions we're addressing. We've decided to go on the premise that they are not going to eat us or smack us around.

That first summer Robin and Michael followed the whales to Robson Bight, where Robin captured a rarely seen moment in the life of the mammal we were studying—a salmon kill:

As the bottom loomed up from the depths, I caught a flash of silver erratically ascending towards me. Halting with unbelieving eyes, I gaped as a large salmon writhed vertically past me in the water column. I have viewed salmon underwater only on the rarest of occasions and had never before been approached by these skittish animals. This fish was obviously disoriented and, although it did not display any physical injuries, I felt the whales (which had just exited the bay) were responsible.

When I reached the shore, I was downstream of my intended destination as a result of the heavy tidal current. I had to grope the final leg of my journey along an intertidal rock face, but I made steady headway to the bay and I abruptly came face to face with another salmon. This one, cagier than the last, eyed me nervously from a tidal pool that was intermittently landlocked on its seaward side. With each flood of waves his security was threatened, and as my presence meant impending danger, this very displaced fish rushed against an incoming surge and swept past me.

Alerted by these fish, I entered the bay searching for more. Sure enough, there against the gravel in the shallows of the shore shimmered two salmon. These fidgety fish raced back and forth across the shoreline. Seeing me, they halted abruptly. As my camera hand was engaged in filming this spectacle, my other hand was poised ready to punch one of these delicacies onto the beach, but both fish gained open water and left me floundering in the breakers.

Robin's encounter hinted at the answer to one of the greatest mysteries of a killer whale's life: how does a massive 8-ton whale catch a slippery, quicksilver 20-pound salmon? Scientists theorize that some cetaceans are equipped to stun their prey with sound. Robin's description of the disoriented salmon was the first eyewitness account I'd ever heard of. It reminded me of the time the Marineland dolphins had acoustically "buzzed" me when I'd gone into their tank after my hydrophone. I believe those dolphins were being gentle with me; they didn't try to stun me at full power. Did the whales really use some form of sonar "stunning" to catch dinner? Other researchers have seen mother dolphins disciplining their babies with a quick, powerful buzz. Dolphins also use intense sound to sexually stimulate each other. There seems to be no end to their acoustic talents.

Robin's early encounters with orcas convinced him that jumping in and out of the water in front of a pod, trying to film them, was a flawed way to record their intimate lives. It disturbed the whales and exhausted Robin. Hauling his camera-laden, wet-suited, lead-weighted body in and out of Johnstone Strait all day left him completely wiped. A remote-controlled camera, he thought, would leave the whales undisturbed and capture their most private behaviors. But first he'd have to match technology to the idea.

Robin shopped his notion among Vancouver's world-class submersible manufacturers. Jim McFarlane, president and founder of International Submarine Engineering (ISE), understood Robin's passion for invention because he shared it. McFarlane gave him permission to rummage through the company's parts department and take what he needed. Living out of the back of his Jeep, Robin spent a month prowling through heaps of gears, platforms, hydraulics, wires, and hoses until he'd fashioned an odd-looking but serviceable remote-controlled platform on which he could mount a camera.

Jim McFarlane was bemused by Robin's invention. "How does it feel to own a Cadillac?" he asked, as he examined the contraption. "What do you mean?" Robin said. "Well," McFarlane explained, "that's what it's worth, in parts value." The two men shook hands over a shared vision of exploring the mysteries of the undersea.

Robin mounted a video camera and a 16-millimeter film camera side by side on the platform. Both could pan and tilt via remote-controlled hydraulics. The video fed a live picture to the surface; when whales appeared, Robin could trigger the film camera from the surface. (Given the prohibitive cost of film stock, he wanted to save every frame for whale action.)

Soon after Robin perfected his setup, he and Michael returned to Robson Bight to solve the mystery of the rubbing rocks:

My day usually started with a morning dive on the remote system to mount the cine-camera and inspect the unit for obstructions, (heaven forbid) leaks and other abnormalities. On the first inspection dive, my attention was directed to an area adjacent to the camera platform because of its striking lack of vegetation. Surveying this 10-by-25 meter clearing, I discovered that the flat gravel bottom was entirely scarred by long furrows and circular concavities.

Resting belly down alongside one of the deeper troughs (my gloved hand just fitted it), I began to see how the puzzle fit together. The whales were responsible for this! They had kept this bed of gravel clear of vegetation by such vigorous and regular rubbing on the seafloor that the kelp could not establish holdfasts. The extent and regularity of this activity was evidenced by the condition of the disturbed gravel.

It was a full day later when the whales returned. Peering out from the blind with one eye watching the underwater scene in the video monitor and the other on the approaching whales, I could barely contain myself. Were they chasing fish? Would they notice the metallic lump in the kelp? I waited. Then, directly behind the remote, a whale surfaced, blew, dove and headed over the underwater platform. There he was! I hit the roll film switch on the control panel and stared. So, that's how they did it! This "fim" (immature male or female—sex unknown) rolled onto its side as it descended to the gravel. Then, swimming laterally on the bottom, it scraped its body as it powered along.

This was what Robin and Michael wanted Jeff and me, "the scientists," to see that day. They had glimpsed the hidden life of killer whales.

After a few days with Robin and Michael, I continued north to Alert Bay. The harsh weather kept me grounded most of the winter—no whale encounters for me. Robin and I continued our courtship by phone, executing a cautious investigation of each other's lives and desires. I wasn't the wittiest or most beautiful woman in Robin's life. But we both wanted the same thing—to be with whales, watching and listening twenty-four hours a day. Robin was the eyes, I was the ears. Mike Bigg encouraged our alliance. After weeks of phone conversations, Robin and I made a plan to drive to San Diego together to collect my stuff. We talked and laughed all the way down the coast. I fell in love with his Canadian accent and the way he said, "You sure got a lotta jam, woman!"

We stopped by Marineland and spent a night together with Orky and Corky. With his filmmaker's eye, Robin spotted details I'd never noticed, like the way Corky always surfaced in exactly the same spot while doing laps and the fact that Orky's eyes were a slightly different shade of brown than Corky's.

In the early blush of dawn beside the Marineland whale tank, Robin asked me to marry him. I paused and thought that I'd better savor this. I'd always wanted children but hadn't been so keen on the bitter trace of ownership that came with the idea of marriage. I trusted Robin, though.

"Yes," I told him. The whales took no notice of us.

Chapter 9

R obin and I said our vows in a forested glen near his house in Duncan. Both of us managed to calm the fears of our mothers—his, that her son was marrying a Yank; mine, that her daughter was marrying a man whose basement home wasn't even carpeted. My sister Suzanne covered Robin's cement floor with salvaged carpet, and my mother filled the barren corners of the house with daffodils. Friends and family arrived on the blustery spring day to see my brother Wade give me away. The ceremony went off without a hitch once we convinced Robin's neighbor to shut off his chain saw.

We drove and took ferries north to the remote Queen Charlotte Islands for our honeymoon. When we returned, we went shopping for a boat. Our plan was to find a live-aboard vessel to use as an orca research base camp. I had a 30-foot motor sailboat in mind, but Robin had bigger plans.

"If we get a small boat, we're going to have to get off her to work," he reasoned. "So we might as well get a big boat we can earn our living with."

After prowling the docks of Vancouver, he fell in love with a big-shouldered, sturdy old girl named *Blue Fjord*.

At 65 feet her shadow could have swallowed two of the sailboats I'd had in mind. She was big and beamy, with a wide fantail stern. The *Blue Fjord* rode the wind and waves like a duck, parting the water neatly around her. The current owner ran the *Fjord* as a salmon charter. He was selling the boat (we realized later) because he saw a major overhaul staring him in the face. *Blue Fjord* had been built in 1939 for the Canadian military to rescue pilots shot down over the Pacific. She was built strong as a bull out of cedar decking and 4-inch fir beams, and it took a lot of sea to push her around. Forty years after her christening, though, she bled a thin rust stain out of every fastening in her body.

"That's how you know there's still some metal holding her together," her owner assured us, as Robin and I eyed the coppery stains striping her side. "It's a good sign!" In all his life, it's doubtful the man had met two lubbers more gullible than the pair who stood before him that day.

By selling Robin's half of the Duncan house and borrowing some cash from my family, we scraped up enough money to take over the *Fjord*. We were about to discover the first law of boat ownership: that's not the end of your boat payments, it's only the beginning.

The upper deck leaked. The transmission, which hadn't been serviced in ten years, marinated in a corrosive orange soup. The generator didn't generate. The freezer never froze. The batteries were shot. Once we got the generator working, we discovered that its muffler had been mounted above the waterline, which turned it into a dandy amplifier. When we powered up, half the province knew it. While it might be true that the rust rivulets indicated that bolts still held the ship together, they did nothing to inspire confidence in her seaworthiness. After weeks of scrubbing, we finally went into town and bought ten buckets of rust-colored marine paint. Problem solved.

Despite the *Blue Fjord*'s mechanical and aesthetic handicaps, we rarely had a problem lining up charters. The previous owner's client list came with the boat, and we soon found ourselves with a summer's worth of work. We guided vacationing businessmen up to the salmon-rich waters on the central coast north of Vancouver Island, ferried research scientists up to the Queen Charlotte Islands, acted as a viewing platform for yachting fans at the Swiftsure race, and assisted with the sea trials of Jim McFarlane's submarines. Much as I've lived my life as an equal of my male colleagues, I made a deal with Robin: I'd attend to the domestic side of the business if he'd manage all things mechanical. This rescued me from the diesel hell known as the engine room, but it did not save me from the nightmare of the oil stove.

Designed sometime in the late Mesozoic era, the *Fjord*'s only source of cooking heat was a dial-less stove controlled only by a cryptic brass knob that metered its flow of fuel. The stove had a mind of its own. Every third day it spewed out soot balls that left black smears wherever they fell. I'd have to lift the top and vacuum it out with a shop vac, leaving me looking like a London chimney sweep. Since heat came from the stove's side, not the bottom, I had to relearn cooking as if it were a foreign language. During our first charter, a load of Vancouver businessmen infected with salmon fever and tanked on Labatt, I baked a beautifully browned cake and put it aside for dessert. As our guests finished their stew, I tipped the cake neatly onto a plate for frosting. Instead of falling cleanly off the pan, it oozed. Raw batter globbed to the bottom. Furious, I grabbed for the pastry, intending to launch it straight into Hakai Pass. Before I could reach it, Robin snatched it away, lopped off the bottom with a knife, and covered it with canned whipped cream. For the rest of the trip, every night's dessert came disguised under a full head of white topping.

The charter business quickly lost its romance. Some guests were enjoyable, but too many others needed baby-sitting. They drank too much, fell out of their bunks, and got surly if the salmon didn't show. To free up staterooms for the paying customers, Robin and I slept on a wooden platform suspended by chains in the wheelhouse.

I made a tactical error early on, fixing the toilet the first time it got clogged and thereby becoming the de facto plumbing expert. The endless hours of cooking, cleaning, bed making, and guest hosting were made more difficult by the fact that I had become pregnant soon after Robin and I were married. The sleepiness was the worst; some days I'd conk out in the middle of a chore and wake up an hour later with the plunger still in my hand.

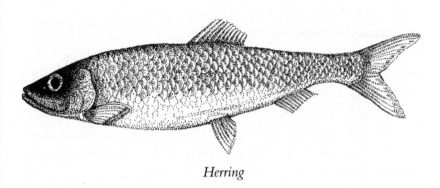

Herring

Besides those days of frustration, there were moments of unexpected bliss. It was exhilarating to navigate the Inside Passage in the *Blue Fjord* when she was up and running, her bow cutting a frothing sea. With more boat beneath the waterline than above, she was enormously stable and solid in every sea. Together in the *Fjord* Robin and I braved spectacular weather that we would never have ventured out in with another boat.

I was growing accustomed to our floating home. There was no "going home." Home was wherever we happened to be. Living in the wilderness made fieldwork easier, of course, but there was also a sense of rightness in adopting a nomadic lifestyle in order to study a nomadic creature.

Toward the end of that summer, we motored back to Johnstone Strait, following the tall blows of Eve and her A5 family. They were at home now, and so was I. We had timed our arrival in the strait to meet a crew from the ABC-TV show *The American Sportsman*. Through Robin's contacts in the underwater film world, we'd been hired to set up a base camp and assist with the filming of a show in which they hoped to feature *Jaws* author Peter Benchley swimming with killer whales. The "crew" that came was a small army—more than twenty producers, directors, assistants, cooks, and people whose jobs we never did figure out. For a remote wilderness like Johnstone Strait, it was the equivalent of a full-scale invasion.

Benchley himself was a real trouper. I was seven months pregnant at the time, and he went out of his way to look after me—even though it was my job to look after him. Robin's remote-controlled underwater platform carried ABC's monstrous camera.

Around this time the orcas brought a new fad into the strait: stay away from divers. For some reason the whales began to avoid Robin when he free-dove with them. It was as if a law had been passed, which all whales obeyed. This meant any underwater footage would have to come from Robin's remote platform. The entire ABC crew spent days sitting around a smoky fire on a damp beach waiting for the whales to show. Benchley wrote notes for his next novel, I studied a manual on childbirth, and Robin tried to keep the various electronics working. Benchley's wit kept the atmosphere light; even a joke-impaired dolt like me was able to enjoy his endless stream of quips.

Whales or not, Robin was in absolute heaven. Directing and filming the underwater segments of the show was Stan Waterman, a legend in marine photography. After operating a dive business in the Bahamas in the mid-1950s, Waterman began putting his underwater exploits on film. By the 1960s he was producing TV specials for National Geographic and collaborating on films such as the 1968 shark classic *Blue Water, White Death*. Working alongside Benchley, his friend and neighbor, Waterman shot nearly a decade's worth of *American Sportsman* shows and worked as codirector of underwater photography on the film adaptation of Benchley's novel *The Deep*. Stan brought with him a new, cutting-edge breathing system. Since whales consider bubbles a threatening gesture, Waterman wanted to try this new device designed by the British navy that allowed commandos to dive without producing a trail of telltale bubbles. The diver's exhaled breath passed through a scrubber, which removed the carbon dioxide and returned a small amount of oxygen to the diver's main supply. It was an early rebreathing device. Robin was so thrilled to try it that he waived his salary, taking the rebreather in payment instead. Watching from the boat, I found that I hated seeing Robin and the others slip beneath the surface with no bubble trace. The way they just vanished left me cold.

Peter Benchley had to leave the shoot before we were able to capture the money shot of the famous author cavorting with whales. In television, though, technological magic and sleight of hand often substitute for luck. We ended up putting a skinny production assistant in Benchley's wet suit and shooting him from behind. The illusion worked perfectly—viewers believed they saw the *Jaws* author finning alongside the wild orcas—although anyone who's worn a wet suit three sizes too big in icy water can sympathize with the poor shivering crew member named Larry that we pulled out of the water that day.

As autumn came on, I experienced my first real coastal storms. The brief westerly gales of summer had been mere puffs compared to the howling fury of a southeaster. One night we took shelter in Growler Cove, well ahead of a storm forecast to reach hurricane force. We anchored on the side that looked most protected, but my confidence faltered as I watched the salmon fleet anchor on the opposite side.

The pitch of the boat shifted, waking me just after midnight. I shook Robin awake. Lifting his head from our wheelhouse bunk, he could see the fleet's anchor lights.

"Look," he said proudly, "all the other boats are coming in here where—oh, shit bags!" and leaped out of the warmth. They weren't moving to us; we were moving to them. The storm had dragged our anchor into deep water, where it dangled unattached to the bottom. The above-deck cabins acted as sails to the screaming wind. I wondered which would be worse: hitting land or scudding out into the full force of the storm.

Instead of firing up the engine, my captain went out to stand by the anchor winch. With utter calm, he simply waited, then released the cable when he sensed we were in position. The anchor grabbed, and *Blue Fjord* snapped into the wind, snubbed like a wild horse. As Robin snuggled his freezing body against the warmth of me and the unborn baby, he drifted off to sleep while I sat up the rest of the night.

The next day I had visions of going into labor during a similar storm, delivering the baby with a doctor's voice fading in and out on our ancient VHF radio. "Just push a little more, Mrs. . . . who is it again?" For the time being, at least, I needed a place to nest.

"Rob," I said that afternoon, "I need to go south."

Robin and I moved the boat south to Victoria, minutes away from Victoria General Hospital. We tied up to the colony of live-aboards at the foot of Fort Street, as warm and family-minded a community as any I've ever lived in. There were old men, families in hand-me-down clothes, and young guys kicked out by their girlfriends. On the dark, stormy nights when the floats heaved and boats leaped wildly against their mooring lines, the marina live-aboards made regular rounds, checking on the boats of neighbors and complete strangers alike, replacing lines and repositioning fenders in a spirit of true community.

The baby came. As dawn broke on a snowy December morning, Robin and I greeted the most adorable tiny bit of human life, our little Jarret. As I checked out two days later, I felt as if I should let someone know that I had no idea how to take care of this infant. I worried that the health nurse assigned to us would find our live-aboard life so appalling that she'd take Jarret away. (As it turned out, she was thrilled with the *Blue Fjord*. A few years earlier she'd lived aboard a boat herself.)

Our wintry life adapted to the crazy clock of Jarret's needs. Robin wrote film proposals for grant-making foundations; we both designed ads for Victoria dinner cruises and tried to keep up with the constant flow of diapers without the aid of a washing machine.

We fed the *Fjord*'s woodstove with scraps from a nearby furniture factory.

A few weeks after Jarret's birth, I noticed a growing assembly of twinkling lights outside the steamy galley windows where I was bathing our tiny boy. I wiped the window clear and saw a bobbing pod of kayaks with candles stuck to their bows. A glance at the tide calendar thumbtacked to the wall brought a smile to my face. Exhausted and doused with spit-up, I wrapped Jarret in a blanket, called Robin to the door, and swayed in wonderment as a flotilla of carolers serenaded us on Christmas Eve.

Chapter 10

~ ~ ~

Soon after Jarret's birth, Brad Andrews phoned from Marineland. Corky was in labor.

I'd been aware of her pregnancy. Robin and I had arranged to attend and record the birth, and I still wanted to study the development of language in a baby whale. Leaving the *Blue Fjord* in the care of friends, Robin and I packed Jarret, the cameras, and our recording equipment into Robin's ancient Jeep and drove hard and fast for Los Angeles. We barreled south without phoning in for updates. I couldn't have stood to hear that I'd missed another birth en route.

We arrived in early March 1982 to find two whales, not three, swimming in the tank. "False alarm," Brad told us. (Brad had taken over as chief curator after Tom Otten moved on.)

Corky was definitely pregnant. We just didn't know exactly how far along she was or when she'd give birth. Robin, Jarret, and I settled in, thinking we'd be there for maybe a week before the birth and a few weeks after. We rented a 16-foot camper and towed it to a far corner of the Marineland parking lot. Robin and I lived by the tank, taking turns cooking and sleeping back at the trailer. Robin filmed the beautiful, mysterious dawn maneuvers, capturing the sensuous spiraling and entwining of the whales' morning courtship. I took notes and made recordings of everything. The days stretched into weeks.

Jarret thrived. Instead of living isolated with his parents on the *Blue Fjord,* he became the mascot of the Marineland staff. He cooed and drooled at the rousing music that accompanied the whale and dolphin shows and swung his chubby fists at the colorful banners snapping in the wind. When he was tired, he snuggled contentedly into my chest. Our observation booth perched on the flat stucco roof of one of the concession stands—prime pigeon territory. Jarret loved watching the pigeons preen, court, coo, and strut just inches away from him as his mom watched the whales.

Without the pull of gravity, pregnancy doesn't stretch a whale the way it does a human. Watching Corky move effortlessly through the water, a 400-pound baby hidden inside her, I thought back to my own recent pregnancy, to the aching joints and the tiny feet pressed against my lungs. I admired her species' ability to harbor so enormous an infant.

The lack of a weight-bearing pelvis has had a profound influence on the evolution of cetaceans. The hips of human mothers have spread wider through thousands of years of evolution to accommodate the growth of our children's brains. Structurally we've reached an impasse: our skeleton can support no further spreading of the female hips. Since human evolution favors large brains, natural forces have found other means to continue the trend. Chemicals released late in pregnancy loosen a woman's joints so her pelvis literally pops apart as the baby's head passes through. Our babies have also adapted well: they're born with a soft spot on top of their heads to allow their brains to continue growing outside the womb. Babies are born with such large brains that their heads are too big for their bodies, leaving them unable to lift their heavy skulls on their own.

A whale's birth, however, isn't impeded by its mother's frame. The infant passes entirely through soft tissue, which has allowed its brain to expand with unrestricted ease. With no pelvic limitation, it might yet continue to expand.

Day after day, night after night, I watched and waited. During this intense series of observations, I became acutely aware of Orky and Corky's daily rhythms. If they were highly active on one morning, they were less so the next, alternating daily. Their "private" life ended with the arrival of the first trainer, and at that moment they ceased their creative, interactive behaviors. I soon noticed that no two shows were identical. The whales never performed with rote precision.

Their daytime activity peaked just before each show as they viewed the assembling crowd, often speeding around the tank with their heads out of the water. During the shows they didn't exactly turn subservient and dependent. They constantly tested the trainers. Corky wasn't supposed to do any aerial maneuvers in the later stages of pregnancy for fear she might concuss the baby, but she periodically rebelled and took off around the tank leaping higher than normal. This drove the trainers wild. They tried everything to stop her, but her leaps seemed to be made not so much to express joy as to assert some sort of control over her own actions.

If Corky grew sulky, the trainers used Orky to bring her in line. By cutting back on his rations, they inspired him to "have a word" with his recalcitrant mate. If a large portion of the orca brain is dedicated to deciphering the world by sound, then these whales' brains were going to waste. As I watched a trainer empty a bucket of fish into Orky's maw, I couldn't help but contrast the scene to the memory of Top Notch churning the waters of Johnstone Strait in pursuit of salmon.

Watching an endless succession of whale performances did give me a measure of respect for Orky and Corky's trainers. They never just stepped out and did a show. Before each performance they discussed the mental state of the whales and adapted the routine accordingly. They knew that they were dealing with intelligent, complex creatures—their equals, in the context of the show. A number of times I heard the head trainer tell his charges, "You've got to let Orky save face." That meant, if the whale repeatedly refused a cue, the trainer should give him a lesser command, reward him, and leave it at that. Each session had to end on a positive note. That care contributed significantly to Marineland's ability to keep the two whales alive under such inhumanely cramped circumstances.

As much as I loathed Orky and Corky's confinement, I found myself in a moral dilemma. The staff at Marineland had bent over backward to let me conduct research. They gained no advantage from my work; they let me in out of respect for science and our friendships. They also cared deeply for the whales. The last thing I wanted to do was betray them. Was I the kind of person who turned on her friends, or was I someone who did nothing in the face of an obvious wrong? I was immobilized.

As our vigil continued, I got my own taste of captivity. Robin and I rarely left the park together. Renée and John Gale stopped by occasionally, but their lives kept them busy. Once a week Robin and I went out to brunch. It seemed as if we'd be inspecting Corky's underside forever. When Princess Diana gave birth to her first son, "Prince William" was suggested as a name for the unborn whale. Early one morning I secretly revealed my breast to Corky as my tiny son nursed in a wishful attempt to help the mother-to-be with what lay ahead. Corky pressed the side of her face to the glass window and scanned us with her liquid brown eye.

As the second month came and went, Robin returned to Canada. He'd lined up work, and we couldn't afford to cancel the jobs.

On June 18 I thought I saw a shiver. It darted across Corky's back like a horse ridding itself of a fly. As she lay still on the surface, her dorsal fin expressed the tremor as a slight wiggle. Then her entire body bowed with the first contraction.

As afternoon faded into evening, the contractions continued. Her waters broke. Watching through an underwater viewing window, I saw a pale, whitish fluid stream from the orca; now her contractions brought squirts of rich milk. With Marineland staffers gathered round, I spent the night watching and recording, baby Jarret asleep in a basket at my feet.

At two in the morning, a pair of tiny tail flukes appeared, folded together like butterfly wings. The infant's tail flapped listlessly as Corky swam. Each contraction brought a little more of the baby out before it slid back in. Corky was laboring to pass her infant at the dorsal fin, the widest part of its body.

Why didn't the baby move? Was it dead? Was its umbilical cord pinched? Were we watching another tragedy unfold? None of us dared speculate.

Then, in an underwater rush of blood, the baby was born. As it emerged from the enveloping red cloud, its dorsal fin flat against its back, its flukes remained folded. It sank for a few seconds, then began wriggling. Corky spun around and nuzzled her newborn. With her mother's contact, the baby sprang to life. Mother and daughter rose to the surface together for the baby's first breath.

The instant Corky released her lungful of air, the calf snapped her tiny blowhole open, too. Encoded deep within the DNA of whales, there is a message: breathe with your mother. With astonishing precision, the two blowholes opened and closed together again and again. Clearly the compulsion for synchrony in an orca's life begins at this moment—its very survival depends on it. While Corky led her baby to air, the infant wasn't sure where the water ended and the air began. She clumsily thrust her head high out of the water to be sure her blowhole was clear before opening it.

Corky's signature breathing pattern stopped the moment the baby swam free. Now she breathed as often as the baby needed air. Without the sound of Corky's exhalation at the surface, I believe the newborn would have suffocated. How was it that Corky so easily choreographed her movements to meet her newborn's need for oxygen, when the act of nursing had proved to be so unfathomable?

Then came the moment of truth. Would Corky remember her training and know how to nurse her calf? Brad Andrews directed the staff not to interfere. This was Corky's moment alone.

The baby's fate was sealed within its first hour of life. With no attending females to push the calf down to Corky's mammaries, the baby immediately became fixated on Corky's head instead of her mother's underside. Corky reinforced this misdirected instinct by turning headlong toward the baby to keep it from hitting the tank walls. Swimming at all was difficult for the newborn; swimming around a circular tank was completely beyond the baby's ability. She smacked the wall with her fragile, acoustically sensitive lower jaw, once, twice, and again. A round wound appeared. We stood watching the drama unfold, silent, knowing there was little we could do.

I recalled something an orca researcher had once told me. Recounting the time he'd seen Corky's wild relative Kelsy give birth, researcher Jeff Jacobsen said, "There were so many females, Alex, there was no telling who the mother was. They all touched that baby over and over." Another researcher observed three orcas pushing a newborn high above the water balanced across their noses.

There simply weren't enough whales in Marineland's tank to hold Corky's newborn aloft. The slogan "It takes a village to raise a child" was never more true than in orca society.

Corky did remember her training sessions with the model calf. She rolled over a few times to present her mammaries to the baby, but by that time it was too late. The baby hesitated, her head sweeping back and forth as if lost. Then, as Corky righted herself, the baby spied her mother's face and rushed to it. Like her doomed siblings stacked in the parks' freezer morgue, this baby had fatally imprinted on the wrong white spot. Milk flowed from Corky with every thrust of her tail, but her calf tasted none of it.

The activities of the ensuing days were depressingly familiar. Corky's trainers kept giving her the underwater cue to present her mammaries. She rolled, but the infant ignored her mother's white-highlighted nipples. One of the trainers bravely entered the tank, grasped the nine-foot whale, and tried to guide her to Corky's mammaries. But as long as a human had hold of her baby, Corky kept her face locked on the infant, swinging her body out of the way and completely obscuring her mammaries. At two days the baby made her first sounds, probably a cry of hunger. Nursing my plump baby while watching Corky suffer the slow starvation of her own threw me into a tailspin. This was deep and delicate torture. As long as she remained in captivity without the assistance of the females in her pod, Corky had little chance of raising a healthy nursing calf.

Eventually Brad Andrews ordered the tank drained. Orky lay over on his side in the shallow water, but Corky remained upright. She scooted around like an enormous tadpole to stay near her baby, which swam freely in the 3-foot-deep water. When the head trainer tried to guide the baby to nurse, Orky swung his tail at that moment and nearly snapped the man's neck. Trainers waded into the tank to attach a mechanical milking machine to Corky. They were desperate to get real whale's milk into the baby—especially the vital colostrum, which precedes true milk production and helps the infant fight off infections.

If there was one subject in which I had become expert during those weeks waiting for Corky to give birth, it was nursing. Milk, I knew from my own baby, can't be extracted from a mammal just by applying suction. There's a chemical interaction between baby and mother that releases it. I spoke to the trainers about this essential "let-down" response, but they had no idea how to induce it. Farmers sometimes play music to cows while they're hooking them up to milking machines; it relaxes them enough to let the milk flow. But nobody knew what would relax a killer whale lying panicked in a draining tank.

Finally they resorted to tube feeding. Every few hours, around the clock, the trainers threaded a long tube down the baby's throat and poured an experimental brew of cream, whipped fish, and vitamins into her stomach. They drew on every bit of knowledge concerning the content of marine mammal milk, but the database was scant.

After the baby had been force-fed for three days, I had to return to Canada. John Gale agreed to continue recording the baby, and I still hoped against hope that this young whale would survive. The baby ultimately lived for forty-seven days. The tube feedings kept her alive. Then one day Corky began hitting the baby, hard, in the belly, until the staff thought she would kill her.

When trainers next went to feed the baby, Corky showed aggression toward humans for the first time. Unwilling to risk human lives, Marineland officials decided to take the baby away from Corky.

John Gale gave me the news over the phone: "The baby died a couple of days later in a separate tank."

"The weird thing is," John told me, "the autopsy revealed the kid's insides were full of gas. Do you think Corky could have been trying to burp her baby when she was hitting it?"

We know that whales can see inside one another with their echolocation. A pocket of air would reflect sound better than all the tissue and bones around it. In fact, it would flash as brightly as a mirror. Hard as the Marineland staff had tried, their best-guess formula was too harsh for a baby whale's delicate digestive system.

I hung up the pay phone and plopped down on the seawall in front of the *Blue Fjord*. My gut twisted with a shot of adrenaline. Now I knew what it would feel like if someone took my baby from me while I was trying to save him.

Chapter 11

$\mathcal{S}$ hortly after getting married in 1981, I met a whale named Miracle at Sealand of the Pacific, a small marine park in Victoria. Miracle was still quite young in whale years—about five—and I was drawn by the chance to work with an orca that might still be developing its language skills. Little did I know the effort would end in tragedy and bitter conflict.

Mike Bigg had first spotted Miracle four years earlier, on July 4, 1977, in Nanaimo Harbour directly across the Strait of Georgia from Vancouver. He judged her to be just over a year old. She swam inside a boom of loosely floating logs, which was no place for a whale. Bigg took photographs of her dorsal fin and saddle to add to his catalog. As he scanned the water, Bigg noted an odd thing: the infant swam alone. It was rare enough to see a lone adult whale; in his six years of research, Bigg couldn't recall ever having seen a lone baby. He assumed the whale's family must have been nearby but out of his sight.

The thousands of flyers that Bigg and his team had sent out in the early 1970s asking people to phone in whale sightings produced what he called "Keeners," people who diligently phoned Bigg with every whale they spotted. This network of Keeners remains one of Bigg's greatest legacies to whale research in British Columbia. What began as a group of people spotting whales from their seaside windows broadened to include whale-watch skippers, pilots, tug captains, commercial fishermen, lighthouse keepers, and people in every form of craft on or above the water. As the coast began attracting whale researchers, they, too, became active contributors to the network, providing accurate identification of the whales they encountered. Today this network has spread from one end of the coast to the other. Each of us may get only a glimpse of the nomadic orcas as they range over their expansive territory, but by phoning our sightings in to Bigg's office, we can pick up on what others have seen.

For two weeks after his initial contact with the lone whale, Bigg received a number of calls describing a baby killer whale moving north along the eastern coast of Vancouver Island. He marked the reports on a chart of the inland water. In fourteen days the whale traveled 125 miles.

On the afternoon of August 2, a sport fisherman named Bill Davis set out in his skiff to do a little salmon fishing in Menzies Bay, near the town of Campbell River, about 125 miles northwest of Nanaimo. As the late-summer sun sank behind Vancouver Island, Davis spotted a small whale floating in the darkening water. Its back was covered in patches of brown slime. As he approached it, the whale retreated beneath the water, wary but not spooked. Davis reached into his bait bucket and threw it a herring. The young orca wolfed it down and begged for another. Davis emptied his bucket. The whale was famished.

Davis returned to feed the sickly whale several times over the next week. Word got out, and crowds gathered. Davis, realizing that the orca needed more than just his herring, called the Vancouver Aquarium, which put him in touch with Mike Bigg. Bigg alerted Bob Wright, owner of Sealand of the Pacific, which had one killer whale but was looking to add another. The two of them, together with Jay Hyman, a veterinarian visiting from the New York Aquarium, flew up to Menzies Bay to examine the struggling orphan.

It didn't look good. Bullet holes riddled the orca's body. The telltale gashes of a propeller wound cut deep into her back. Given the whale's emaciated condition and badly infected wounds, Jay Hyman could do little more than predict the animal's imminent demise. Bob Wright decided to buck the odds and truck the calf south to his Oak Bay Beach Hotel, an old Victoria landmark famous for its saltwater swimming pool.

As the most British of all Canadian cities, Victoria loves nothing better than a heartwarming animal story. With Miracle recovering in the Oak Bay's intensive care pool, local newspapers and television stations ran daily updates on her condition. The city held its breath as the little whale, now named "Miracle," lived up to her billing by blooming back to health.

After Miracle had spent three months in the pool, Sealand moved her to a specially constructed net pen in the ocean next to Haida, the marine park's longtime captive killer whale.

After hearing about my research on whale vocalization at the University of Washington conference, Sealand's administrators invited me to spend time with Miracle. They wanted to know if Miracle was picking up language from Haida. I hesitated. My emotions about captive whales were pretty raw from Corky's birthing trials, but I still held out hope for learning something from very young orcas about the development of their language. Since Miracle had arrived too young to have acquired a whale dialect, I was as curious as the Sealand staff to see if she'd picked up anything from her male companion. And I had to give Bob Wright and Sealand credit. As troubling as it was to see another whale brought into captivity, without their costly rescue, Miracle would have died off the coast of Vancouver Island.

Miracle and Haida were kept in two separate net pens below a series of low docks from which Sealand visitors could observe the whales. The Sealand staff thought it best to keep the young male and the infant female safely apart. "He's like a logger who's been in camp a little too long, if you know what I mean," a staff member told me.

By the time I reached her, four years after her rescue, Miracle had grown strong enough to perform in short daily shows: she'd open her mouth to let a trainer clean her teeth with a giant toothbrush, that sort of thing. I pitched a tent on the dock to record her vocalizations night and day. She was an adorable, affectionate little whale who exhibited extremely strange behavior. After every show she rushed over to a particular spot and banged her head against the underside of the dock. She did it so often that her melon had become badly bruised and spongy.

When we were alone, Miracle lay still beside me. I wanted to watch what she was doing, but she had the same curiosity about me. I was watching a whale watching me. My hair and toes especially fascinated her. As I sat on the railing, watching her stare at my toes, I'd wiggle them for her entertainment. I offered her control over my feet. When she wanted to see me wiggle them, all she had to do was wave her pectoral fin. She caught on immediately. Cruising past me, her eye ringed white with excitement, she'd roll to one side, expose her little fin, and flash a wave. In response I'd remove my boots, climb on the fence, and wriggle my toes. Running my long braid through her teeth caused her eyelids to droop dreamily as she gently pressed her teeth around my hair, her jaw shuddering slightly. At night I stroked her as she lay beside my tent. This lone baby whale craved too much attention for me to maintain a passive scientific observer relationship.

The head banging concerned me. Whenever I pulled my hand out of the water, Miracle started in with the bumping. After puzzling over it for weeks, I remembered what a calf does to its mother before nursing: it bangs its head against her mammaries. The contact probably stimulates the milk to flow, the let-down response. This baby was desperate for contact with her mother. The attention of a human could momentarily alleviate her need, but as soon as my hand withdrew, she returned to the last sensation she remembered of her mother. Moments after nudging her mother, she would be filled with sweet, rich milk and a sense of comfort and security. If only Corky and Miracle could have met.

What the staff at Sealand didn't know was that Haida's ability to "teach" language to Miracle was extremely limited. He'd been captured from a pod of southern resident whales in Washington State in 1968, and I didn't know the normal dialect of his pod. But whether he'd been taken too young to learn his pod's full repertoire or had lost his vocal range during more than a decade of captivity, the fact remained that Haida made only a single call. Miracle had learned it, as it turned out, and the two called back and forth quite a bit.

Haida's situation at Sealand wasn't exactly equivalent to Orky and Corky's world at Marineland. Haida still swam in the waters of his natural habitat. He didn't suffer from chlorine in his water or endure long cross-country truck transfers. He could probably even hear the distant calls of his pod mates, on occasion.

But unlike Marineland, Sealand made almost no attempt to educate the public about the whale it was watching. Every working day Haida performed a skit in which a trainer pretended to pour gasoline into the whale's mouth. Haida would then imitate the sound of an outboard motor as he swam around his enclosure. This was even worse than SeaWorld's "Shamu Goes to College" act.

The greatest contrast between Sealand and Marineland, though, was the lack of any "save face" policy among the Sealand trainers. The older trainers were careful with the whales, but one younger staffer often took pleasure in exerting his human dominance over Haida. When the orca refused a command from this trainer, he would refuse to give Haida an alternate cue, instead leaving the hungry whale to brood for an extended time-out. When Haida finally did obey, the arrogant trainer walked away with a "Guess you know who's boss now" swagger. This enraged Haida. The whale slammed his tonnage against the platform where the trainer had been standing, then raced around the tank breaching. Down at the far end of Miracle's separate pen, I rose and fell on the swells of Haida's anger.

Although her trainers wouldn't allow Miracle any contact with Haida, she did have a pen mate—a fur seal named Shadow. One day I came out to the pen and couldn't find Shadow, although I could hear him breathing somewhere beneath the dock. Peering through the wooden slats, I caught sight of his dark outline. He'd slipped past Miracle's net but remained caught behind the main net encircling the park.

Concerned that Shadow or Miracle might become entangled between the two nets and drown, I alerted the staff. They rolled their eyes: not again. In her boredom Miracle apparently pulled at the net with her teeth, tearing seal-size holes in it. Shadow often discovered the holes and got trapped between the two nets. What was important to Miracle wasn't so much the hole itself as the response it elicited. Holes needed mending, and that meant sending divers down.

Miracle loved divers. Robin dove with her once to gather film for a TV show called "News from Zoos." Unlike the wild whales, which Robin could usually barely see, Miracle played with him like a giant puppy. She examined him head to toe, then yanked his flippers off one by one, effectively immobilizing him. When he dove to retrieve them, she pulled on his gloves and eventually tugged them off, too. She worked herself into such a frenzy that he had to get out for his own safety. When he tried to calm her down by playing a little flute tankside, she tried to grab that as well.

One day I returned to find Shadow gone. He had finally drowned between the nets. While the inner and outer nets usually hung down with a space between them, the tide sometimes swept them together. With net billowing all around him, Shadow had been unable to find the surface.

Realizing that Miracle could easily die the same way, I wrote up a report and sent it straight to Sealand owner Bob Wright. I told him about Haida's abnormally stunted vocabulary, Miracle's head banging, the dangerous situation with the nets, and what I'd seen of Haida's mistreatment at the hands of one of the trainers.

The report was not well received. I heard nothing from Bob Wright, and my relations with the Sealand staff turned frosty.

A few weeks later Miracle drowned between the nets. Sealand immediately claimed that someone must have cut her inner net, allowing the whale to become fatally entangled. It was a blatant attempt to divert attention from the fact that Sealand's nets couldn't safely hold marine mammals.

Sealand immediately wanted to capture two whales to replace Miracle. But times had changed. When Haida had been captured in the late 1960s, he'd been an anonymous member of a nameless population. But by the early 1980s, every orca in the northern and southern resident communities had its own identity. We knew its mother, its family, a little of its history. A wondrous thing happens when an animal moves from population status to individual standing: it can no longer be mistreated with impunity.

No one was willing to let Sealand take a whale. Researchers in the north were determined to protect their pods, citing reasons why this whale and that whale weren't good candidates for captivity, and researchers in the south were no less adamant.

The state of Washington's secretary of state, Ralph Munro, sent a letter to Canada's minister of Fisheries and Oceans, Roméo LeBlanc, on August 11, 1982. "I am writing you to respectfully protest the proposed capture of 2 killer whales, Orcinus orca, that has been requested by a Victoria aquarium." Munro stated that the United States and Canada share the whales of Puget Sound and that those stocks had already been decimated by live captures. Washington State had a long-standing policy prohibiting the harassment or capture of local orcas. "Our Governor and Attorney General successfully sued the United States government and SeaWorld to prevent further captures in our waters. No captures have taken place since."

The Nuu-chah-nulth Tribal Council, representing thirteen tribes in the area of Victoria and western Vancouver Island, put out a press release: "Killer whales are sacred animals. Today many of our people own the Killer Whale crest, and we perform ceremonial dances using shawls displaying the Killer Whale, and our most sacred dances use whistles that imitate Killer Whale talk. Due to the outstanding Nuu-chah-nulth Land/Sea Claims over most of the waters of the West Coast of Vancouver Island, the Tribal Council believes it is in a unique position to protect whales that frequent their aboriginal territorial waters. . . . No one owns the Killer Whale and No Killer Whale should be held in captivity."

Robin offered a compromise in an article he wrote for the Victoria paper *Monday Magazine.* Why not capture a whale for five years, he said, and then return it to the wild? In the face of so much opposition, Sealand realized that it had better make some concessions and expressed interest in the idea. Sealand was issued a permit for two whales, in exchange for Haida's freedom. Haida must be released "within 90 days following the successful capture of the second whale or before the 1st day of October, 1982, whichever is sooner."

As the date set for Haida's release neared, the marine park said less and less about setting the orca free. Haida was a perfect candidate for release: he'd never been taken out of his home waters; all Sealand had to do was drop the nets surrounding him. I looked forward to seeing if he would rejoin his pod and regain his use of language. But in a bizarre turn of events, head trainer Cees Schrage noticed that Haida did not appear his usual self on D day—Friday, October 1— the day he was supposed to be turned free. Cees noticed that he wasn't paying attention, "his mind seemed to be elsewhere." Cees just had a gut feeling that something wasn't right, reported Victoria's *Times Colonist.* Because of Schrage's concern, a blood test was done that day. The results were "normal." Sealand veterinarian Dr. Alan Hoey said, "There was nothing, no way of knowing." Haida died two days later. Angus Matthews, the park manager, said, "The timing was a hideous coincidence." I found the "coincidence" deeply disturbing. With friends we held a candlelit wake for the whale, who perhaps knew more about his circumstances than any had realized.

Haida's was the fifth death at Sealand in twelve years. He was towed out to sea and sunk.

With Haida's death Sealand was free to proceed without any capture-and-release nonsense. On February 20, 1983, the federal minister of Fisheries signed another permit for the capture of two whales from the big southern resident L pod. It had been nine years since the last whale capture in British Columbian waters. Curiously, the permit prohibited the capture of any white whales. It went on to specify that the whales must be between six and ten years old, not nursing or pregnant, and they had to be either one male and one female or two males. The whales could be neither sold nor bartered away. The permit also contained an extensive clause regarding Sealand's educational responsibilities, an attempt to rationalize the taking of wild whales. In all of British Columbia, there were only about nine whales that met the permit's stringent requirements.

Sealand set up its capture nets in Pedder Bay, just around the corner from Victoria. The same bay had been the site of a successful Sealand capture a decade earlier. In 1970, Sealand owner Bob Wright had gone hunting for a mate for Haida. Scouting the water of the Victoria shore, he spotted a rare white whale swimming in a pod of four normally colored orcas. Wright is a man who knows a tourist attraction when he sees one. He directed the Sealand boats to fix a net at one side of the entrance to Pedder Bay. Using seal bombs (underwater explosives), the fishermen drove the whales deep into the bay and closed a net around them. At the end of the day, Sealand held five whales. Two females were taken to Sealand: a calf they named Nootka, and the white one, who became Chimo. Two other females and one male remained in Pedder Bay awaiting their sale to other marine parks.

Nootka and Chimo refused to eat for three weeks. The three orcas held in Pedder Bay wouldn't eat either. Graeme Ellis, who was working for Sealand at the time, offered the orcas every kind of fish he could get ahold of—salmon, herring, and lingcod. Nothing suited them. Finally, on the twenty-fourth day of Nootka and Chimo's captivity, Haida pressed some herring against their mouths through the net. They accepted the fish and broke their fast.

The starving Pedder Bay orcas had no such guide. Two months passed. Graeme Ellis wondered how long they could survive without food. After seventy-five days the older female made a run at the net and got stuck halfway through. Emaciated and exhausted, she drowned.

The Pedder Bay male, who'd been dubbed Charlie Chin because of the jut of his lower jaw, tried to rip through the net with his teeth. This time the net held. On day seventy-eight Charlie Chin took El-

Two Pacific white-sided dolphins engaged in the spectacular aerial play for which this species is known. Photo by Alexandra Morton.

Steller sea lions nervously eyeing a pod of killer whales in Kwatsi Bay, where the orcas prey on them. Photo by Alexandra Morton.

Siwiti, a young female killer whale, breaches alongside my boat. Photo by Alexandra Morton.

Taking accurate notes is the cornerstone of field science. Photo by C. Bennett. (Courtesy of Alexandra Morton)

lex, Jarret, and Robin in Cramer Pass, 1984. Not all days are equally inspiring for the whole crew! Photo by Tove Laundry. (Courtesy of Alexandra Morton)

A5 pod rescues me when my boat is lost in the fog, 1980.
Photo by Alexandra Morton.

Yakat and Kelsy, sisters from A4 pod, who despite many losses of family members continue to survive as a pod. Photo by Alexandra Morton.

Steller sea lions at their winter hangout at Eden Island. Photo by Robin Morton. (Courtesy of Alexandra Morton)

A humpback whale breaches in front of my house. The comeback of humpback whales of the eastern Pacific is a rare success story. Photo by Alexandra Morton.

Robin Morton filming killer whales
in Johnstone Strait in 1986.
Photo by Alexandra Morton.

My floathouse, Christmas, 1990.
Photo by Alexandra Morton.

'sitika's spectacular son Blackney demonstrates the enormous capacity of his lungs.
Photo by Alexandra Morton.

Clio having a bath in my boat's sink, 1997. Photo by Alexandra Morton.

Eric building a boat, 1998. Photo by Alexandra Morton.

lis's salmon by the head and moved up alongside the remaining female, vocalizing. She took the other end of the fish in her mouth. Together, the two whales circled the enclosure in tandem, the fish held perfectly still between them. Finally they broke it in two and ate it. Charlie Chin came back to get another fish and gave it to the female. After she took hold of it, he returned and got one for himself.

It wasn't until years later that Graeme Ellis helped discover that these whales weren't resident fish eaters at all. They were transients. And they ate only mammals.

Transient orcas are the same species as the fish-eating resident orcas, but over the years we've gradually uncovered the distinct nature of the two orca cultures. Transients eat only warm-blooded prey like seals and sea lions. They talk less, breathe less, and travel routes distinct from those of the residents. All these differences seem based on the fundamental difference in diet. "It's as though the two had agreed on some sort of treaty," Mike Bigg once said. " 'I'll eat one kind of food, you eat another.' This way they can stay in the same area and not compete."

Because they're not as common as residents and their movements are harder to predict, our knowledge of transients has been slow to accumulate. During his surveys of the northern and southern communities in the 1970s, Mike Bigg found transients—who did not belong to either of the resident communities—difficult to get close to and photograph. Years would pass before he recorded a second sighting of some transients (hence the name). Photographs of the elusive whales revealed slight, but unmistakable, differences in their physical makeup. Their dorsal fins were more pointed; their saddle patches reached farther forward on their sides and had smoother edges. These distinctive characteristics could mean only one thing: residents and transients didn't interbreed often, if at all.

After years of research, it became apparent that transients were the only whales attacking and eating other marine mammals. Resident whales ate only fish; transients went after bigger game like porpoises, seals, and sometimes even birds.

Chimo and her relatives had almost certainly never eaten a fish in their lives. They weren't refusing Graeme Ellis's food; they simply didn't see it *as* food.

The sharing of that first fish, following the drowning death of the female, gave Ellis a remarkable insight into the mind of a transient. The whales can eat fish, but they choose not to. Was the eating of fish taboo, repulsive, or just too alien to consider? Whatever the reason, the surviving male grasped the situation. Rather than simply swallowing a fish to save his own life, he made sure that the last surviving member of his family lived, too. Haida had been similarly compelled. He'd helped two transients, orcas with whom he'd never have associated in the wild, when their survival was at stake. When synchrony is elemental to life, you'll accept any partner, no matter how mismatched.

The two survivors in Pedder Bay escaped eight months after their capture. Someone secretly weighted the net at one corner, allowing the two orcas to slip back into the wild. I've watched their progress over the years; at least three babies have been born to the female since their traumatic encounter with humanity.

Chimo the white whale survived for only three years at Sealand. She died in 1972.

Robin and I decided to document Sealand's Pedder Bay capture. My research hinges on comparing how whales use sound in contrasting activity states, and I'd never recorded wild whales in distress. Moreover, Robin and I felt that if wild whales were going to be captured for the public's pleasure, the public should know what that capture really looked like.

None of this came as good news to Sealand officials, who knew that the whale capture would be an unpleasant spectacle. The more eyes—and cameras—watching, the worse it would be for the marine park.

Sealand was nothing if not media-savvy. It planned an end run and executed it perfectly. While we waited outside the trap set in Pedder Bay, Sealand cut a deal with Icelandic whalers to have three orcas flown in to the Victoria airport in the dead of night. They had those whales swimming in Haida's old pen before anybody at Pedder Bay even got word.

With the arrival of the Icelandic whales, Robin and I moved the *Blue Fjord* to Oak Bay, just outside of Sealand. I'd never heard Icelandic whales and was curious about their dialect. I also wanted baseline data on the new orcas in case their vocabulary atrophied as Haida's had. Because the orcas were in nets, not tanks, I could easily pick up their sounds on a hydrophone dangled from the *Blue Fjord* at anchor in Oak Bay. The first night I listened to the three Icelandic whales cry for hours, far from their mothers and home.

Sealand was in no mood to have me collecting more data on their whales. After our monitoring of the Pedder Bay site, Robin and I had become personae non gratae at the marine park. After we had recorded the Icelandic orcas that first night, Sealand ordered a couple of employees to tie a boat to the dock between us and the whales and leave its engine running.

"I don't believe it," I said to Robin. "They're drowning out the whale calls with engine noise."

I was less concerned about my recordings—now nothing but Evinrude whine—than about the young whales. For them this was like living under the glare of klieg lights.

That night I woke to the sound of an outboard just outside the wheelhouse door. I cracked the door open and caught a Sealand boat in my flashlight beam. The driver was reaching for my hydrophone line with a pair of wire clippers. Startled by the light, he wheeled and raced for the dock. This was becoming absurd.

"I'm loading up," said Robin. Where others might reach for a gun, Robin always reached for his camera. He snapped a fresh roll of film in place and went prowling the portside rail but found nothing. An hour later, with both of us dozing in the wheelhouse, we heard another outboard approach. (The hydrophone could pick up an engine from the moment it started up a mile away. We had more warning than Sealand imagined.) Robin crept onto the deck and hid. We waited until the boat came alongside and—flash!—got prime footage of the chief curator in his Sealand cap maneuvering up to my hydrophone with wire clippers.

The next morning a young fellow came out and began circling our boat in a skiff, overloading the hydrophone and letting us know that our presence was not welcome. "Now they're sending out a lackey," Robin commented, watching the anxious youngster circle the *Blue Fjord*. "We must be sinking in priority." We would have left, but now it was blowing a gale.

That afternoon things got worse. Robin caught sight of a diver coming up from under the *Blue Fjord*. Before Robin could reach him, a speedboat swept in, collected the diver, and sped off with the frogman's leg still pointed skyward.

Let me tell you something about Robin Morton: if you wanted to piss him off, mess with his boat. "Shit bags!" Robin flew into the cabin, as angry as I'd ever seen him.

Convinced that the diver had sabotaged our hull, he suited up and went over the side to inspect the boat. As soon as he hit the water, another boat approached from Sealand. With my husband in the water and a reckless propeller homing in—and a toddler in the wheelhouse and my mind set on edge by two sleepless nights—I grabbed a flare, the nearest attention-getting device at hand. I planned to summon the Coast Guard. The flare gave its intended message.

"Don't come any goddamn closer!" I screamed. The boat turned away.

Robin bobbed to the surface. "It's the anchor," he shouted up to me. "They rolled it up in the chain." This would allow the boat to drag anchor into the beach and a dozen yachts at anchor inshore of us. Sealand showed that it, too, could send a message: Time to weigh up.

That afternoon I went ashore in the Zodiac. Robin's old buddies at CHEK-TV had come out to interview us; as a result, a teacher at the Oak Bay School asked me to give a talk to the kids on whales while we were in the area. But before I could reach the third graders, I was met by members of the local constabulary as I hit the beach in our Zodiac. They'd got a report of a woman waving a gun around in the bay.

Once I told them the situation, they were quite sympathetic. But there wasn't much they could do for us. "You're not in violation of any laws," one of the policemen told me, "but clearly things are escalating. It might be best for everyone if you moved on." It wasn't a threat—more of a plea to avoid a confrontation by making discretion the better part of valor.

I agreed. The wind that had kept us at harbor had died down, and we were doing no good for the whales. Ten years later those three whales became the first captives to kill a human. Three babies raised in complete isolation from whale society, they grabbed a young woman after she fell into their enclosure. They tossed their screaming victim like a seal; eventually she drowned. A year later Wright sold the trio and their two calves to SeaWorld for a reported $5 million. The public outcry against capturing whales in British Columbia had been good for the market. Haida had cost Wright $5,000. The Icelandic whales had been procured for $200,000 apiece. With their coming of reproductive age, that price had risen to more than $1 million each.

Robin and Jarret and I raised anchor and pointed the *Blue Fjord* toward the cold, rough waters of the north, where we hoped to find welcoming neighbors and magnificent wild whales. And, just maybe, our permanent home.

Chapter 12

R obin and I needed three things in a home port: whales, mail service, and playmates for Jarret. He was now two, and it didn't seem fair to raise our boy in ship-bound isolation. Our charter business paid the bills and allowed us to make a living on the water, but it didn't allow for the life we wanted. Running a boat had turned into a full-time job. I began referring to the *Fjord* as "the other woman" because she was so demanding. Her silent threat, *fix me or I'll sink,* ensured that she always got what she wanted. We recaulked her decks, sandblasted her hull, reroofed her, reboomed her, and repaired the freezer more times than I could count. Between the charters and maintenance, we had no time or money for whale work.

My patience for charter work finally ran out on a summer day in Port Alexander, off the northern end of Vancouver Island. I was making lunch for an IMAX film crew, slathering mayonnaise on slices of bread. When the sharp retort of whale blows reached my ears, I looked up to see an assemblage of G clan whales passing us in single file and the girlfriend of an IMAX crew member taking *my* Zodiac out to see them.

"That's it for me," I told Robin when we finished the charter. "I'll plan the menu, do the shopping, and hire a cook, but there's no bloody way I'm going to be trapped in that galley by sliced white bread ever again."

Robin surprised me by agreeing. "I'm bent over in the engine room, where I can't even see daylight, much less pick up a camera."

So when a group of anthropologists chartered the *Blue Fjord* for a run up to the Queen Charlotte Islands, Robin and I made a pact to stay north, find a spot of our own, and begin the life we had dreamed of. Without Victoria's high berthing fees, we figured our whale photographs and Robin's underwater film business could support all three of us. If things turned desperate, we could always pick up a charter.

We bought as much film and audiotape as we could afford and stocked the pantry with dried beans, rice, pasta, a few spices, and a tofu press. I would've loaded the freezer, too, but the *Blue Fjord*'s refrigeration system tended to work at random intervals, and I didn't want to poison the whole family. I canned corn, tomatoes, salmon, and pickles. We repaired the fishing rods and laid in a new supply of hooks. If all else failed, we'd catch our supper. In Victoria I bought shirts, sweaters, pants, and shoes two and three sizes too big for Jarret.

Since there weren't any good outdoor clothes for toddlers, I laid in a supply of ripstop nylon, bunting, flannel, and wool cloth. I bought an old hand-cranked sewing machine and made Jarret a winter wardrobe. My sister-in-law Colleen helped us make a canvas cover for the forward third of our new family-sized Zodiac to give Jarret some protection from the wind. There was no telling when we would see a city again.

There are two main bodies of water between Vancouver Island and the Canadian mainland. There's the relatively placid Strait of Georgia, around which is clustered most of the population of British Columbia, and then there's the northern water.

Whenever I listened to the marine radio weather report, I could count on the wind exhausting itself as it traveled south. If it blew 30–40 knots on the northern tip of Vancouver Island, it was 20–30 knots in Johnstone Strait and 10–15 knots in the Strait of Georgia. Cruising on calm waters up the eastern side of Vancouver Island, we passed the town of Nanaimo, its plumes of pulp-mill effluent billowing like a slow-motion explosion. Small beach homes dotted the low-lying shoreline. Children and dogs played on sandy beaches.

After two days of travel, we reached the town of Campbell River at the northern end of the Strait of Georgia, where Vancouver Island and Quadra Island pinch the strait, forcing the tide to run through Seymour Narrows like a turbulent river. The southern island's last outpost, Campbell River calls itself the sportfishing capital of the world. The waters surrounding the town bob with gleaming white whalers, massive steel purse seiners, elegant double-ended gill netters, and commercial trollers bristling with their long trolling poles. The smell of fish mingled with the spicy, cloying scent of wood rendered to pulp, a reminder that the island's dominant industries were—at least in 1984—still alive and well.

After Seymour Narrows the coast changes. Sandy beaches are replaced by sharp-cut rocks and steep, forested mountains. The forests widen, the towns vanish, and the beach homes disappear. While it's possible to swim in the ocean south of Campbell River, a dip in the water north of that point will take your breath away.

We traveled for two more days along the steep, rocky shore, accompanied only by the deep green forests of cedar, spruce, hemlock, and fir rising up from the water. Occasionally the Vancouver Island mountains split into a wide valley, allowing a river artery to flow from the heart of the island to the ocean.

We cruised through Johnstone Strait keeping our eyes peeled for whales, but it was too early—only June—and the orcas hadn't yet arrived. The strait seemed unnaturally quiet without their echoing blows.

The anthropologists from the Royal British Columbia Museum in Victoria who would be chartering the *Blue Fjord* were planning to put steel reinforcement rods down the back side of totem poles at Ninstints, an ancient Haida village in the Queen Charlotte Islands. The Haida considered the poles, carved out of the soft native red cedar that surrounded their villages, an organic art form that was designed to decompose. Museum curators, however, are in the business of preservation. They couldn't stand the thought of those magnificent poles falling, to be reabsorbed by the earth.

The previous year the curators had scraped away dirt from the base of the poles and replaced it with gravel, to better drain the rainfall and slow the rotting process. This project stood in contrast to an earlier generation's idea of preservation. In 1957 the Museum of Anthropology in Vancouver had come to Ninstints to remove several poles and take them south for exhibition in the big city. It seemed hopeful to me that a culture that had so recently destroyed the artists now went to extremes to preserve their art.

Having driven up the island, the anthropologists joined us at Port Hardy, the most northerly town on Vancouver Island. We loaded their mountain of camping, boating, and pole-restoration gear aboard the *Blue Fjord* and set off in the early afternoon.

Our troubles began immediately. The tide had run slowly away from us all morning. So when we backed away from the harbor floats, we ran aground on a mudflat that wasn't marked on the chart. The anthropologists were so busy stowing their gear, they hardly noticed—the first time. I quietly slipped into the Zodiac and motored over to a tug captain loading groceries at the end of a nearby dock. He grumblingly agreed to pull us free.

Moments later the *Blue Fjord* was freed. But the old boat never could back up straight. Before the tug captain could return to his groceries, we found ourselves once again parked, our keel driven deep in the soft mud.

"I oughta just leave you here!" growled the disgusted tug skipper. This time I noted worried glances exchanged among our passengers.

Fortunately the tug captain pulled us off. We departed from the tip of Vancouver Island and headed across the open waters of Queen Charlotte Strait. This exposed body of water, dotted with rocky islands, yawns gradually wider to meet the open Pacific. In early evening we skirted around the desolate Cape Caution, a dark headland exposed to the whims of the open ocean. With the approaching solstice stretching daylight past 10:00 P.M., we motored up the wild coast and pulled into the deserted coastal cannery town of Namu just after midnight.

After a few hours' sleep (interrupted by the thumping of otters gaily exploring our decks), we set off at five o'clock the next morning. The Queen Charlotte Islands, a collection of 150 jigsaw pieces, form a huge wedge pointed at Vancouver Island. They're actually the peaks of an undersea mountain range and a glacial refugium. The Queen Charlottes are one of the few places on the British Columbian coast that escaped the crushing weight of Ice Age glaciation. Pollen and fossils found on the islands predate life on the mainland.

Our plan was to cross Hecate Strait at its widest point to reach Rose Harbour, near the southern tip of the islands. Or rather, that was Robin's plan. I wasn't too keen on it. On the clearest day the strait is so wide there that the islands remain under the horizon line until you're more than halfway across. If you miss your mark, you'll chug straight into the open Pacific without enough fuel to get home. Robin saw it as completely logical: the shortest distance between two points is a straight line. By going straight across, we'd save a full day of travel and gallons of diesel.

We ran on a compass bearing the whole way. Fog socked in the strait most of the day. The *Blue Fjord* rolled in light seas, its decks heaped high with inflatable boats, metal scaffolding, tents, boxes of food, and a haystack of bags. What worried me was a big metal outboard engine jammed against the outer wall of the wheelhouse cabin, a few inches from our brass compass. I'd heard stories about big metal objects' throwing a compass off, so when it came my turn to steer, I kept a bearing 5 extra degrees north. Better to make landfall farther up the islands, I figured, than not at all.

Just as darkness began to fall, one of the anthropologists spotted a faint horizon miles away. The wind was coming up, and I was ever so glad to have the islands finally in sight.

And then the engine died.

"What's going on?" I asked Robin. My eyes bugged out with panic.

"She's overheating, so I shut her down," he told me. He shot a look of confidence to the passengers. *No worries.*

"Try and keep her into the wind," he mumbled to me. Wrench in hand, he disappeared into the engine room.

As we tossed in the early swells of a coming storm, the land seemed to recede before my eyes. I'm sure Robin was down in the engine room for only a few minutes, but they were some of the longest minutes of my life. Finally I heard the sweet sound of the Gray Marine (what everyone on the coast calls a "Jimmy") diesel engine fire up. An hour later we felt our way through the dark into Rose Harbour.

From 1911 to 1942 Rose Harbour operated as one of the premier whaling stations on the northern Pacific coast, turning hundreds of blue, right, sperm, humpback, and fin whales into bonemeal, blood meal, baleen, meat, and oil. In light of the overpowering stench of decaying and rendered whale, the irony of the town's name (it was chosen in 1788 in honor of George Rose, a prominent member of the British Parliament) made it the butt of many a joke.

Today Rose Harbour's beach is composed almost exclusively of ground whalebone and rusting metal. Both the station and the remains of its prey decay together, shuffled and reshuffled twice daily by the tide.

Early the next morning I made coffee and gazed out over the bay. A lone gray whale blew and rolled to expose her barnacle-mottled back to the morning light. Her deep, sonorous breaths had punctuated my dreams all night. I watched the whale sift through the bones of its ancestors for crustaceans buried in the seafloor. Oystercatchers filled the air with shrill calls, darting in and out of spartan rock nests camouflaged in the outcroppings. The blood, oil, and stench of rotting whale and diesel were gone. The bay was tranquil again. It supported the very life it had worked to exterminate. No matter how permanent our endeavors, nature will reclaim them. When we leave, the balance between life and death will be struck once again.

Leaning totem

Ninstints was a place of great sadness. When the First Nations of British Columbia settled on this coast, they unerringly picked the richest, most spectacular places to live. Ninstints was no exception. The remains of the once-thriving village, known as "Place of the Red Cod" by the Haida, lie curved in a semicircle around a small bay dotted with islands. The continental shelf narrows into a mere sliver along the west coast of the Queen Charlotte Islands, allowing a banquet of open-ocean sea life to reach the village. With its abundance of food and its easily defended coastline (enemies had to brave

Dall's porpoise

some of the strongest winds in North America to reach the little island), the Haida outpost flourished for fifteen hundred years.

The Haida were a fierce people; they're sometimes referred to as the "Vikings of the Pacific." In the late eighteenth century, they attacked four European trading ships that had come to the northwest coast looking for sea otter pelts. In a retaliatory raid the chief of the Haida and fifty warriors were killed—but the Haida's troubles were only beginning. In 1862 the Haida were nearly wiped out by some smallpox-infested blankets they'd been given in trade. In 1884 the thirty surviving members of the village relocated to the most northerly island in the Queen Charlotte archipelago. Nearly a century later, in 1981, the United Nations recognized the Ninstints village site as a significant record of human culture and designated it a World Heritage Site.

In 1984 Ninstints's only remaining residents were the totem poles that stared silently out to sea, surrounded by a deep carpet of moss. Tiny deer the size of dogs grazed among the poles. A few beams from a 50-foot longhouse remained propped up at one end. I could scarcely imagine crossing Hecate Strait from the mainland in canoes, but that's what the Haida did. Evidence of their passage can be found in the poles they left behind, decorated with the crosshatched tail of the beaver; the wide, toothless grin of the frog; and the lolling tongue of the grizzly bear—all animals found nowhere on the Queen Charlotte Islands.

Both Rose Harbour and Ninstints spoke of death. The whales died for their oil; the people died for simply being Haida. One society left magnificent towers of art; the other, its bleaching bones.

After dropping off the anthropologists, the *Blue Fjord* had just enough diesel to get back to Port Hardy, so we left her at anchor in Rose Harbour and took the Zodiac out on a home-hunting mission. The area absolutely burst with life. At Lascoone Inlet the Pacific littleneck clams were so tightly packed that they couldn't close their shells without clamping onto a neighbor. I dug them out with a teaspoon. In the Zodiac we surfed a huge ocean swell down to the weather station at James Point, where we were greeted by a Steller sea lion colony roaring on the rocks. At the top of hundreds of stairs, the lighthouse keepers were delighted to see us—to see anybody, really. The two couples who tended the lighthouse proved to be cautionary tales. Both couples lived on the rocky outcropping and were rarely separated by more than a few hundred yards. And yet each referred to the other couple as if they lived in Vancouver. A set of strict, arcane rules kept the peace in the common work areas in the lighthouse, which was eerily neat and clean. I realized that there might be such a thing as too much isolation.

The landscape took our breath away, but the area was so remote, we couldn't even receive any Coast Guard stations on our marine radio. There were few whales and no children. Obtaining groceries and mail would require a several-hundred-dollar expedition. We loved the place, but I knew the Queen Charlottes wouldn't work for us.

We considered Namu, the old cannery town on the mainland coast. It had docks, whale-rich waters, and shelter, but no children. Rivers Inlet had whales and a few people, but it was a wind tunnel with little area to roam safely. Seymour Inlet, just south of Cape

Caution, looked intriguing, but its narrow entrance created one of the fastest menacing tidal currents on earth. Port Hardy, the old Vancouver Island fishing and mining town, was too big. Sointula, a Finnish fishing community on Malcolm Island, had children and whales in summer, but its surrounding waters were open; we'd never get out in winter. We began to realize that what we were looking for wasn't going to be easy to find.

Robin and I pored over our marine charts, sizing up every headland, cove, and passing bay like a pair of nesting geese. One question loomed in our minds: where did the whales go in winter? When we found the answer, we suspected that we'd also find our home.

After the Ninstints charter we rejoined the whales in Johnstone Strait and temporarily suspended our search for home. After the succession of tragedies I had witnessed among captive whales, it was sheer joy to be enjoying the high summer season with the wild orcas again.

The orca year revolves around the seasons of salmon. In the early 1980s we knew that the A pods, on which my fieldwork focused, came to Johnstone Strait in mid-July to feed on salmon returning to spawn in their home rivers. They stayed in or near the strait as wave after wave of returning pinks, sockeye, chinooks, coho, and chum poured into the channel between Vancouver Island and the mainland. Near the end of November, the salmon all but disappeared, and so did the orcas.

The A pod is actually made up of three subpods, each containing five to fifteen family members. The variation within their common dialect was so slight that I was able to work with all three groups for my language research. Their range begins just south of Campbell River and runs north along the British Columbia coast to the Prince Rupert area. They've never been seen in the Queen Charlotte Islands, but they do venture out to the west coast of Vancouver Island and into the open Pacific.

We spent quite a lot of time with Nicola, the sixty-year-old grande dame of the northern community and matriarch of the

A30 subpod. In 1984 Nicola traveled with her thirty-seven-year-old daughter Tsitika and four grandchildren.

Just as the people of the northwest coast had established hereditary lands, the whales also showed a complex pattern of dominion. One couldn't call them "territories" because no one ever saw patrols, disputes, or the warring that occurred among neighboring communities of many animals. It became increasingly apparent, however, that some system of dispersal guided the placement of orca pods on the British Columbia coast.

Nicola appeared to be the hereditary matriarch of Johnstone Strait. This was evidenced not by her displacement of other whales but rather by the way she greeted them. Her family was generally the first to arrive at the strait in early summer. The deep curves of mother and daughter, flanked by the boys, sliced into the area just a few days ahead of the early pink salmon runs.

Robin, Jarret, and I fell into the rhythm of Nicola's family. For a week they swept back and forth, riding the strait's favorable tides. We followed them for 9 nautical miles as they swung west into Queen Charlotte Strait. When the whales got within a mile of an arriving pod, they let the newcomers approach. The two pods then mingled in an intense tangle of fins. They pushed and slid along one another in sensuous physical contact. The youngsters popped up and down, chasing, splashing, and rolling side by side with their mothers. "Hey, Jarret," I said, calling him out from beneath his canopy. "You gotta see this." Robin rolled film, I recorded their tumultuous calls, and we all watched in awe as the whales piled up in such a small piece of ocean.

How do you raise a two-year-old boy on a Zodiac? You keep him happily busy. We stowed thousands of dollars' worth of film and sound equipment aboard the *Blue Fjord,* but the most important pieces of equipment in either boat were Jarret's LEGOs. He was an avid builder, creating planes and spaceships while Robin and I worked with the whales. The *Blue Fjord*'s rails were high enough to keep Jarret from tipping overboard, and I sewed sleeves onto his life vest so he could wear it as a coat. The *Fjord* was big enough for him to move about, but the Zodiac was another story. To make our research boat comfortable for Jarret, I strung a hammock of shrimp netting across the bow under the canvas canopy, complete with windows, for him to take shelter in. Around the perimeter of this triangular wedge-shaped hammock, I tied nylon stuff sacks filled with warm bedding, clothing, and toys. I stockpiled toys when we went to town, and every few days I hid a little surprise for him to discover. Jarret's Walkman played *The Wind in the Willows* and Winnie-the-Pooh books on tape. His mother-sewn outerwear was crude but effective. I made sleeping bags, vests, pants, and coats to keep his little body warm. I commissioned a local craftswoman to make him a pair of tiny sheepskin boots. Since we rarely saw any other children, Jarret was never made aware of the true strangeness of his wardrobe.

He was remarkably tolerant of our life-style. I once overheard someone ask Jarret where he'd grown up.

"I was raised in a Zodiac," he said matter-of-factly.

When Jarret was in the Zodiac, he got top priority. I learned this the hard way. Spending frustrating days attending to his needs while continuing to watch the whales always led to tears, poor notes, and a bad day in the boat. The trick was to give him my full attention, solve his dilemma, and work with him awhile, then turn back to my own work once he began to ignore me.

Jarret had an extraordinary intensity and an ability to focus that was sorely tested in the Zodiac. His tiny hands searched for the exact piece he needed as the thumping waves made the whole LEGO pile jump out of his lap. Every once in a while, he poked his head out to ask, "When are we going to a beach?"

We moved from one anchorage to another all summer and into fall: Growler Cove, Alert Bay, Double Bay, Freshwater Bay, Bauza Cove, Forward Bay. I became more familiar with the salmon cycles of the whales' lives and with the dialect of the A clan whales. The *pituuuu* call still fascinated me, particularly its role in facilitating synchrony. One afternoon as we drifted in the open waters of Queen Charlotte Strait, I made the call to a whale passing close to the boat. It was Eve's son Top Notch. He dove and reappeared seconds later beside the boat, his enormous head rising 8 feet out of the water. He seemed to be having a look at who, or what, was in the boat.

I don't know exactly what I said to him, but I had the impression it was something he understood. A fishing boat sped over to assist us—the skipper thought we were being attacked. I was thrilled, and so was Robin, although the photographer in him couldn't resist chastising me. "Don't ever speak to a whale again," he said, "unless I have film rolling!"

In typical orca fashion, my "speaking" to them never elicited such a response again. I imagined them thinking, "Yeah, yeah, we know you can do that. Show us something new."

In August millions of sockeye salmon funneled through Blackney and Weyton passes en route to their spawning rivers. We floated above their backs, their silver sides shimmering and glinting over the dark waters as they made their distinctive multiple leaps as far as the eye could see. Unlike chinooks, which schooled along the shoreline, sockeye congregated in the open-water tidelines. Sockeye are the long-distance runners of the salmon world, traveling hundreds of miles up their natal streams to spawn. Some of the sockeye that passed beneath our boat were bound for mountain lakes in Idaho, nearly 1,000 miles from the coast. Years ago the sockeye returned to their rivers in massive schools. I once read a story about a Canadian fisheries officer in the 1930s eating his lunch beside a quiet salmon stream. Suddenly the sockeye came home. The warden heard a roar and watched the sheer mass of the incoming school raise the level of the stream.

Orcas will eat any size salmon, but some pods are known for their predilection for certain types. Kelsy and Yakat, the sister matriarchs of the A4 pod, loved the 2- to 5-pound pink salmon that are also known as humpies. When the chum salmon show up in October, so do the orcas in the G clan, who are notorious dog salmon eaters. "Dog" refers to the chums, who are called that because they develop big, curving caninelike teeth at spawning time. (Years later I crept up to a pool of spawning chum hoping to slip my underwater still camera beneath the surface to photograph them. When I reached the water's edge, I slowly eased the camera into the water. As I neared a spawning pair, the far from shy male turned and sank his teeth into my index finger. Ow! They really use those teeth.) We don't know why the G clan times its arrival with the chum run, although it may be that by October the runs in their northern waters have simply run dry, leading them to follow the chum south.

If the orcas had to pick one species of salmon over all others, though, it would probably be the chinook. In a paper I coauthored with Graeme Ellis, John Ford, Lance Barrett-Lennard, and others, we found that 65 percent of the salmonids eaten by orcas were chinooks, 17 percent were pinks, 6 percent were cohos, 6 percent were chum, 4 percent were sockeye, and 2 percent were steelhead. Canadians call chinooks springs; Americans call them kings; killer whales call them good eating. The largest of all salmon species, chinooks can grow to more than 100 pounds in exceptional cases. They tend to stay close to shore, swimming in and out of rocky outcroppings protected by extensive kelp beds. Chinooks know how to hide from the whales; they use the air-filled stalks of kelp as camouflage, since echolocation can't penetrate the air pockets inside the kelp stems. A chinook-hungry orca will plow through dense kelp beds looking for springs until the brown fronds pile up over his dorsal fin.

When the chinooks were in, we used to watch killer whales push their rostrums into cracks in cliff faces. With their faces against the rock, they'd swim hard against the cliff, pumping with their powerful tail flukes to build waves that crashed against the cliff. Other whales lined up behind the hunter, waiting their turn. We didn't know what was going on until orca researcher Jeff Jacobsen found a 30-pound chinook wedged in a crevasse one day. Apparently the salmon hide in the crevasses, and the whales try to wash them out by creating waves. Jacobsen noted his finding, then gaffed the salmon and invited us to his camp for dinner.

———

It was during the October run of chum that we got our first glimpse of serious sex in killer whales. Before going any further, I should say that when it comes to killer whales, as with other cetaceans, there's sex and then there's sex. Whales and dolphins are highly sensual, sexual beings. I've seen male dolphins drag Frisbees around with their penises; I've seen females insert their rostrums into the genital slits of pen mates and propel them around the tank. All sorts of objects—even turtles—were incorporated into sex play. In the wild, sex play occurs wherever there are partners and plentiful food. Male sex play usually happens in the absence of females. You can't see exactly what's going on but can often glimpse their 3-foot pink penises waving about in the rough and tumble.

Serious procreative sex is another matter. In most cetacean societies males compete for breeding access to females. Male bottle-nosed dolphins are known to form tight coalitions and abduct fe-males. Male right whales produce prodigious amounts of sperm in hopes of washing out the sperm of a previous suitor. We think humpback males might sing to attract females.

With killer whales we still don't know if and how the competi-tion takes place. I once watched a transient female mate with the oldest transient male that was available on three successive days. When a younger male was present, he waited in the wings until the older male departed. While consorting with a male, the female trav-eled an erratic course close by the male of her choice. Privacy is nei-ther an option nor a concern. The families of both whales swam behind, side by side, following the consorting whales' every move.

During the chum run the A12 matriarch Scimitar and her three children joined up with the I2 pod. Instead of swimming close by her sons, Scimitar paired off with the huge I5 male, an old bull with a massive twisted fin whom I named Ulysses.

Over the next few days, Ulysses appeared next to Scimitar when-ever we encountered them. Then, early one morning in the chop of Blackney Pass, Robin and I watched as Ulysses and Scimitar swam out ahead of the other whales. Their families followed a few hundred yards behind, eleven whales rising and falling like a line of cresting waves. We motored quietly behind the intermingled pods and every now and then noticed large milky deposits on the water's surface. This we read as a sign that Scimitar and Ulysses had consummated their relationship; we dared not go any closer.

If we hadn't exactly caught Scimitar and Ulysses in the act, we had been given a clue to one of our unanswered questions: Where are the fathers? They're around, it turns out—in other pods.

Years later this would be confirmed by Lance Barrett-Lennard, a British Columbian marine biologist who studied the genetics of British Columbian killer whales for his doctoral thesis at the University of British Columbia. Using a crossbow, Lance took tiny samples of blubber from whales of different pods and compared their DNA. He discovered that resident whales mate outside their pod but within their community.

I awoke one morning to a strange, distant croaking noise. As I stepped onto the deck of the *Blue Fjord,* I looked up to see a V formation in the sky. The sandhill cranes were leaving their Arctic summer range, headed for Texas and other points south. Later in the week they'd be followed by the snow geese and Canada geese. The birds sparked excitement in me. Winter was coming.

As autumn progressed, the whales became more dispersed. Instead of pacing back and forth in Johnstone Strait, they kept disappearing to the north for days at a time. We turned to the other vessels in the area to track their movements. During summer and early fall, researchers in Johnstone Strait use the VHF radio for daily, sometimes hourly, reporting. We pick one frequency at the beginning of the season and radio detailed records of which whales are sighted and where. In the Johnstone Strait area, Helena Symonds continuously monitors the radio at OrcaLab to collect a detailed record of movements.

The folks at OrcaLab make sure I receive all the sightings in my area, and I do the same for them. Some days we know the location of one hundred whales spread over 80 miles, which helps us understand how they coordinate their society. We now know that the concept of "traveling together" is much broader for whales than for humans. To a human watching from a boat, a young mother and her offspring might look as if they're alone, but my contact with other vessels tells me that she just went around the north side of an island, while granny and the others are on the south side. Conversely I might find that she really is alone, with a report of her sister 50 miles away, letting me know that perhaps her family is beginning to form a new pod.

This late in the year, all the researchers were gone except Paul Spong and Helena Symonds, but there were plenty of others still living and working in the northern waters: commercial fishers, lighthouse keepers, floatplane pilots. Tugboat crews were the best. The captains and deckhands in the *Duncan Foss, Sea Span Cutlass,* and *Captain Bob* kept their sharp maritime eyes open for whale sightings.

On a cold day in late October, Robin and I followed Scimitar and Saddle as they led their families east out of Queen Charlotte Strait toward an unfamiliar sea lion rock at the mouth of Fife Sound. We followed them with intense concentration, anxious not to lose them this late in the season. They were due to depart for their winter grounds any day. Sharky surfaced next to the rock outcropping at Eden Island and gave the sea lion colony such a fright that one of them got pushed into the water. Had the whales been transients, that sea lion would have been supper. As it happened, though, Sharky was as startled as the poor sea lion; as the sea lion scrambled back up the boulder, the young orca rocketed away in fright.

The whales continued eastward, and we followed in the Zodiac, unsure where we were going. As Robin drove, I inched my finger along the chart, never lifting it for fear I'd lose our place.

The whales were leading us into the Broughton Archipelago, where the Canadian coast atomizes into dozens of islands and waterways. Motoring up Fife Sound felt like cruising slowly up the

Amazon; this wasn't uncharted territory, but it was definitely undeveloped, uninhabited, and unknown to us. The deep green of one
island blended into the next, giving me the sensation of entering a
maze. Compared to the broad maritime highway of Johnstone Strait,
Fife Sound seemed remote, private, and full of mystery. And oh, the
silence. I'd never heard silent water before entering the archipelago.

The whales milled in the tranquil channels, corralling salmon in
small, steep-sided bays. Gulls and eagles circled overhead. A young
orca surfaced with a salmon crosswise in its jaws. As we moved
farther east, the channel opened into a huge natural amphitheater.
Snow-frosted mountains rose straight up from the water. A sprin-
kling of islands—the gently sloping Burdwoods—sat in the middle
of the water, giving massive scale to the surrounding mountains.
Robin shut down the engine and let us drift with the tide. I put my
headphones on and heard an extraordinary clarity in the water. No
cruise ships, fishing boats, or distant tugs roared underwater. The
whales' calls echoed five and six times in the stillness. It felt as if
they'd led us to the end of the world.

I spotted a whale's blow a mile away. Through the binoculars, I
saw that the blow was really smoke. The smoke led to a chimney, the
chimney led to a house, and the house led to—water. I pulled the
binoculars away, sighted the house, and looked again. It was no mi-
rage. The house floated.

We'd traveled 40 miles through the rain. Rivulets of freezing
water trickled down my back. We abandoned the whales for the
promise of a warm hearth. As we drew near the house, we noticed
an odd roof that sloped away at all angles. A raft of logs ran together
from the house to the shore. A hand-painted sign near the door said
WINDSONG BARGE. It appeared that somebody had sheared a hobbit-
style hut off at the foundation and plopped it down on a floating
wooden barge. Nearer the shore we could see that these water
dwellers weren't alone. Here and there little shacks bobbed along the
bayshore, buoyed up by enormous cedar logs lashed together with
steel cable. My heart leaped when I spotted, across the bay, the familiar red-and-white lettering of a Canadian post office. At the head of

the bay was a government dock that led up to a grassy area and a broad white beach. Robin pointed to the empty dock. We nodded to each other: moorage for the *Blue Fjord*.

Robin idled the motor and swung the Zodiac alongside the Windsong just as a slight, elegant woman in her thirties came out to take our lines. Two doe-eyed girls peeked out from behind her.

"Who are you?" piped the older girl. She wasn't asking Robin or me. She was talking to Jarret, whose hands were clamped around my leg. "Do you know how to play cards?" she demanded.

Christine O'Donnell smiled and asked if we'd like something warm to drink. Her two daughters shanghaied Jarret as we hopped onto their float. Christine opened her front door and bid us enter her warm, dry sanctuary.

"Welcome," she said, "to Echo Bay."

Chapter 13

Over a simple dinner of rice, chapatis, and canned salmon, Christine and her husband, Jim, filled us in on Echo Bay, formerly a thriving Kwakwaka'wakw village. The neighboring bay had once been known as the receptacle of supernatural power. Pale cliffs above the bay still bear faint red ocher pictographs of a sun and a human face. The broad white beach had been built up by eight thousand years of clam and barnacle feasts. Like so many other First Nations communities, this one was all but wiped out when smallpox was introduced in the nineteenth century. The first white settlers arrived in the surrounding area in 1880 to practice hand logging, a labor-intensive but minimally destructive technique that involved cutting a tree and sliding it straight into the water using hand tools and boats. In 1897 the Powell River Company brought in a steam donkey and began logging the 150 square miles of Gilford Island that surrounded Echo Bay. More loggers arrived with their families. They built floathouses, which aren't the most practical buildings in the world—imagine a house on logs that begin slowly sinking from the moment they hit water—but made sense for the loggers, who could tow their homes from one logging claim to the next. Entire communities floated together, with bunkhouses, shops, single-family homes, and gardens bobbing on rafts of logs.

In the early 1980s Echo Bay consisted of 150 fishermen, loggers, and hippies. As our coats and sweaters steamed dry by the wood-stove, Jim, a bear of a man, told us how he and Christine had fled to

175

Canada from the American Midwest in the early 1970s to escape the Vietnam War draft. After wandering the coast making a living from jobs that ranged from teaching music to running a salmon roe plant, they discovered Echo Bay and stayed to homestead on the water.

Jim and Christine had turned their barge into a lovely home. Outside, everything was crazy angles and rough-hewn cedar; inside, it offered a comfortable living room with a slab of polished wood for a coffee table and worn Oriental rugs, huge lounging chairs, and an enormous steel drum that had been converted into a woodstove. Jim, who had once worked as a photographer for *Life* magazine, had hung his penetrating series of black-and-white portraits of native chiefs on the far wall of the barge next to a number of ceremonial carved masks. They had no electricity but got along just fine with candlelight.

Unlike the loggers, Jim and Christine had settled in Echo Bay for the life, not the work. They did a little of this and that to survive. Jim had tended bar at the nearby Echo Bay Resort for a while, flown seaplanes, and turned himself into a jack-of-all-trades in order to keep the barge afloat.

"Some nights the bar could get pretty wild," Jim said. "All the loggers came in and tried to beat up each other just for the fun of it. It was my job to keep them from killing each other."

Scattered among the loggers and the hippies were a few families that had lived in Echo Bay for several generations. The hippies and the old-time locals generally got along well. The hippies admired the old-timers' hard-won local knowledge; they were the teachers everyone needed when the 17-foot tides and hurricane-force winds hit the archipelago. To the longtime inhabitants, the hippies were often amusing, sometimes baffling, but always good-hearted people.

Christine filled us in on the day-to-day routine. Mail came in by seaplane three times a week. There were no telephones, so the entire town communicated by VHF radio. "We call over channel 16, then usually switch to 70. But don't expect any privacy," she laughed. "People here know what you're going to do before you've done it."

Her two girls, Cedar and Willow, along with thirteen other children from Echo Bay, the two local logging camps, and the nearby native village of Gwayasdums, attended Echo Bay School over at the head of the bay. School boats picked them up and dropped them off every morning.

"In fact, how old is Jarret?" Christine asked.

"Nearly three," I said.

"I thought so. Same age as George and Susie's son Chris. You'll meet them."

Christine had already gone into recruiting mode. Echo Bay is perpetually threatened by lack of children. By 1984 every school in the surrounding communities had closed. It's a common pattern on the north coast. When a school closes, the young families drift away, then the post office closes for lack of business, and finally the remaining families move or die off. In the three of us, Christine saw not just potential neighbors and friends but new life for the community. I find myself doing the same thing to visitors today.

A fisherman named Billy Proctor took the older kids to North Island Secondary School in Port McNeill on Monday morning and brought them home on Friday afternoon, a six-hour round trip. Billy made regular grocery and hardware store runs to Port McNeill, too, said Christine. If you just show up on the dock at 7:30 in the morning, she told us, he'd take you for free.

As Christine tucked Cedar and Willow into their beds, Jarret nestled into my lap and fell asleep.

Who else lived there? we asked when Christine returned. How did they get by?

The only "job" jobs were at Scott Cove, where the International Forest Products company based its logging operation, and at Shoal Harbour, where Whonnock Industries put its timber in the water. Otherwise, said Jim, folks made do. Billy Proctor worked the *Twilight Rock,* a commercial salmon troller, with his sixteen-year-old daughter, Joanie. George and Susie, who lived one bay to the north of Echo Bay, had worked as fisheries guardians for the provincial government, which meant they spent their days counting salmon in local streams. "George's from Austria, and Susie's from Costa Rica," Jim told us. "They make their own saki. Powerful stuff." Bob and Nancy Richter ran a general store at the Echo Bay Resort, where pleasure boaters tied up during the summer. They'd bought the run-down wreck of a marina a few years previously, quit their computer jobs in Seattle, and moved north to restore and run the place.

We talked late into the night. Before turning in, I got up the courage to ask the make-or-break question.

"Are there whales here in the winter?"

"There are more whales here in winter than summer," said Jim, stretching the truth a bit. "But you'll want to talk to Billy about that."

Billy Proctor is a compact, grizzled man in his early fifties who wore a two-tone wool cap with a festive ball on top. We found him leaping out of an incredibly beat-up old speedboat at the post office. A shy man, Billy glanced at us occasionally but preferred to study his feet while talking to strangers.

"Whales?" he said. "Oh, Christ, yeah, we've got whales. They go up Knight's Inlet before a big winter southeast storm. Four years ago there were two humpback whales in Bond Sound in December. I used to know a whale named Joe, lived near Freshwater Bay . . ."

I fumbled through my pockets for pen and paper. My God—the man was the oracle of Echo Bay. We'd never got answers like this. Once you got Billy going, there was no stopping him. He had a photographic memory. Billy could recall every whale he'd seen in the past forty years and, if pressed, probably could have told you about every big fish he'd caught, too.

"Up till 1966 I had never heard the term *killer whale*; we always called them blackfish. There used to be lots of 'em, but the whalers shot a lot in 1967 and 1968. Back in 1945, when I was young, you could see so many blackfish, you'd think you could just about walk across their backs. Robson Bight was their meeting place and where they'd rest. When the sockeye was running, they'd go out to the north shore of Malcolm Island on the ebb tide and play and feed around Bere Point. In winter on the big full-moon tide, they go up Knight's Inlet and stay there for two to three days." I was writing for all I was worth. "When I was a small boy, we lived in Freshwater Bay on the edge of Blackfish Sound. This is where Old Joe, a humpback whale, lived. He would come in on the tide and feed on the big schools of herring that were around then. The herring would be running off his head. He always looked like he was smiling, and he would feed like that every slack tide. When the tide started to run hard, he'd just lay in the back eddy by the kelp and sleep. He seemed so content with his tummy full of herring. I'd row up to him and sit and watch. Oh, he knew I was there, but he never seemed to care. Once I let the rowboat drift right up to him. His eye was open, he could see me, and I reached out and touched him. He didn't care. It was real neat. There was another humpback that lived in Fife Sound. People called him Barney 'cause he had a big barnacle on his back, and a lot of the time he had a buddy, so she was called The Missus." I had no idea that humpbacks had once been part of the local ecosystem.

It had started to rain and my notes were smearing, but I didn't want to move for fear Billy would stop talking. He took no notice of the downpour.

"One day, when I was down in Blackfish Sound, this kayak came alongside my boat and asked had I seen any killer whales. I had never seen anyone like this guy in my life before. He had hair down to his belt and three strings of beads around his neck. A few days later a school of blackfish came along, with an armada of kayaks following them. Leading them was a real odd-looking boat with a guy standing on it, and you know he was bare naked and long hair blowing in the wind, and he was beating his chest and screaming into the wind. I could not believe my eyes. I thought, *'My God, what next?'*"

Billy glanced up at me. "How come you want to know all about whales anyway?"

By the end of the morning, we knew we'd found our home.

After talking with Billy, we visited the floating post office to see if we could get a box number.

"Oh, that's all right," said postmistress Nancy Richter, a tall, confident woman with brilliant red hair. "We don't have numbers here. Just names. That's enough."

Robin, Jarret, and I sped out of Echo Bay with our hearts singing. We'd found what we were looking for.

Before we could settle into Echo Bay, we had to retrieve the *Blue Fjord,* which we'd anchored back in Double Bay, on the north side of Hanson Island. We motored back into the open water of Blackfish Sound and Johnstone Strait, where we were waylaid by the A and G clans hunting the autumn run of dog salmon, heavy with eggs and spawn. (Our rule of thumb was, Never pass up an orca at hand.)

Every now and then the orcas would be joined by a school of Dall's porpoises, who liked to speed alongside the whales. The first time we saw them, we thought they were fleeing a whale attack, but as Robin filmed the "hunt," it became apparent that the porpoises were chasing the whales. The porpoises tended to cluster around one whale and zip around its head in tiny bursts of spray. We're still not sure if the porpoises do this purely for fun or if it's some sort of foraging technique, with the porpoises taking advantage of the whales' powerful echolocation to stun the fish or picking up the orcas' salmon scraps. (Salmon are too big for porpoises to consume on their own.)

What puzzled us was the porpoises' seeming nonchalance in the presence of killer whales. Had these been mammal-eating transients, the porpoises would have been attacked and eaten. The porpoises must have been able to tell the difference—but how?

The fall of 1984 blessed the British Columbia coast with a true "Indian" summer. Between storms the sky turned electric blue and lit up at night with stars brilliant enough to navigate by. We had fallen in

Bowhead whale

love with Echo Bay on a rainy day; on a warm autumn afternoon, we absolutely swooned. The snaking white beach set off the green water and surrounding evergreen hillsides like a string of pearls on a velvet gown.

Every morning before Robin and Jarret stirred, I rose, wrapped myself in two layers of wool, and went out on the back deck to light the Coleman stove for coffee. Perched on the ship's railing, I listened to the poetry of ravens conversing across the bay. A puff of smoke, followed by the incense of burning cedar, signaled the awakening of Christine O'Donnell and her household. I breathed deeply. These eight-thousand-year-old sounds and smells couldn't have been more alien to the proper colonial brick world in which I'd been raised. And yet I had never known a more perfect home.

We'd tied up the *Blue Fjord* to the wharf at the head of the bay, where the schoolchildren tumbled out of the school boat every morning at 8:50. With their excited chatter and brightly colored jackets, they resembled a tiny flock of birds. As newcomers, we were the children's—and the town's—chief objects of curiosity, and every morning they peered through our windows and waved hello with mittened fingers.

Most of the children came from logging families at the Interfor camp, but others were from families looking for an alternative to living "in town," which is how Gilford Islanders refer to any outpost of civilization bigger than the microcommunity of Echo Bay. I expected children raised in such a remote area to be shy, but these kids were open, approachable, and exuberant. Once they heard why we were there, they barraged us with whale stories. "We see whales *all* the time. They're okay. Once I saw a whale chase a duck. I saw a *hundred* whales on the way to town. Have you ever seen a whale jump? That's the coolest . . ." We wrote down their sightings and asked them to help our research by calling us the next time they saw whales. They loved that.

The *Blue Fjord*'s batteries lasted about four days before our lights began to dim. We recharged them by cranking up the Lister, our obscenely loud diesel generator. This wasn't a problem in the wide-open spaces of Johnstone Strait, but in cozy Echo Bay it proved embarrassing. The place is named Echo Bay for a reason. Sound skates across the bay, bounces off the pictograph cliff, and resounds back into the bay. When it was running, the Lister sent the school-children scurrying past with hands over their ears and set the locals' teeth on edge. After a couple of weeks, we and our generator were in danger of wearing out our welcome.

In typical north coast fashion, the problem was solved with a dose of generosity. One morning when we visited the post office, Bob and Nancy Richter made us an offer we couldn't refuse. If we kept an eye on the resort while they did some traveling, we could tie up to their dock and plug into the generator they kept behind padded soundproof walls. Thus was the community spared the *rat-a-tat-tat* of the boorish Mr. Lister, and we, the enmity of our new neighbors.

Robin, Jarret, and I went out in the Zodiac every day, determined to encounter and identify every whale that came through the archipelago. We had no idea of their travel patterns, so we covered as much water as we could. Freezing cold didn't slow us down; only a real storm kept us in for the day. We became experts in outerwear and underwear, adopting a layering system to blunt the wind that sliced at us as we traveled at 20 knots in the open Zodiac: long underwear, turtleneck, thick flannel shirt, down vest, and a blinding yellow exposure suit made of quarter-inch high-density foam. We moved stiffly like robots, but at least we stayed warm. Jarret played under his customized canopy, tucked into sheepskin boots and his homemade wardrobe. When the water turned rough, I folded him into my arms and served as a human car seat. On the coldest days Jarret remained in Echo Bay to play with Chris Jahn, whose parents, George and Susie, generously looked after him.

What we did not find, to our frustration and chagrin, were all the whales that Billy, Jim, and the schoolchildren had seen.

With Robin standing at the pilot station and me facing backward to scan for whales, we explored the hundreds of islands and passages of the Broughton Archipelago. The eastern shore of Vancouver Island is fairly low and contiguous, but the mainland coast is a ragged maze of inlets, channels, passages, and bays that cut into steep mountain ranges. Dozens of islands insulate Echo Bay, from the open waters of Blackfish Sound and the Queen Charlotte Strait. Some are rocks that disappear at high tide; others stretch several miles across and support thriving populations of deer, wolves, black bears, and mink. We often spotted bears turning over beach rocks at low tide. On their favorite beaches the bears rotated the rocks so often, you'd find barnacles growing on all sides.

Every morning we faced a decision: which direction? Some days the wind dictated our answer, but more often we just guessed. For three weeks we set out searching for whales, and for three weeks we found nothing.

We stopped at every logging camp, fishing camp, and floathouse to ask if the residents had seen whales. We met some mighty nice and mighty strange folks. The children in a family living in a huge beached boat were so wild that they crept around in the background, peeking out at us suspiciously. People were often suspicious when Robin and I, clad in our official-looking matching yellow suits and driving the well-outfitted Zodiac, approached their boats. One day we pulled up to a little tug called the *Gale Winds* towing a floathouse. It took a fair amount of yelling to get the skipper's attention. At last the door flew open, and there was Bobby Lamont, a wiry old cuss, sitting at the wheel wearing nothing but his underpants.

Finally on the twenty-first day: "Robin! Whales!"

We were speeding back to the *Blue Fjord* near dusk, around three in the afternoon. Looking north toward Mount Stevens, my eye caught the soft gray plume of a blow.

Robin spun the Zodiac and pulled the throttle back to an idle. Three whales rolled smoothly from behind the rocky point. In the dimming light we couldn't identify them, but from the extreme pointiness of their dorsal fins and small pod size, we figured they were probably transients. In a desperate attempt to bring something away from the encounter, Robin mounted a flash on his camera and clicked off a roll of film. We got twenty-four blurry shots of the flash reflecting off the whales' black, wet backs.

A few days later I rose for Robin's thirty-first birthday. I had breakfast in bed planned. As I primed the stove with the thumb pump, five quick retorts echoed across the bay. *Kwoof, kwoof, kwoof, kwoof-kwoof.* A bolt of adrenaline flashed through me. I whirled around to see a fin disappearing to the north.

Robin and I scrambled to dress Jarret, provision for the day, and toss everything in the Zodiac. We were sure to lose them if we didn't hurry. The whales maintained their course, moving slowly toward Tribune Channel. They took no notice of our approach as we passed the scattering of floathouses just beyond Echo Bay, but as soon as we followed them into the deserted reaches of the channel, one of the whales broke away and dashed back to our boat. Robin and I watched the water turn black as the female orca glided beneath us. With one eye swiveled up to observe us, she swam the length of our boat before porpoising back to her mother. A few seconds later she returned to have another look.

It was Sharky. I had the distinct impression that she was surprised to see us here. Whale following was normal behavior for humans in Johnstone Strait, even near Echo Bay, but not in Tribune Channel.

Just ahead of us I spotted another familiar dorsal fin.

"Good morning, Saddle," I said.

Robin snapped the film magazine onto his sleek Éclair 16-millimeter movie camera while I lowered a hydrophone over the side. I flashed Robin a smile and gave him a thumbs-up. The sounds of Saddle and her daughter Sharky and her five-year-old son, A15, bounced off the steep walls of the mainland and into my ears. We'd done it: we'd found A pod in winter. This was what we'd dreamed of when we first met. With Jarret in my arms, I turned to Robin and beamed. "Happy birthday."

Never before had I seen Saddle and her immediate family travel without other members of the A clan. Robin and I scanned the water all day long, expecting to see the blows of Eve, Stripe, Top Notch, and other members of the A5 pod. But they never came. All winter long we encountered family after family broken down into its smallest divisible matriarchal unit, mothers and offspring. Eve came through Kingcome Inlet with her sons Top Notch and Foster, and the matriarch Licka brought her daughters Havannah and Sonora as well.

Clearly the big gatherings of cousins, aunts, uncles, and other more distantly related members of the northern resident clan were unique to summer. During winter the fish eaters resembled the mammal eaters, with their smaller, quieter groups and less boisterous behavior.

The reason for this winter fracturing became apparent as we continued to encounter the whales. The whales fished differently in the cold season. Rather than feasting together on huge runs of salmon in the tidelines of deep water, they now investigated the shallow kelp forests. As they plowed through kelp beds, I hypothesized that they were looking for rock cod, bass, flounder, sole, and the occasional chinook salmon. (Figuring out what they're eating has always been one of the challenges of studying killer whales. With other large mammals, it's often as easy as examining scat. Whale researchers don't have that luxury unless we're very quick with a net.)

I was also fishing to feed my family. Robin and I usually jigged a couple of times a day from the Zodiac, so that by the time we got back to the *Blue Fjord,* we had dinner in hand. On a good day we brought home salmon; but rockfish was delicious, too. We always had to be careful with the rockfish. Their sharp, poisonous spines could puncture the Zodiac or the spare fuel tank. If they pricked your skin, you'd be in for a couple of hours of discomfort. I often wondered how the whales, with their soft, pink mouths, dealt with these prickly morsels.

We ate the white flesh of rockfish and used the heads and skeletons to trap crabs and prawns. When I caught a fish, I generally stayed in that spot until I caught my fill. The whales, I noticed, had a different strategy. They rarely stopped moving. As they hunted, I heard the sound of kelp stalks snapping as the orcas' dorsal fins popped them free of their anchors. They never lingered, even if the eating was good, so no spot was ever completely cleaned out. They were conservationists by nature.

Winter days are short up here. Daylight doesn't arrive until after 8:00 A.M., and darkness falls as early as 3:45. Robin and I hadn't realized how little time there was going to be each day to find and follow whales in winter. It usually took a couple of hours to find them, and some days it seemed as though we'd have to leave twenty minutes after our first encounter in order to make it home before it turned pitch-black.

To overcome the strictures of daylight, in late December we decided to follow the whales at night. As Licka and Eve and their families moved eastbound through the darkened Sutlej Channel, we followed them by shutting off the motor to listen for their blows.

The whales led us into a long dogleg bay called Greenway Sound. We followed with our motor at a low purr as the orcas moved deeper into the dead-end sound, which cuts Broughton Island nearly in half. I dropped the hydrophone in the water, fixed the headphones around my ears, and heard the most wondrous sounds. Whale calls ricocheted back and forth off the steep, convoluted shore of Broughton Island. Each call echoed five and six times. The clarity was like nothing I'd ever heard. There wasn't even a trace of motor noise. With each echo the whales' spotlight beam of echolocation broadened into a surround-sound effect, outlining the boundaries of their environment. As the calls echoed in waves of dying intensity, every member of the whale family could utilize this shared illumination of Greenway Sound and the fish it contained. The calls created a deep melody that played on and on and on. Lying on the floor of the Zodiac, looking up at the winter moon, I let the sounds work their magic on me and felt a warm rush of contentment fill my soul.

I couldn't have designed a better study site than the Broughton Archipelago. The area seemed to be an important part of the A pod's winter range. Because my research relied heavily on correlating behavior with sound, the smaller the pod, the more precisely I could record both sound and motion. The tiny winter units of A pod proved to be ideal. And of course, the purity of whale sounds in the archipelago's many channels, inlets, bays, and sounds proved to be exquisite.

The archipelago also turned out to be fertile ground to study the most intimidating and elusive of killer whales: the transients.

Our brief observation of the porpoises playing among the resident orcas had piqued my interest in transients. It was nearly impossible for humans to separate transients from residents without getting close enough for dorsal fin identification. I wanted to find out how the other mammals whose lives depended on it could so readily pick up on the difference.

I knew from my seasons on Johnstone Strait that (once I found them) resident whales were relatively easy to track, because they traveled highly predictable routes. Transients were another story. After more than twenty years in the field, I find myself still challenged whenever I follow these cunning ocean hunters.

Early that winter Robin and I came upon two of the most famous transient orcas moving north through Blackney Pass. Flores (T13) and her son Pender (T14) were two of the first transients ever photographed when they were captured for the oceanarium trade near Seattle in early 1976. By the mid-1970s the people of the Pacific Northwest had grown so strongly opposed to whale captures that public outcry forced their captors to release Flores and Pender a few weeks after their capture. They weren't completely freed, however. In a barbaric act of science, a collar attached to radio transmitters was slipped over the whales' dorsal fins and attached with stainless-steel bolts drilled right through the fins. The bolts were secured by corrodible nuts, with the idea that the nuts would disintegrate in about a year, allowing the packs to slip off. In the meantime scientists hoped to receive detailed information about the two whales' movements.

The whales were released in April 1976, but the packs transmitted data for only ten days. During that time the whales traveled about 68 nautical miles a day at about 2.8 knots. They reached a top speed of 16 knots and dove for as long as seventeen minutes. This was interesting information, but it could have been obtained without cutting holes into live whale flesh.

When Flores and Pender were next sighted three years after their release, the packs had disappeared. The nuts hadn't corroded, though. Flores's dorsal fin had swelled horribly, and two deep wounds appeared on Pender's fin. Somehow the bolts had been pulled straight through to remove the pack. I wondered if the whales had done it for each other. Because the integrity of Pender's fin had been breached, the whole fin tilted backward.

Transients are expert stalkers. They have to be; their prey is intrinsically more intelligent than resident orca prey. Fish don't learn to evade killer whales as easily as mammals do. Mammals live longer than fish and have the capacity to learn from their elders. A mother seal teaches her pup that when you see or hear an orca, you go silent and immobile or head for high ground—the nearest beach or rock. As a result, transients are masters of stealth, vocalizing rarely, if at all, while hunting. They hide their essential echolocation clicks in the general ocean noise by using more random sequencing and longer intervals. They also learn to hide their blows out of sight from potential seal or sea lion prey. One transient male I've come to know over the years, Kwatsi (T20), had a disconcerting habit of surfacing right behind my boat. No matter how I tried to alter my course, his 5-foot fin stayed right behind my engine. After a while I realized what he was doing: Kwatsi was using my boat and its engine noise as a moving hunting blind.

To let the transients know I wasn't hunting them, I made my movements obvious and predictable. The whales knew every time I turned toward or away from them by the pitch of my outboard motor. I learned to resist speeding up when they blew, even though I was dying to get close enough to photoidentify them. I kept the boat speed constant and steered closer to them, very slowly. The whales knew where I was and what I was doing, and they learned that I wasn't going to lunge at them.

Right from the start, the transients showed that they could ditch me anytime they wanted. They're acutely aware of their surface appearance and what clues a mammal might take from their distance and position. Sometimes I'd see them surface while moving westward, then realize some time later that they'd feinted a move west, then dived and swam invisibly east. They rose quietly, hidden in a kelp bed or behind an island, and blew so softly, I often missed the sound completely. They have other ways of getting rid of me that I have never figured out. They simply vanish.

Because we never saw transients join in the summer whale gatherings, there was a natural temptation to classify them as the "outcasts" of orca society. But the more information I and other researchers gathered, the more we realized that the transients weren't outcasts but rather members of a different society.

Years of Shamu shows have conditioned the public to think of killer whales as pool toys. Resident whales, with their matriarchal societies and fish-eating ways, dovetail nicely with that false image. The transients, however, are nothing like Shamu. While they can be gentle and patient, these orcas are responsible for some of the most violent kills in the waterborne world. That doesn't make them bad. That's just the way they are.

Following a group of feeding transients can be an unnerving experience. I'd expected to see spectacular roiling-water kills, but transients aren't always flashy. Most of the time they'll take a seal underwater, dispatch it in a matter of moments, and move on. Sometimes all you'll see is a group of transients milling on the surface and a flock of seagulls dipping down to scavenge the scraps. At first I was blind to these subtle signs of a kill, but gradually I learned to recognize the evidence. Trailing at a safe distance in the Zodiac, I'd come upon the remnants of their meal in bits and pieces: tiny pencil-eraser-size chunks of seal fat, a telltale slick of marine mammal oil, and the pungent fishy smell unique to seals. On one occasion I found an entire severed porpoise head, its upturned jaw frozen in a ghoulish lifeless smile. Transients pop the meat and fat off the body of their prey, letting the bones and internal organs sink to the bottom. Through the hydrophone, I could hear them literally tearing their prey apart.

There's a term for what they're able to do: *deglove*. The best way I can explain it is to say that while following in the wake of some feeding transients one day, I picked up what looked like a latex porpoise mask. The transients had degloved its head.

On another day I steered the Zodiac over to a chunk of debris bobbing in the wake of some milling transients. I leaned over the side of the boat and scooped up a chunk of lung attached to an intact mammalian heart, still beating.

One late November morning during that first year in Echo Bay, I spotted a group of whales cruising by the resort dock. Robin had just boarded a seaplane to Vancouver, where he hoped to drum up funding for two films about the seasons of the orcas and the water dwellers of the Echo Bay community. The rain poured down like a broken water main. I radioed Susie and asked if Jarret could spend the day with her and Chris; I didn't want to subject him to another day of pelting rain.

I counted eleven whales, a big group for transients. They flowed together, separated, and regrouped, which made it tough to get an accurate count. When I don't know which whales I'm with, I count them by age and sex: how many females, how many males, how many youngsters, how many mother/baby pairs. These demographics can help in later putting together which families were present. By their sharply pointed fins and closed saddles, I knew these were transients.

They swam north past Scott Cove, where a pile of shattered trees was burning at the log dump. They took me past Viner Sound, a deep V cut into the Gilford shoreline, a watershed pockmarked with logged clear-cuts. We turned into Tribune Channel, which cuts Gilford Island off from the mainland. I was so engrossed, glassing each fin for identifying marks, that I scarcely noticed where they were leading me. When we arrived at the western opening to Kwatsi Bay, the lead whales stopped and hovered on the surface for nine minutes, just breathing. Gradually all eleven whales collected there, breathing, not moving forward. What were they up to?

When orcas go down for a long dive, they show more of their backs than usual. One after another, by silent cue, each of the eleven rolled into this type of dive and vanished. I clicked the stopwatch the moment the last whale slipped beneath the surface. I'd once seen Steller sea lions lounging on a ledge partway into Kwatsi Bay, so I suspected the whales were on the prowl for them. I repositioned the Zodiac in the middle of the bay.

I glanced at the stopwatch. Ten, eleven minutes passed. My eyes flicked between the red, glowing numbers and the dim, rain-soaked scene. Did I miss the surfacing? Maybe they'd crossed Kwatsi Bay or gone back the way they'd come.

Twelve, thirteen minutes. The drizzle became a downpour. A trickle of water wandered down my back and made me shudder.

Fifteen minutes. As I looked up from the watch, a wall of white water erupted near the head of the bay. In the froth I glimpsed patches of black and white and a tawny brown. A sea lion somersaulted through the air like a rag doll. The whales had found what they were looking for: Steller sea lions unprepared for attack.

I watched three sea lions in various stages of being killed. The orcas exploded to the surface in high, arcing dives and whacked the sea lions with their enormous tail flukes. Others rammed the sea lions head-on. Their strategy was, hit too hard and fast for the sea lion to get a bite in. The sea lions bunched together, slashing at the orcas with their teeth. It was no contest; the orcas vastly outnumbered and overpowered them. Still, this was not a quick kill. Steller sea lions weigh more than 1,000 pounds, and it took nearly forty-five minutes for the whales to subdue them all.

The sheer power of the scene awed me. After more than five years of research, I had until now never truly realized the power of the killer whale. I sat there feeling amazed and blessed that the orcas never loosed this power on humans.

Through my earphones came the sounds of orcas tearing the sea lions apart. The whales moved so fast, they shook the sea lions out of their skin.

In complete contrast to the violent behavior I was seeing, the whales' calls were soft *heee aaaw*s and a faint, eerie rapid-fire call completely new to me. These accompanied the gunshot cracks of water cavitating. The mammal-eating whales are commonly more scarred than the fish eaters; it's my guess that many of those wounds are earned at moments like this, in mortal conflict with the canine teeth of the Steller sea lion. During the attack the whales kept their sounds soft and catlike. Once the sea lions were immobilized, however, the whales turned up the volume. Their sudden loudness startled me. I spun around, expecting to see another group of whales closing in on the attack. But there was nothing there. Then I realized: once the transients had caught their prey, they could afford to be as noisy as their fish-eating cousins.

If Robin had been with me, we would have moved close to film the spectacle, but I was content to record their sounds from a distance. Recently a harbor seal had jumped into a Zodiac to escape transients off Victoria. I did not see how my boat would remain afloat if one or several 800-pound sea lions decided to come aboard.

I turned for home in the dim, drenched evening. Skimming down the final reach of Tribune Channel, I recalled a passage in Jane Goodall's book *In the Shadow of Man*. If she had abandoned her fieldwork after only ten years, she wrote, she would never have witnessed chimpanzees engaged in war. That observation radically altered her understanding of who chimps were and what they were capable of.

While I'd known that transient orcas killed and ate sea lions, I drove home with a new understanding that night. It's one thing to read about predators and prey. It's quite another to witness the transaction at its purest, most brutal level. Observing that kill changed my relationship with the whales. They had become infinitely more real. I had witnessed the raw exchange of energy that gave the transient orca its place in the ecosystem.

As a child, I had loved the idea of the food chain. It made perfect sense, unlike the tangled complications of human society. Some species ate, other were eaten; everything was clear and well defined. As an adult, I found that this chain becomes both more miraculous and more difficult to accept. Death becomes so much more terrible once you yourself have given birth. But the tangled relationship among all of earth's life-forms is a beautiful mathematical equation. The grand total of a sea lion's ability to suckle, swim, forage, and live within a community had just been transferred to the transient orcas. The whale, in turn, used this accumulated energy to create heat, movement, and intelligence—in other words, life.

I came away from Kwatsi Bay horrified by the slaughter. To the sea lions, nothing could have justified the attack. To the orcas, it had been the means to another day of survival. Death lends itself to life. Life sets the stage for death.

Chapter 14

A bout the time we settled into Echo Bay, the Royal Canadian
Mounted Police began asking people in the coastal communities of Vancouver Island to watch out for strangers with no obvious
means of support who showed up in expensive boats loaded with
green garbage bags. They were looking for drug smugglers. We fit
the description perfectly.

Most folks in the archipelago traveled in open fiberglass skiffs;
ours was the first inflatable in the area. Robin transferred his cameras
between the *Blue Fjord* and the Zodiac in green garbage bags as a
cheap way of protecting them from the rain. Our modified inflatable, with its bow canopy, welded-aluminum containment boxes,
and VHF and loran C antennas, looked to be outfitted for more than
your usual day trip.

"My God," a fisherman once exclaimed upon seeing our rig, "a
live-aboard Zodiac."

We had no apparent day jobs, and no one had ever heard of
whale researchers sticking around for the winter. The police who
prowled the archipelago kept a wary eye on us.

The local grapevine crackled with news of our presence. "What
do you think of the drug dealers who moved into Echo Bay?" a shop-
keeper in Port McNeill asked one of our new neighbors. The RCMP
patrol boat *Perkes* became a familiar sight off our bow. The blue-and-
gold cutter often roared up and gave us a friendly five-minute interro-
gation. Since the deck of the 45-foot *Perkes* was a good 8 feet above

the sea-level Zodiac, Robin and I often felt as if we were conducting conversations with the undersides of the officers' black shoes. Jarret was always in the boat with us, which made us wonder what a heartless, desperate picture we must have seemed, running drugs with a toddler.

Robin and I were mostly amused by the scrutiny, and after a while we started asking our own question: "You guys seen any whales today?" After a few months we fell off the RCMP's radar screen, and we were sad to see them go before we could turn them into Keeners. The *Perkes* would have made a phenomenal spotting boat.

I've never failed to be amazed at the generosity of people in the archipelago. Whenever we showed up on a stranger's porch or float late in the day, he or she would insist that we stay for dinner or bunk for the night. We met Steve Vessely that way. Steve is a bearded, wiry man in his fifties who works as a watchman at a logging camp and lived in a double-wide trailer way up in Wakeman Sound, a large branch off Kingcome Inlet.

Robin, Jarret, and I discovered Steve's place while following the transients Flores and her son Pender one winter day. The whales were foraging silently, but they were both on the same breathing schedule. I noticed that when they started blowing, they gradually moved toward each other. I couldn't detect any calls and began to suspect that they were using the sound of each other's exhalation to home in on each other after separating during their long-cycle dives.

The mother and son probed every nook and cranny of the shoreline for food. The seals hauled out on land watched the whales warily, their necks outstretched and their bristly whiskers tweaked forward sniffing for whale scent. We drifted within a few feet of several beached seals, which normally will send them into the water. These seals wanted nothing to do with the water as long as those orcas were around, though. I was beginning to suspect that the local marine mammals knew to avoid killer whales that were quiet—if they had the opportunity.

Since we were almost an hour's run from Echo Bay, we radioed

Steve to see if we could spend the night at his place. That way we could stay with the whales until the last moment of dusk. (It's a simple equation: the more you're with whales, the more you see.)

We'd actually heard plenty about Steve before meeting him. He'd often call Billy Proctor on the VHF and provide what I liked to call the Wakeman Report, a mix of weather update, fish and grizzly report, and social commentary given in Steve's unique dialect of salty English. Today Steve still calls me when he sees whales to tell me what "those black sons of bitches" are up to in the northern inlet. If children are around, we change the channel; if they're not, we turn up the volume.

Steve and his wife, Reta, invited us in for the night. "I'll meet you in the pickup down at the log dump," he said, "and yer better tie that pretty little boat of yers up good, because it can howl like a bastard up here."

Tying up an inflatable could be a challenge, because steel bolt ends, splintered logs, bits of sharply frayed cable, and other spiked objects often threatened to pop the craft. We dealt with these rugged tie-ups by affixing an assortment of tough bumpers to the boat. We were never worried about theft, though, and the ignition key never came out of its slot.

Over a hearty meal of pork chops, mashed potatoes, and canned beans, Steve regaled us with tales of his colorful past. He was a bank robber in his younger days, and a pretty good one, known as the "Bicycle Bandit." Steve's specialty was the two-wheeled getaway. While the local cops screeched around looking for him, Steve quietly pedaled away down the back alleys. "Never caught!" Steve told us. "Until one of my %#*%@* friends ratted on me."

Nowadays Steve acts as the unofficial guardian of the Wakeman River watershed. One of the reasons the Wakeman Report rarely fails to entertain is that the weather up there punishes our faithful correspondent relentlessly. Our weather in Echo Bay comes in from the moist, temperate coast, but Wakeman Sound reaches far enough inland to attract colder systems from the Canadian interior. Freezing winds funnel down the Wakeman River, hit one shore, and career back and forth across the sound with such chaotic ferocity that it's nearly impossible to anchor a boat. When we get a skiff of snow in Echo Bay, Steve will be climbing out his windows because the snow's too deep to open the door. You'd have to be as tough as Steve to survive up there; it's a hard country of big grizzlies, big wolves, big trees, and big tides. "I came here," proclaimed Steve, "to get away from the goddamn human race."

As rough, tough, and crusty as Steve is, he's also an incredibly dedicated caretaker of his place. Steve's no saint, but he lives with Wakeman Sound, not against it. When I call him the guardian of that territory, I mean *guardian*. If you go up there and fish inside the proscribed boundaries or set a crab trap too close to the river, he might threaten to send a load of buckshot over your head and make you think twice about how badly you want to land that salmon. Out here river mouths are the banks. They're where all the riches are stored; they pump life into the world. The Wakeman River provides spawning ground for 250,000 pinks, 5,000 cohos, 18,000 chums, and 1,000 chinook, which feed the whole ecosystem, from trees to grizzlies. If every wild place had a watchman like Steve, there would be a lot more of them left in the world. As we watched Jarret entertain himself with Steve's wolf's-head rug, our host's eyes softened for a moment. He looked into his glass of whiskey and said, "I love this place. I really do."

We left at daybreak and found Flores and Pender not far away, exiting Bellisle Sound on the far side of Kingcome Inlet. They were retracing exactly the previous day's route.

While resident whales usually looped through the archipelago, we were starting to notice that transients commonly backtracked like this. I couldn't interpret it as good hunting strategy—confronting prey already alerted to their presence. I was beginning to wonder if this behavior might be socially driven, allowing for interception of any missing pod mates or other transients who might be following in their wake, a way of staying together without sound. Or was it simply a way to find their way out of the mazy archipelago? Transients cover thousands of miles of coastline, sometimes not returning to an area for ten years or more. Despite the enormous capacity of their memory, it seemed possible that they might not remember the ins and outs of every inlet on this side of the continent.

In early 1986 Robin's dream job finally came through. The National Film Board of Canada agreed to fund the two projects Robin had been pitching for months: one film about orcas and another about life on a floathouse.

"They went for it!" he hollered, waving the letter and dancing a jig on the dock at Echo Bay.

Filmmaking may be the world's most overromanticized profession. Magazines and TV shows portray filmmakers as hip young people living the glamorous life. That may be the case on a Hollywood set. But for wildlife documentarians, it's a grueling struggle that breeds its own strain of insanity. Because everything is beyond the filmmakers' control, their only recourse is to risk life, limb, and their spouses' wrath to get the shot.

First we had to find the whales. Then the light changed (assuming there was any light at all). If the whales and light cooperated, the gear went south. A miraculous whale performance could happen 6 feet from the camera, but if the batteries ran low, the wrong lens was mounted, or a hair caught in the gate that guided the film past the lens, the scene was worthless. Dampness, a change in temperature—any one of a dozen things could destroy what had been painstakingly caught. If one of us dropped a canister of exposed film, pinpricks of light would appear on every frame. I drove the Zodiac while Robin filmed and found that even the quirks of the boat worked against us. When the inflatable's stiff throttle and steering wheel showed up as midshot jerks, he'd howl with frustration. I came to see every frame of good film as a gift from heaven.

Over time we began to understand the whales' patterns of movement. We learned to read the tides and no longer made blind guesses as we headed out each morning. In winter both transient and resident sightings came in sets. If we saw them once, we'd likely see them again within thirty-six hours.

The orcas travel with the tide in the major marine arteries along the coast, but when they come to the inlets to sleep or forage, they move against the tide. Whales don't have a sense of smell. They lack the essential brain component, the olfactory bulb, to process odors. But they do have extremely sensitive taste lobes protruding from the edges of their tongue. In the same way that terrestrial predators hunt downwind in order to hide their own scent and gather information on what lies upwind, orcas hunt and sleep against the tide in order to taste what's coming their way.

The seasons became more predictable. In April and May a little fish called the eulachon spawns in rivers at the head of Wakeman, Kingcome, and Knight inlets. A type of smelt, the eulachon is so rich in oil that it was once a major trade item for First Nations people on the coast. Routes through the coastal mountains were known as "grease trails" because of the importance of the nutrient-rich oil rendered from the fish. Eulachon were so rich in oil, in fact, that their dried bodies were burned for light, hence their common local name, *candlefish*.

As the eulachon schools coalesced into the narrow inlets, seals, sea lions, and chinook salmon followed on their tails. Just as the local human tribes coveted the rights to these fish, killer whales appear to have established a similar hierarchy of access. While resource defense, the impulse to guard one's home territory and food supply, is a fairly common behavioral trait in nearly all animals, it's curiously absent in whale and dolphin societies. The closest I've come across is the way in which some pods exclusively fish certain runs. Only members of the A pod, for instance, showed up in the archipelago during the eulachon run. The orcas didn't eat the eulachon directly; they were after the eulachon-fed chinook. I learned to expect Eve and her relatives soon after Steve Vessely reported the first eulachon sighting in Wakeman Sound.

That same spring Robin and I began to notice a curious thing.

The male orcas in Kingcome Inlet seemed to swim with the tips of their fins just barely showing above the water. They looked like little black sharks zigzagging up the inlet. Chris Bennett, a local fishing lodge owner and legendary spring salmon fisherman, knew what was going on.

"Glacier melt," he told me.

So much water runs off the local glaciers that it stains the inlets an opaque turquoise green. This gritty, silt-laden freshwater layer fouls up the salmon's delicate gills, so the fish congregate about 6 feet down from the surface, along the ceiling of glacier water. The orcas respond by moving up to find these fish cruising near the surface, snapping up the salmon made fat, tasty, and highly nutritious, from feeding on eulachon oil.

In summer the orcas liked to leave Johnstone Strait and enter Fife Sound at the beginning of the ebb tide to forage for fish. After passing Echo Bay, they arranged themselves into a resting line. Once they entered Tribune Channel, the whales moved forward side by side with their pectoral fins touching. In the quiet, sheltered waters of the channel, the whales then performed one of the most common and fascinating bodily functions in the animal kingdom. They slept.

In 1964 John Lilly first noticed that captive dolphins seemed to sleep with one eye open. A few years before I went to work for Sam Ridgeway in San Diego, Ridgeway had produced evidence that dolphins sleep a half brain at a time. Of the three stages of sleep, Ridgeway found that the deepest level occurred in only one brain hemisphere at a time for periods up to two hours long. Interestingly, REM (rapid eye movement) sleep, which is most often associated with dreaming, has never been recorded in dolphins. Dawn Goley, a researcher at Humboldt State University, later confirmed Lilly's observations and Ridgeway's findings by documenting that captive dolphins close one eye at a time while "sleeping."

It appears that dolphins and whales alternate the sleeping hemispheres in their brains a number of times during a rest period.

Goley found that during their seven hours of nightly sleep, dolphins changed formation to keep their open eye fixed on their schoolmates, not searching for predators. (We shouldn't extrapolate too much from this; her study subjects were in a tank, where there were no predators.)

Whales become extremely vulnerable when they sleep, as Robin and I discovered one day while studying them in Tribune Channel. We had run far ahead in the Zodiac, then shut off the motor, dropped the hydrophone, and waited for them to pass by on their "sleeping" run. Once Tsitika and her family fell into formation, they generally slept for the next 25 miles, making a semicircumnavigation of Gilford Island.

A sleeping whale pod is a spectacular sight. Coming straight on to you, they raise a forest of fins and blows across a broad swath of ocean. From the side their fins arc to the surface like a succession of ebony bowed blades. I realized that whoever had carved the multi-finned whales on the Alert Bay totem poles must have seen orcas sleep.

A sleeping orca usually takes one long three- to five-minute dive, then surfaces for five or six short dives before rolling deep for another long dive. Some whales seem to need less air than others and will skip a breath. Another researcher, Janice Waite, has coined the term *superbabies* for youngsters who often hold their breath longer than their mothers.

As they came toward us, the sleeping whales seemed not to notice the Zodiac floating in their path. Stillness came over the water as the pod submerged. Robin checked his watch and signaled three minutes, four minutes, five. Suddenly the waist-high fin of a female appeared off our port side. As I listened to her breathe, I caught sight of a black male fin rising from the depths, heading straight for our boat. "No-o-o-o-o you don't!" That fin would have pitched Robin and me overboard and sent tens of thousands of dollars' worth of equipment straight to the bottom of Tribune Channel. I grabbed a paddle and slapped the water as hard as I could. Startled by the sound, the whale rolled to his right, just avoiding the bottom of the

Zodiac. I felt ashamed and made a silent promise to be more responsible with my boat.

When they weren't being rudely startled by the likes of me, the whales usually stirred from their resting state as they approached the rough waters of Knight Inlet. As temperatures climb during the day, the air over the archipelago's inlets heats up and rises, which sucks in cooler air from the open ocean. Tribune Channel enjoys the shelter of low-lying mountains, but Knight Inlet, which cuts almost 100 miles inland, sees the worst of this effect. As we approached the inlet, Robin and I stowed and tied down everything that needed to stay dry. We'd take one last look at the mountains reflected in the channel's mirrory surface, then grit our teeth for the westerly whipped whitecaps of Knight Inlet. I squatted on the floor, braced my back, and held on tightly to Jarret (who promptly fell asleep). The effect was as immediate as turning a corner. The whales, roused and refreshed from their nap, exploded over the steep, curling waves and made their way back to the wide waters of Queen Charlotte Strait.

Robin and I thrived on these explorations of the Broughton Archipelago. Through most of 1986 he filmed to his heart's content. Our freezer no longer had room for food: it was solid with 16-millimeter film awaiting the signing of his National Film Board contract and its subsequent release of funds for processing. With the promise of the film board's backing, Robin hit his stride. Zodiac Canada lent him a new top-of-the-line 25-foot inflatable. With its twin 50-horsepower engines, it flew across the water so fast I couldn't breathe if I stuck my head over the visor. With its speed and a comfy sleep-aboard fiberglass bow cover, we could go out twice as far for twice as long. When it came to camera work, the new Zodiac was as stable as a barge.

Robin got some amazing shots. He filmed grandmothers communing, males engaged in play sex, and calves cavorting in kelp. He filmed the blood flowing from an old bullet wound reopened in

Charlie Chin's dorsal fin. He filmed a young female with sport-fishing gear embedded in her dorsal fin. He filmed whales at dawn, whales at sunset, and during all hours in between.

Once we discovered the Broughton Archipelago, we became more and more reluctant to return to Johnstone Strait. Though there were far more orcas there in summer, in the mid-1980s the exploding whale-watching industry began turning the strait into a circus. The whale-watching pastime that Bill MacKay and Jim Borrowman had founded in the old *Gikumi* was on its way to becoming a million-dollar industry. Whenever a whale jumped, a dozen tour boats homed in like flies to a wound.

Although the visitors were shooting orcas with lenses, not rifles, I and a number of other researchers viewed the growing industry with alarm. Many of us simply left the area to remove our boats from the mounting pressure on the whales. Graeme Ellis and John Ford went north to the central coast, Robin and I retreated to the inlets, and still others moved ashore for land-based observations. We all knew that the long resting lines were particularly vulnerable to disruption and wondered if the whale-watching boats weren't disrupting the orcas' sleep patterns. The problem becomes cumulative. Everyone thinks he or she has a right to get close to the whales, and a lot of folks who come up to the northern waters of Vancouver Island have only one day to spend with the whales. Kayakers, who believed their lack of engine noise reduced their impact, often approached orca resting lines at close range, startling the sleepers. Americans who had already seen their own orca grounds in the San Juan Islands overrun by whale tours warned us to limit the number of charter operators before it was too late.

The whale watching wasn't all bad, though. Whale watchers hired whale boats, which meant good-paying jobs for a region that often saw its most promising young people lured to Victoria and Vancouver by the promise of a decent wage. The industry also gave wild whales an economic value, which has, sadly, often become the only hope for a species trying to survive in this industrial age.

Some folks argued against regulating the industry on purely

ideological grounds. Although Mike Bigg hated regulations, he became one of the leading voices demanding that the government restrict water and land access to the "rubbing beaches" area around Robson Bight. Paul Spong and Helena Symonds became strong voices over the radio, coaching dozens of boats a year on whale etiquette. They wanted people to learn how to see whales without running them over. If people wanted whales to keep coming back to the places they can be seen, people were going to have to learn whale etiquette. It was that simple.

I have learned to listen closely to the stories people tell about the strange creatures they encounter up here. There's valuable information to be had; you just have to train your ears to hear it. Most people don't know the names of the different whales, but they're pretty good at describing what they've seen. If someone reports "a pod of baby killer whales," I usually translate that as a group of Dall's porpoises, the 400-pound black-and-white cousin of the smaller harbor porpoise. Sometimes it becomes a game of twenty questions. "Did you see the tail?" I'll ask. If they did, then you can rule out minke whales, which don't lift their flukes when they dive. "What about the dorsal fin? The one on its back?" Orca dorsals are huge, of course. Humpback whales have a small dorsal; gray whales just have small bumps down their backs. It's crucial never to offer any suggestions as to what people saw, just ask specific questions.

Sometimes two eyewitnesses can look at the same creature and describe two completely different animals. One day Robin and I met two fishermen on the dock at Minstrel Island, a winter vacation spot not far from the confluence of Tribune Channel and Knight Inlet. They were wide-eyed and eager to tell us what they'd witnessed. Out on the water at the crack of dawn, they'd seen an enormous whale.

"Sucker had a 9-foot dorsal," one of them said. That got our attention.

"What color was the fin?" I asked.

"Black," said one man.

"No, it was white," said the other.

Killer whale dorsals never grow taller than 6 feet, but there had been a pod of orcas photographed more than twenty years ago with white splashes on their fins. I tried to pin them down on the color.

"Definitely black," said the first fisherman.

"I don't know what the hell *he* saw," said the second. "It was definitely white."

Clearly something was out there—of whatever pigmentation. Robin and I packed our campsite, climbed back in the Zodiac, and headed toward Queen Charlotte Strait. It didn't take long to solve the mystery. A mile west of Minstrel Island, we spotted tall, palm tree–like plumes of mist rising and falling in the familiar pattern of a breathing whale. As we got closer, we identified an adult humpback lying on its side, smacking the water with its pectoral fin. Robin and I laughed out loud when the whale raised its fin. Both fishermen were right: the fin was about 9 feet long, black on one side and white on the other.

The next day we told Billy Proctor about our humpback encounter. "That's great," he said. "Used to be humpbacks all over the place here twenty years ago."

"Where'd they all go?" I asked.

"Remember that whale Barney I told you about? He used to go into Viner Sound every day to feed. We all liked him, but there was a lady that lived in Viner, and she hated whales. I guess she musta been afraid of them. You know sometimes they went right under our houses and scratched their backs on the logs. That kinda shook things up.

"Anyway, she decided to get rid of them whales. In 1952 she phoned the whalers out at Coal Harbour and told them there was some whales around here. Six of them lived up in Knight Inlet, and it was the same in Kingcome Inlet.

"Well, the whalers came in and went up Knight and came out towing the whales lashed to the sides of the boat. I will never forget that day. It was in August. I was trolling in the mouth of Knight Inlet, and I seen the old *Nahmint* coming out towing all the old whales alongside. I just about cried.

Humpback whale

"That was the last of the humpbacks in the mainland. Never was the same without Old Joe puffing along the kelp beds of Flower Island waiting for the slack tide to fill his tummy. I used to think a lot about Old Joe and Barney. They'd grown to trust humans, and then they up and get shot by a human. It just never seemed right to me. But that's the way life is sometimes."

According to western Canadian whaling records, a total of 24,862 sperm, blue, fin, sei, and humpback whales were killed between 1908 and 1967. Over that time the size of the whales killed decreased significantly, and the number of pregnant whales declined to such an extent that not a single pregnant sei or blue whale was killed after 1960. Those findings suggest a destruction of whale populations to the point where whales weren't maturing and having as many offspring. Whaling all but ceased during World War II, and after the war only the Coal Harbour station on northern Vancouver Island started up again. Although the market for whale products continued to shrink, the industry stayed alive until 1967 because of a deal between a large provincial fish company, B.C. Packers, and a Japanese firm to ship frozen sei whale meat to Japan.

The archival whaling records confirm the existence of the small inshore populations of humpbacks that Billy Proctor remembered. Those small groups of whales were scattered coastwide and were wiped out one by one as they were discovered. During the winter of 1907–8, a single whaling station in the Strait of Georgia accounted for the deaths of ninety-seven humpback whales in three months. They took them all. According to archival records, the humpbacks Billy Proctor had known around Echo Bay were members of one of the last inshore populations of humpbacks in existence.

Fortunately the humpbacks have mounted a small revival in recent years. I have documented a steady increase in humpback whales since my arrival, including whales that are coming back yearly. I photoidentify them by the undersides of their tails and distribute the photos to whale researchers in Alaska, Mexico, and Hawaii. Some of the whales have become familiar enough that I've given them names: Maude, Iwama, Galen, and Houdini. The humpback may yet become one of the Pacific coast's great comeback stories.

Chapter 15

___ ___ ___

On the morning of September 16, 1986, the three of us awoke wrapped in the silence of fog. We had set up camp the previous night on the beach at Bere Point, a spot on the north side of Malcolm Island that the whales always pass by before entering Johnstone Strait. The Spanish galleon that Jarret and Robin had built out of driftwood the day before still stood on the beach awaiting its christening.

In the Zodiac we switched on the radio just as a commercial fisherman, tending his gill net, reported whales entering Johnstone Strait about 20 miles south of us. Robin fired up the boat and navigated by compass and luck. He pushed the engines to high whine. We shot around Pulteney Point and into Broughton Strait, the heavily trafficked passage between Port McNeill and Sointula, skimming fog-blind over the water. Robin's fearlessness knew few bounds. I clung to the dashboard and thought, "Man, this is way too fast."

As we moved into the strait, we spotted the distinctive mechanical sails of the *Alcyon*. The *Alcyon* served as the floating base for a Cousteau Society crew that had been filming whales in the strait. The ship's futuristic sheets, which looked like a set of gigantic white PVC pipes slit lengthwise, had become a common sight that summer. An onboard computer regulated the sails, adjusting to every shift in airspeed and direction. Every time I came upon them, I smiled at the row of tiny men's bikinis snapping dry in the breeze on the ship's railings.

When we'd met in July, Robin had offered to lend a hand with the underwater shots, but the Cousteau photographers had confidently declined. Two months later, on their last day in Johnstone Strait, they excitedly waved us over. Their thick French accents made it difficult for Robin to understand them, but my years of rearing under Jacqueline Baldet allowed me to translate. The underwater shoot hadn't gone as well as they'd hoped. Now they wanted to know if Robin had any footage to sell.

Robin shot me a wry smile. "Oh," he said, "I think I might be able to part with a minute or two."

For Robin this was the ultimate validation. In eight years of filming, he had compiled a total of three and a half minutes of killer whales underwater. That doesn't seem like a lot, but it was an eternity compared to what everyone else had. Robin was on top of the world. As we left the *Alcyon,* he turned to me with a great beaming smile and said, "Let's get another three and a half minutes."

We caught up to A5 pod south of Hanson Island. The matriarchs Eve and Licka, along with their sons and daughters, lazily followed the same run of river-bound sockeye that the purse seiners and gill netters had come out for. In midafternoon the whales disappeared into Robson Bight.

In 1982 the provincial government had agreed with Mike Bigg and a host of other conservationists and declared Robson Bight an ecological reserve, which protected the increasingly famous rubbing beaches and a sliver of the surrounding Tsitika River watershed against logging and development. The government had established an exclusion zone around the beaches to allow the whales some relief from humanity's aggressive interest and noisy motors. Robin had donated the use of his footage to help promote the creation of this whale haven.

We stopped at a spot just east of the rubbing beach and waited for the orcas to exit the reserve. Robin pulled on his orange dry suit and snapped a fresh film magazine onto his camera. He slid the camera into the underwater housing, carefully greased the O-ring seals, and methodically tightened the hatch, each bolt a quarter turn in series to increase the pressure evenly. He strapped on his fins, spit into his mask to prevent it from fogging, put the rebreather between his teeth, and slipped into the water. I moved the Zodiac a few meters away—out of the shot—and turned my attention to Jarret.

Robin set up about 30 feet offshore. As Jarret drew in his coloring book, I idled the boat against the tide and kept an eye on Robin treading water near a kelp bed. Now and then he'd look over at me for an update: See anything? Nothing, I waved back. Robin and I had developed a personal semaphore language necessitated less by distance than by the peculiarities of his equipment. In normal scuba gear, Robin would have spit out his mouthpiece on the surface to conserve air in his tank. But with the rebreather, his prized souvenir from the *American Sportsman* shoot, he didn't have to worry about wasting air. Once Robin activated the rebreather, the mouthpiece stayed in, and his mouth shut, to keep the entire system recirculating properly.

The fog burned off in late afternoon, leaving only a few white ribbons floating through the steep fir forest that rose up from the beach. To the west commercial fishermen set their nets and complained about the day's catch over the radio.

Finally a fin. Eve broke the surface and moved toward Robin's position. We exchanged signals. Robin waved and ducked under.

Eve dove toward Robin, then abruptly emerged from the water and charged back toward me. She surfaced beside the Zodiac in her flight, paused, then disappeared into the deep. Her movements struck me as strange, like a film played forward and reversed. She shouldn't have resurfaced so soon. She shouldn't have needed that second breath so soon after the first. I couldn't put my finger on her behavior. I looked around for her sons, Top Notch and Foster, but found them nowhere. No other whales appeared. I looked toward shore, expecting Robin to surface and give me a "Where the hell'd they go?" signal. He didn't.

I sat and waited. Jarret worked his crayons across the paper. Robin's voice ran through my head. "Whatever you do," he'd said to me time and again, "don't blow the shot." It had taken him eight years to get three and a half minutes of film. For all I knew, he could be getting the next three and a half at that very moment. If I moved the boat, I'd ruin it.

One minute and another and another. Eve did not reappear, and neither did Robin. Her sons were nowhere to be seen. Between me and the beach lay nothing but calm water.

Don't blow the shot.

My blood ran cold.

Don't blow the shot!

"The hell with this," I thought. "I'm going in for a look."

I sidled the Zodiac into shore near Robin's last position. Moving a propeller in on a diver who isn't producing any bubbles is always an iffy proposition. There's no way to know exactly where he is and no way to keep him from surfacing straight into the blades.

I cut the motor and let the boat drift to eliminate the danger. As the green water cleared, I saw seaweed, kelp, starfish, and the rocky floor.

And I saw Robin. He lay prostrate on the bottom, staring calmly at the sky. His arms stretched up as if reaching for me. The re-breather was not in his mouth. He did not move.

"Mayday! Mayday! Mayday!" I hollered into the radio. "Man on the bottom at rubbing rocks."

"I have a husband in the water," I thought. "And I have a boy in the boat." The boy was four years old. If I left the boat, the tide would take the boy. The tide was already taking his father.

There was a rope. I tied one end to the tow post and the other around my waist. The water was cold, but Robin wasn't too deep. I had just enough breath to unhitch his weight belt. On my second dive I pulled him to the surface by my feet. I gasped, as much at the cold as for air. The rope unraveled from the boat. I called to Jarret to retie it to the tow post. I could hear him saying "Tow post. Tow post," trying to remember what the tow post was.

Robin's face was so very pale. I tried giving him the kiss of life. He was cold, so very cold.

A numb peace settled over us. It felt as if Robin did not want to be revived. It felt for just a moment that there was a crack open between two worlds. I sensed the same coming and goings as I had at Jarret's birth.

Jarret found the tow post. I wrapped the line around Robin and swam to the boat. The Zodiac's pontoons rose nearly 3 feet from the water. I climbed up the engine to get back in. Robin's body was too heavy. It stayed in the water.

I pressed Jarret against me, hugged him to my soaking clothes and dripping hair and tried not to let him see.

Other boats heard our mayday. Bill MacKay and Jim Borrowman heard it way up in Fife Sound. Bill later told me that his guts ached, because he had emergency oxygen equipment on board the *Gikumi* but knew they were two hours away. Christine O'Donnell heard it in the Windsong Barge and remembered that the two of us had talked a few days before about how lost we'd be if our men were gone. The Coast Guard wasn't sure what had just come out of their radio. They'd heard my call but wondered where the "rubbing rocks" were. I thought, "My God, people as far away as Japan and Germany knew about the rubbing rocks." I screamed across the water to the fishermen setting their nets, but the roar of their engines drowned out my voice.

Help arrived thirty minutes later. The *Chilco Post,* the Fisheries Department boat that I had encountered years ago on my first day in Alert Bay, pulled up alongside. David Bain, a young whale researcher, came aboard to help. In the way that strangers can sometimes lead you through moments of trauma, he saw us through the next few hours. David joined Jarret and me in the galley while the crew of the *Chilco Post* brought aboard Robin's body. I never saw him again. A crewman offered me a dry sweatshirt and pants. I went to change and found that he'd given me two shirts. I put my wet clothes back on. The cook fed Jarret cookies, and David entertained him with stories.

Up until then I'd kept it together by focusing on the minute-to-minute business of the rescue and keeping Jarret safe and calm. With my son finally in safe hands, I stepped onto the deck and slumped against the wall and let it go.

The Royal Canadian Mounted Police arrived. A policewoman interviewed me. At that point they thought that a whale had killed a man. I was not so sure. Even if Eve had wanted to hurt Robin, she hadn't been near him long enough for any sort of altercation. I described the spot where Robin went down, and they dispatched a diving team to recover his camera and rebreathing gear. The film counter indicated that Robin had rolled film.

Days later when they developed the film, all they would see was a setup shot of kelp strands swaying in the current. Robin never shot a single frame of Eve. A naval inspector found a slightly clogged valve in the rebreathing unit. Had his oxygen cut off abruptly, Robin would have bolted for the surface. Instead, the valve malfunction let him continue to breathe a mixture of recycled air—but as the scrubbing mechanism broke down, he inhaled more carbon dioxide and less oxygen. Our brain has no warning mechanism for this sort of thing. We just kind of drift off. It's what happens when people commit suicide by shutting themselves in the garage with a running car.

Robin had a habit of holding his breath when he rolled film. It steadied the shot. With his body already starving for oxygen, he saw Eve, stopped his breath, and blacked out. He fainted and then drowned. The whale didn't kill Robin. The sight of her did.

The ambulance took Robin's body to the hospital morgue in Port Hardy. David arranged for us to stay the night with Bill and Donna

MacKay in Telegraph Cove. Jarret met their son Tyson, who was also four. They began a lifelong friendship. Bill offered to call Robin's parents.

"No," I told him. "I'll do it."

I did. Afterward I wished that I had let Bill.

I couldn't make sense of anything. How could a man so fit, confident, and at home in the water drown at a depth of 30 feet? This couldn't be happening. I kept repeating the events over and over as Bill and Donna put a blanket over me, put a cup of rum tea in my hands, and kept me company most of the night.

Late that night I put Jarret to bed in the MacKays' guest room. As I tucked him in, he looked up at me with a question. "If Daddy's dead," he said, "how are they going to fix him?" His face completely expected good news. I could not give it to him.

"They can't, Jarret. They can't."

Chapter 16

The newspapers eulogized Robin as a leading British Columbia filmmaker. He would have loved that.

My mother flew out to be with me. Robin's family held a memorial service at the Newcombe Auditorium in the Royal British Columbia Museum in Victoria. The next day Jarret and I rode a bus north to Port McNeill. I held Robin's ashes in a box on my right knee, and Jarret fell asleep on my left. I sat there in a warm bus on a cold day and felt the dead father and the living son connected by a circle of life through my body.

I lay awake at night thinking about how I could have saved his life. I should have checked on him earlier. I should have thrown that stupid rebreather overboard. I feared and distrusted a world that had suddenly turned cruel and random. I sat by the fire thinking and reading about death. I wrapped myself in despair. Was it possible that events this big could be a mistake?

When I finally fell asleep, I dreamed about him incessantly. Robin came back in my nights, always rummaging around the *Blue Fjord* looking for something. I apologized for selling his camera. We were broke, I told him, and needed the money. He smiled warmly. While he never said anything, the message was always, "Don't worry about me. I'm fine."

Were it not for Jarret, I would have slumped in a corner and not moved for two years. Every morning I woke up to a little boy who needed breakfast and lunch and dinner and snacks and stories and trips to the beach and a mother who functioned at some level of normalcy. The logistics of a four-year-old's life pulled me through.

Jarret and I scattered Robin's ashes on the sea in a place where we had often waited for whales. We moved off the *Blue Fjord* and into the floathouse that Robin had hired Billy Proctor to pull onto a spot of land we leased from Bob and Nancy Richter. Robin's brother Cal and his partner, Colleen, ran a water line to the kitchen, built a woodshed, and helped me put the house in working order. I gutted the *Blue Fjord* with an eye toward selling it. I spent long days on my knees in the bowels of the ship, emerging in the late afternoon looking like a woman who'd taken a grease bath. It was miserable work, and it suited me. I knew why mourners through the centuries had worn garments of anguish, rubbed ashes over their bodies, cut their hair. You want to tell the world, I am beyond happiness. It's both a warning and an appeal.

Without knowing how to mourn, scouring the *Blue Fjord* became my ritual. I washed and scraped and sanded every dark corner and then painted the whole thing white. The black insides of that boat became my skin. I felt guilty eating and breathing now that Robin no longer could. I wore his coveralls. The black smudges on my face were an honest declaration of the blackness within. It felt right to pour my labor into the *Blue Fjord,* this object that Robin had loved so much that he couldn't bring himself to leave it. It felt right to make it beautiful again.

That winter I held close all the things that carried traces of Robin. The clothes that held his scent. His undeveloped film. His son. The boat he cherished. Everything except the whales.

By God, was I ever done with whales. It was clear that Eve hadn't hurt Robin. But she hadn't helped him, either. I kept my hydrophone on to take comfort in the sounds of the sea, but I stopped listening for whale sightings on the VHF. I knew that my anger was irrational. But there were two beings in this world who could have saved Robin: Eve and myself. And I was mad at both.

———

The Zodiac blew away in a December storm and was never found. I sold a few things to make grocery money and bought a used 16-foot fiberglass Hourston, which I named the *Inlet Westerly*. Bill MacKay and Jim Borrowman drove the renovated *Blue Fjord* to Telegraph Cove and arranged to move her to Nanaimo, where she might find a buyer. Once again Mike Bigg came to my rescue. He and Graeme Ellis were sitting at their desks at the federal Department of Fisheries and Oceans' Pacific Biological Station in Nanaimo one day when a fellow came in and said he wanted to get into the whale-watching business.

"Oh boy!" Mike told him. "Have we got the boat for you."

And so we made it through the winter, surviving on kindness found in unexpected places.

In February, five months after Robin's death, I spotted a whale through the window. I absently picked up a stopwatch and began taking respirations. He was a big male transient, but I couldn't identify him from the house. Storm-force winds whipped up the water and pelted my window with rain. I sat in my slippers, sipping coffee, watching him pace back and forth across the passage. I had never seen a whale stay in one place for so long.

The storm worsened during the night. The house shuddered under near-hurricane gusts. The next morning I went to the window to survey the damage. And there was the whale, still circling. I put on some rain gear and walked down to the beach and got in my boat and motored out to look at him. As I approached, the transient slowly moved away. By now I recognized his fin from the ID catalog. It was F1, a lone transient who had several large tears in his fin. I'd never encountered him before.

As I followed, the orca did nothing spectacular. He moved away from my house and began meandering sedately into Tribune Channel. But he got me off the beach. Sitting there in a boat again, listening to the sounds of a whale blowing for the first time since Robin's death, brought me solace I hadn't felt in months. A familiarity and a closeness to Robin settled around me. Every once in a while, I caught a fleeting sense of Robin's presence, and never as great as that morning. I realized that I couldn't control what had happened to Robin but I could control my response. Gradually, over the next days and weeks and months, I stretched a tightwire over the chasm of Robin's death. I fell off often at first, and then less and less. Soon the wire became a rope and then a bridge.

I began to emerge from grief, profoundly changed. My world began to move again. But I still had a lot to learn about surviving as a woman in the wilderness.

Chapter 17

Single women don't last long in Echo Bay. They get married or they leave. Since I'm an American immigrant, folks around Echo Bay naturally assumed that it wouldn't be long before I hit the road. But it was different for me. I wasn't here because of my husband's work. My work was here, too. And so was my life. My dad offered to come, pack us up, and take me home, but this was the only home I wanted.

Jarret thrived on the rugged life of the coast, and despite—or perhaps because of—the sometimes painful reminders of Robin that this country held, there was no place I would rather be. Robin left me with everything I needed to carry out my life's work. I wasn't going to throw his precious gifts away.

To dispel the premature reports that I would be moving out, I got on the VHF and called a neighbor who'd been feeding the rumor mill with news of my imminent departure. "This is my home," I told her, "and I am not leaving." Since people up here are incorrigible radio eavesdroppers, I knew that word would get around.

A few days later I woke up to find nine logs tied anonymously to the beach outside my house. Firewood. No bouquet of roses ever looked so pretty, burned so long, or so clearly delivered its welcome message: Glad you're sticking around.

As much as our friends and neighbors tried to help out, Jarret and I found ourselves quickly slipping toward beggar status. Larger communities might sustain a widow, but it was all that people up here could do to maintain their own homesteads, let alone look after a mother with a young son. I had to become self-sufficient—and now.

First things first. We needed heat. A winter's worth of firewood sat on our beach, but Robin had never taught me how to run the chain saw. Too dangerous, he said. Well, now I had to learn. It was a matter of survival.

I took the saw to Kayak Bill, who happened to be working at Echo Bay Resort at the time. A true nomad, Bill had earned his name by living most of his adult life out of a kayak. He traveled up and down the coast, living off the land and sea, spending years at a stretch in parts unknown. Every once in a while when Bill needed some money, he'd find a job and build a cabin nearby, which he always decorated with his own paintings. Wondrous images of the coast hung from the walls of his cabin, which he'd situated not far from mine on Bob and Nancy Richter's land. Bill smelled permanently of wood smoke, his long hair and wool hat matted together into a set of northwoods dreadlocks. Nancy was always plotting ways to get him into a tub.

"Bill," I said, holding up the saw, "can you teach me how to run this thing?"

Bill didn't believe in making a fuss over anything. "Set the choke right here," he said, "then pull the starter cord until it fires." He handed back the saw and left me to my own devices.

That saw bedeviled me. My arm still ached days after pulling the starter cord. It wasn't just a matter of pulling—you had to kinda throw the saw down while yanking upward at the same time. At some point in all this flailing about, the saw's spinning blade of razor-sharp teeth would spark to life inches from your kneecap. Now and then the cutting bar got pinched so tightly in a log that I had to chop it out with an ax. The chain flew off several times. Because I didn't sharpen it properly, it spiraled through the log instead of cutting neat slices. One time a neighbor who'd watched me make little headway with a thick cedar round came over and discreetly took me aside. "Here's your problem," he said, trying not to bruise my ego. "Somebody put your chain on backwards."

As Jarret's only surviving parent, I found myself operating under new rules of risk. I cut wood only if the weather was calm enough for a floatplane to fly me to the hospital. I'd seen enough scars on some of the locals to know what a bucking saw could do.

Once I conquered the chain saw, I worked on my splitting technique. In this part of the world, the men are maestros with a maul, and most are happy to give you tips on proper strategy and form. One day I found myself cutting up a thick log of gnarled fir on the beach near the Echo Bay school. Fir can really warm a house—few woods burn hotter—but if it grows with a twist, it can be nearly impossible to split. I sectioned the log easily and then tried to quarter the rounds. The wood greeted my maul as if it were an anvil, bouncing it straight back at my face. All afternoon I flailed at the fir, desperate to beat a rising tide that threatened to float all the rounds out to sea. Near tears with frustration and exertion, I began tying the uncut rounds together to save them from drifting away.

Along came Jack Scott. An affable logger in his seventies, Jack looked at me and said, "Sweetie, you're going about this all wrong." I panted and leaned on the maul. "You gotta cut this bastard grain," he said. I had no idea what he was talking about.

"Here, give us a try." In his enormous grip, the maul looked tiny as a hammer. Almost quicker than I could see, Jack lopped off the twisted outer edge of one of the rounds instead of cutting it like a pie as I'd done.

Then Billy Proctor showed up. "Aw, Jack," he said, "I'm not gonna let you have all the fun."

Billy had his own method, which he demonstrated on a round near the water's edge. The mauls flew in a fury. As their friendly competition continued, I ran around and scooped up the chunks. The job got done in no time. I beat the tide, learned to split bastard grain, and Jarret and I luxuriated in the warmth of burning fir deep into the winter.

I learned to use other tools of survival. Robin had kept an old .303 rifle in the boat—a guy had once given it to him in lieu of a month's rent at his house in Duncan—but I'd never touched it. That changed the night a bear came knocking at our door.

I'd spent the day canning salmon, which involved filling both the cabin and the surrounding wilderness with the rich aroma of steamed chum. Jarret and I had gone to bed with our kitchen shelves groaning under a homesteader's pride of pressure-cooked fish. Then I awoke to a dull thump. *Thud. Thud. Thud.* Somebody was pounding on the wall. I sat up and listened. It was coming from the wall at the head of my bed. I groped for the flashlight, pressed it against the window, and lit up every hair of a black bear nose pressed against the other side of the glass. Kelsy, our sweet-natured golden retriever, had turned into the snarling, drooling Hound of the Baskervilles.

I blasted the air horn at the bear, which made him at least drop to all fours. I rummaged through the kitchen and found the biggest knife. I thought, "This is stupid. I'm gonna take on a bear with a *knife?*" I knew that Robin had kept a rifle in the house, but I had no idea where it was or how to use it. I might pay for that ignorance with my life.

The next morning the bear tried to break into a neighbor's house and was killed. I took my rifle to Chris Bennett's place, and we spent the afternoon putting bullets into a target he'd drawn up. That night before going to bed, Kelsy and I walked the property. Holding the rifle in one hand and a flashlight in the other, I felt a surge of liberation run through me. I would no longer cower under the covers.

By the fall of 1987, Jarret and I had figured out how to survive in Echo Bay. Jarret started grade one at the Echo Bay school, a one-room schoolhouse with twelve kids from grades one through seven. For an only child the atmosphere was ideal; Jarret already knew most of the children, and they looked after him like older brothers and sisters—for better or worse.

After rowing Jarret to the school dock in the morning, I divided my time among homesteading, whale work, and writing. Most wildlife researchers leave home to conduct their fieldwork, which forces them to maintain both a home and a life in the field. By living in the field, I only needed to support my son. There's not much to spend money on out here—no parking meters, restaurants, bookstores, or movie theaters. I started growing most of our vegetables and fishing for our meals—salmon, cod, crab, clams, halibut, sea cucumbers, and sea urchins. My income from writing and selling photos usually sat below the poverty line, but we wanted for nothing.

My life revolved around Jarret, the tides, and the passage of whales. While I continued to record the A-pod whales that had drawn me to Canada, Mike Bigg encouraged me to collect as much data as possible on the transients that were frequenting my area.

"You're the one seeing transients, Alex," he told me. "You're getting to be an expert on them." I hadn't thought of it that way and had been forwarding all my observations on transients to him. What had got me to Echo Bay had been a single-minded purposefulness. With Mike's suggestion, however, I broke out of that pattern. My focus drew back to include an increasing number of players in the ecosystem around me.

Mike's advice about the transients was simple: measure the differences between resident and transient behavior and see what the numbers said. The division of one species into two distinct forms living side by side is highly unusual in the animal world. The types of differences between these two whale groups—diet, language, social system—generally arise only when a species becomes geographically separated into two populations with no contact between them. The estrangement between resident and transient orcas more closely resembled the behavior of human tribes.

The questions of how and why this happened were a rich source of debate between Mike and me. When Robin died, I not only lost my husband; I lost my partner in orca research. Whenever I'd witness some new and strange activity, I could describe it to Robin, and he'd return my enthusiasm. Nobody in Echo Bay knew whales as Robin had. Fortunately Mike Bigg was just a radio call away. After every noteworthy sighting, I always phoned him on the autotel, a kind of radiophone at the post office. I dubbed it the "autohell," because the signal invariably faded and cut off. In fact, if the signal didn't cut, I found myself rambling on, actually forgetting how to say good-bye. Though he was busy with his own work, Mike always made me feel as though my sightings were of vital importance. We bantered about the arcane details of whale behavior, and I sent him regular reports on the transients.

With Mike's help I cobbled my research into one of the first scientific papers on the behavior of transient orcas. We found that the differences between residents and transients appeared entirely based on the different survival strategies necessitated by their choice of food. A whale that ate fish could afford to be vocal; form big, splashy groups in summer; bear a large family; travel predictable routes; and breathe loudly and frequently. A whale that ate animals that were constantly on the lookout for its approach, on the other hand, had to be quiet and unpredictable, keep its family unit small, and quietly hold its breath. The discovery of these two "sympatric" species (animals that live in the same area but don't compete for food or habitat) may be unique in the animal world.

In my early years I had thought of the resident orcas as being the "norm" and the transients as an aberration, but in fact, the transients may have preceded the residents by thousands of years. During the last major glaciation period, salmon populations took refuge in the Columbia and Skeena Rivers. As the glaciers began receding about ten thousand years ago, the salmon slowly fanned out into the newly etched river courses. About thirty-five hundred years ago, the forests of British Columbia had created a habitat favorable to salmon, cooling the riverbeds with their lush canopies and metering out consistent levels of rainfall runoff. The coast's torrential rainfall no longer scoured river bottoms and sent fragile salmon eggs tumbling to the sea. We suspect that the mammal-eating orcas may have been here all along, throughout periods of glaciation, and the fish eaters joined them, perhaps coming in from the western Pacific, once the salmon population grew large enough to sustain them. Lance Barrett-

Lennard's genetic research has revealed that transient orcas are actually more closely related to Atlantic Ocean orcas than to the resident orcas that share their same Pacific waters.

I find it remarkable that no lusty young orca ever wandered over to the other side for a forbidden tryst, but the genetic record is irrefutable. Something in the nature of these two races of killer whales has caused them to remain separate after thousands of years of interaction.

Over the years I've learned never to say that killer whales "always" do anything. I've deduced too many rules of orca conduct only to see those rules contradicted time and time again. Whales tailor their responses—to humans, prey, the tide, one another—to each specific circumstance. They don't merely rely on instinct. They're intelligent; they learn.

That ability to adapt and strategize is never on more dramatic display than when a group of resident orcas encounters a group of transients. Sometimes the transients will move undetected through a group of widely spaced residents. Other times I've seen transients turn and leave Johnstone Strait the moment they heard the call of residents. On one occasion Graeme Ellis witnessed a group of residents with a newborn baby chase and attack some transients who had come too close for comfort.

Ellis's observation raised an intriguing question: do transients sometimes kill resident babies? Are they partly responsible for the nearly 50 percent mortality rate among young orcas? We don't know for sure, but Ellis's observation suggested at least the existence of strong animosity between the two types of orcas. The residents drove those transients into a bay with a ferry terminal. The fight broke up when the ferry departed, so we don't know how it would otherwise have concluded. Ellis thought it possible that the residents were trying to force the transients to strand themselves on the beach.

I witnessed a similar encounter myself. On the morning of Canadian Thanksgiving Day, when I should have been inside cooking up my contribution to the community potluck, I found myself following about forty members of the A pods, swimming west through Sutlej Channel, just north of Echo Bay. I recognized that this could be the last time I might see many of them until the next summer. They were clearly in high spirits. Small knots of whales splashed and surfaced all around me. I looked down to my notepad to record a few observations, and when I looked up, they had vanished. What had been a channel roiling with whales a moment ago had turned lifeless.

I shut down my engine and called Kelsy to attention. Her ears could pick up much finer clues than mine. When she heard a whale blow, her ears perked up, and her nose pointed toward the orca. We waited. Her head jerked. "Good girl," I said, and restarted the motor.

The whales had swept up against the southern shoreline. They were tightly bunched and moving fast. Their behavior had changed. There was no splashing about. Babies tucked in close to their mothers, and the entire pod swam so near the dark shoreline, it was difficult to see them. I followed right behind as they poured into the first bay they encountered, Greenway Sound.

The whales formed a solid line. I dropped the hydrophone over the side and recorded deep gorillalike grunts, a sound I'd never heard before. With each breath the whales surfaced facing a different direction, as though defending themselves in all directions. When they came up facing me, I looked upon an imposing sight, a threatening phalanx of fins standing like the spear tips of a medieval army. Their sounds were so threatening that I removed my headset and prayed that this had nothing to do with me. What could have caused such an extreme reaction?

Kelsy perked her ears in the direction opposite the whales. As I swung around, I caught sight of four new orca fins slicing eastward against the far shore of Sutlej Channel. I reached for my binoculars. Now there was no doubt about the reason for A pod's strange behavior: transients. I recognized the four interlopers as Kwatsi's family, the T20 group. The transients must have revealed their presence to the residents with an acoustic signal—but why had three pods of forty residents taken evasive action to make way for only four transients? What did they have to fear from the mammal eaters? Or was it fear at all? Maybe it was distaste, xenophobia, or some other emotion entirely unique to killer whales.

Two observations have made me question the orca's capacity to even sense fear. The top ocean predator may have little need for this sentiment. Once out with the whale sisters Kelsy (the whale, not the dog) and Yakat, and another time with transients Kwatsi and family, I watched something that gave me pause. When a logging company wants to remove a forest from a slope too steep to build a road access, it uses large double-bladed helicopters to pick up the logs and drop them into the sea. The company builds a floating rectangular corral, called a boom, chains it to the shore below the cut block, and that's where the helicopter releases each load. Like clockwork, 60-foot trees come flying down the mountainside on the end of a cable and drop with a gargantuan splash into the water every four to five minutes. The concussion of so much weight hitting the water has killed bottom fish and brought them floating to the surface. The noise can be heard underwater for miles. A heli-log dump is a lethal place for any marine animal to be.

Despite this, on two separate occasions, I have watched orcas swim right through these dumps. The first time was frightening. Yakat and Kelsy crossed from the Gilford Island side of Tribune Channel to the mainland and deliberately approached a heli-log operation. They surfaced just outside the boom as a several-ton log crashed deep into the water. When it became clear that the whales were planning to dive through this foaming cauldron of logs falling from the sky and breaching back to the surface, I desperately tried to communicate with the helicopter pilot. "There are whales in the dump. Don't drop," I repeated on every radio frequency I could think of. Then I heard the *whump, whump, whump* of the chopper coming back down the hill. Since aircraft use different frequencies than boats, no one heard me, and I watched in terror as the pilot released his load. The log fell heavily into the spot that the whales had just entered. I watched helplessly for blood and blubber. But as the helicopter ascended, I heard the whales blow and spun to see them calmly rolling just beyond the boom. They'd timed their passage perfectly. Perhaps all those bubbles were a light show extraordinaire not to be missed. Maybe they tickled deliciously. The whales could have been looking for dead fish, or was it just curiosity? For certain it had been a dangerous, deliberate, and precisely choreographed move that left me wondering if whales know fear at all.

Transient orcas constantly challenge the animals around them, partly out of a sense of play and partly because their survival depends on adapting to and exploiting any new addition to their environment. Transients have been seen killing swimming moose, trying to wash dogs off a beach, and circling deer stranded on a rock. They kill seabirds for sport.

They've even made me the target of their stealth maneuvers. On one occasion four transients disappeared in Tribune Channel as I was tracking them. I'd failed to identify them, so I sat and drifted in hopes that they might reappear close enough for identification.

Beware what you wish for.

Twenty-five minutes I sat with not a hint of a whale blow. The day was so still, I could hear the wingbeats of ravens flying long before they appeared overhead. Then, without warning, all four whales burst to the surface within inches of my boat. I was surrounded. The blast of their exhalations surprised me off my seat. They swiveled their large brown eyes up at me. This is how they catch sea lions—unaware. If I'd leaned over, I could have stroked their rostrums. The quartet eyed me for a few seconds and then slipped away into the murky, nutrient-rich waters of Tribune Channel. I did not follow—I had made my identification.

I never allow my dog to look over the side at transients for fear the whales will think I have a tasty seal in my boat.

I had a second aggressive encounter a few months later. Jarret and I headed out in my new boat *Blackfish Sound* after hearing whales on the house hydrophone. We spotted a transient family moving fast into Tribune Channel and glimpsed a tiny new infant tucked in among them. The little fellow's spots were still pinky-orange. An extremely thin blubber layer causes this babyhood blush; as the infant fattens up on his mother's rich milk, his insulating blubber thickens and turns the spots white.

Since baby whales often vanish in their first years of life, I felt obligated to photograph the youngster. An accurate record of whale births and deaths is essential to understanding the health and dynamics of wild whale populations, and the best tool for accuracy is the photograph. Too many times I'd heard Graeme Ellis's retort to any casual whale identification: "No picture, no proof."

In my haste I broke one of my own cardinal rules. I rushed. The whales were moving fast, so to catch up with them, I revved my motor. Now I know what happens underwater when you rev a motor. If it's close to my hydrophone, it'll hurt my ears. But I had to get that picture.

Before I got close enough to raise my camera, one of the whales peeled off from the group. It was a teenage male named Arrow, almost certainly the baby's older brother. There was no doubt where he was headed: he came straight at me. He kept his dorsal fin high, in full view. His fin tore the water, and his back plowed a furrow. I watched the water cascade off his head. Adrenaline streaked through me with such force that it shocked my fingertips and scalp. Jarret froze.

I've seen whales at top speed. At this distance I knew there was no getting away from big brother. I responded by turning away from the family, paralleling the young male's course without throttling up. As soon as I completed my 90-degree turn, he dove and disappeared. I continued my course away from the family and glanced at Jarret to make sure that he was wearing his flotation vest. There are no existing reports of killer whales' attacking boats or people in recent times, but I knew that this guy had us if he wanted us. The next few minutes stretched into an anxious eternity. Why didn't he surface?! My body tensed for impact.

Kwoof. "There he is," said Jarret. Arrow had resurfaced by his mother's side.

I guessed he was satisfied by my move. I turned the boat back parallel to the transient pod and slowly motored along. I watched the young male warily and kept a respectful distance—the one he'd chosen for me. After an hour of progress through the channel, the entire family turned slowly toward me. As I stopped, they crossed just off my bow. I raised my camera and captured the day's valuable proof. Jarret and I turned home, having learned our lesson in cross-cultural etiquette. Had he wanted to cause us harm, the teenage transient could easily have flipped my boat. Instead, he came at us with his dorsal fin raised high as a pennant, bearing a simple request: Back off—or else.

More than mating, more than food, more than home territory, it's family around which a killer whale's world revolves. And as with most families, the events that have the most profound effects are births and deaths. In all my years of watching and listening to the whales, the interactions between mothers and children still touch me the most deeply.

I wouldn't want to say that Nicola's A pod family was the dominant group in Johnstone Strait, but when I met them, they seemed to play an important role in the summer gatherings of the northern resident community. Nicola and her descendants are marked by exceptionally elegant fins. Nicola, her daughter Tsitika, and granddaughters Clio and Minstrel all have the lovely, deep-curved dorsal of their mothers. The trait is so strong, it can be faintly detected in the tall fins of one of Tsitika's sons, Blackney. They were the first to appear in the gathering place of Johnstone Strait every summer and seemed to hold the perennial honor of escorting waves of more distant family members into the strait to feed and socialize.

When Nicola died in the winter of 1988–89, however, the family gave up its position of leadership. As with most killer whales, the sixty-two-year-old matriarch's body was never found; she disappeared over the winter and never returned for the summer gatherings. That fall, when Tsitika and her sons came through the archipelago, their movements became much less predictable. Instead of stepping into her mother's role, Tsitika, perhaps distracted by her new baby, often let her sons lead the family. They entered bays and channels where I'd never seen them before. I had the impression that the guys were curious about all the places that Granny had never taken them.

In 1993 I saw an event that further changed the family. Tsitika and her five children came through Fife Sound in a boisterous mood, breaching and leaping. Every few minutes they stopped and milled about. I followed them past the Burdwoods and into Tribune Channel, then saw them stop and huddle in a tight little group in the deep water near a steep cliff. I sensed that something was up. Jarret, now eight years old, had become a crackerjack video cameraman, which gave me the freedom to observe, record sound, and shoot stills. He rolled video while I idled back to the whales.

After a few minutes of roiling action among the tightly clustered whales, we saw the fleetest glimpse of a tiny whale. It surfaced at a 45-degree angle off the rostrum of Tsitika's son Strider. I couldn't tell for sure whether it was a baby orca or a Dall's porpoise. Strider took the little creature on his back several times, but it slid into the water on each attempt. Whatever it was, it wasn't moving under its own power.

The whales grew agitated, surfacing rapidly and making quick changes in direction back and forth. After twenty minutes Strider's younger brother, Blackney, left the group and went to shore. There he pushed his face into a cleft in the rock face, turned, and rejoined the others.

The whales banded close together and swam back the way they'd come. This was highly unusual; whales almost always make the full circuit of Tribune Channel except when they're facing a strong full-moon tide. There was no such tide. The three brothers and two sisters crowded around Tsitika. Their mood had grown markedly subdued—no jumping, no quick surfacing. They seemed intent on getting out of the archipelago, moving fast and silently. Strider was mere inches from his mother. The two must have been touching each other most of the length of their bodies. I kept looking for the baby whale with each surfacing, hoping it was obscured behind the turmoil of fins.

That evening Jarret and I reviewed his video. Clearly there had been a baby orca. We couldn't make out whether it had surfaced alive or been propelled to the surface. Lying awake that night, I realized that after Blackney had gone to the beach, I never saw the baby whale again. When he returned, the whales' behavior had shifted dramatically.

"Oh, my God." It hit me like a ton of bricks. "He put the infant's body in that cleft in the rock face."

At first light I went back to check the place that Blackney had nuzzled but found no sign of an infant. Had it washed away? Had it never been there in the first place? Do orcas bury their dead?

The next day Tsitika returned in the close company of C5, a seventy-year-old matriarch and a contemporary of Tsitika's late mother. They didn't enter Tribune Channel but instead swept past from Fife to Pemphrase. Today Tsitika is a healthy fifty-four-year-old matriarch whom I still see often in Johnstone Strait, but since that day with C5, she has never returned to the waters of the Broughton Archipelago.

Tsitika remained uncharacteristically unsociable the rest of the summer, often lagging behind other families. It was tempting to interpret her behavior as heartbroken sadness, but that would be making assumptions. Any number of things could have produced that behavior; she could, for instance, have been physically ailing.

Tsitika reminded me of the chimpanzee mother Flo in Jane Goodall's fieldwork. Both Flo and Tsitika were exceptional mothers who produced families that became central to the well-being of the larger community around them. Goodall had attributed the family's size and standing to Flo's tender and constant mothering. I felt that the same thing had happened with Tsitika. Other female whales had lost many more babies, but Tsitika's family had five young whales survive to maturity, a family size rarely exceeded in the northern community. None of this group had been taken into captivity, so theirs was a rare intact family. In watching Tsitika, I feel I am witnessing fully realized bonds among family members and the great impact of loss among orcas.

After the terror and horror of Robin's death, I was not particularly keen on returning to Johnstone Strait to work with whales, but there was another reason I began to avoid the place even though this often meant spending days without whales. I found myself increasingly reluctant to add the sound of my outboard engine to the barrage of noise accumulating in that stretch of water. Whale watching, which began in 1980 with one part-time boat run by Jim Borrowman and Bill MacKay, had exploded into an industry with dozens of vessels of all sizes and shapes by the early 1990s. Ten local boats began taking people out to see whales on a daily basis from July through September. This was good for the local economy and helped give whales a reason to exist in the minds of many within the logging community. Then high-powered twin-engine Zodiacs began screaming north out of Campbell River, making the grueling trip up an often rough strait, and many boats, including my old *Blue Fjord,* started including Johnstone Strait and the whales as the focus of multiday trips.

Paul Spong and Helena Symonds responded to the increased pressure on the whales by taking their boat off the water and setting up land-based whale-watch camps. Volunteers from all over the world come to sit in these strategically placed outposts and report information back to Paul and Helena's OrcaLab. Bill MacKay and Jim Borrowman recognized that they were part of what could become a problem for the whales, knowing that whales need to be able to hear one another to feed and socialize. These two men took responsibility for the industry. Working closely with Mike Bigg and later Graeme Ellis and others, they designed a voluntary code of conduct and made it clear to everyone that if you did not abide by these guidelines, you were clearly running a second-class operation. Impressively, this has been largely effective.

The rules are simple: don't charge at the whales, don't get in their way, don't leapfrog with them, stay 100 meters (300 feet) away, keep your engine at low speed and thus quieter when near whales, and don't move toward a resting line of whales. Following Bill and Jim's example, most operators purchased hydrophones, thus introducing their guests to both the marvel of whales talking and the terrible noise we humans make with our boats. No automotive manufacturer would consider making a car or truck that produces as much noise as boat engines make underwater. Such a vehicle would be banned from all townships. However, the shrieking blare of boat engines is contained below the water out of human earshot, and so "quiet" was never even considered.

While Bill and Jim set an example, Paul and Helena see everything with the help of their volunteers, and any boat harassing whales can expect a radio call from them. "The 18-foot white boat with a blue canopy, alongside whales at Izumi Rock, please come back to the *Shachi,*" begins Helena in her feminine voice. I admire her restraint, as she takes the attitude that everyone *wants* to be kind to the whales but may not know how. In addition to the whale-watch fleet, there are hundreds of people in their own small boats, who just want to get a few good minutes of whales on video before returning to fishing. I am certain that many must look all around thinking, "Where is this woman, and how does she know how close I am to the whales?" Most are won over and thank her in the end.

On the few days that I do work among the fleet, I have seen some lovely encounters in which boats, with engines off, drift silently among frolicking whales. But I have also witnessed sickening scenes of one lone pod hounded relentlessly, crowded up against the shore in a blue haze of carcinogenic outboard exhaust. The mind-set, "I'm only with the whales for a few minutes, so I am going to do what I want," may turn deadly for whales as they helplessly attract one small fleet after the next, day in and day out during their prime opportunity. If they don't build up their blubber layer, they will not stay warm through winter. A good friend and colleague, Rob Williams, documented that even at 100 meters, an approaching vessel will cause whales to speed up and become evasive. In fact, he

mused in a research paper, "some tracks of killer whales and the experiment boat (following at 100m) are reminiscent of long-term exposure photographs of moths evading bats." Our need to see the top
predator of the ocean has fostered a predator-prey relationship, where
there was none for this species.

Because restraint is a trait that we, as a group, still can't muster
voluntarily, whale-watching laws with stiff penalties are being drawn
up, similar to those that exist in the United States. It is already illegal
to "harass" a whale, but the term has been so vague that individuals
and industry have got away with just that, to the point of driving
killer whales out of large swaths of territory.

It is important to recognize that even the simplest act of "looking" can too often cause irrevocable change for the very creature we
came to see. Sometimes it is the sheer mass of our presence; sometimes our observations expose a species to hunters or make the creatures political pawns or targets for acts of violence. Sometimes a rare
sighting will trigger a human flocking response and trampling of our
coveted quarry's environment. On bad days I think whale watching
is harmful to whales, but then I hear about the deep emotional response that many, many visitors have to seeing wild whales. The
commercial skippers tell me about people crying, dying children
smiling, and people coming year after year until they are bringing
grandchildren. I have turned around to see forty faces beaming from
the deck of a boat looming above me, all focused on the vanishing
flukeprint of a wild whale. Twenty-five percent of the whales that
died in captivity were found to have bullets lodged deep in their
bodies, illustrating just how many wild whales used to be shot at!
I know that the very best hope for any species on earth today is
that some group of humans loves it, but the line is fine between
guardianship and molesting a species quite literally to death.

Every September Paul Spong and Helena Symonds host a gathering
of orca researchers at OrcaLab. For three days we sprawl around Paul
and Helena's amazing home telling tales of what we've seen the

previous summer and debating the need for limits on whale watching, orca captures, and our own research methods.

Having led Greenpeace's fight for whales in the 1970s, Paul Spong turned his attention in the 1990s to the release of captives. In 1990 Paul and Helena began an international campaign to return Corky to her family in the A5 pod. Their efforts ranged from the small and personal (since Anheuser-Busch, the maker of Budweiser beer, owns SeaWorld, Bud has been banned from the OrcaLab fridge) to the grand and international. The Corky banner, which began as a modest quilt made up of 50-centimeter by 50-centimeter squares of cloth donated by people who demanded Corky's freedom, has since grown into an epic undertaking. At last count the banner's fifteen thousand panels made up a strip more than 3 kilometers long. On Mother's Day 1996, Spong's volunteers displayed the banner from one end of SeaWorld to the other.

SeaWorld, of course, refuses to meet Spong's demand. Corky remains entombed in her concrete tank. She stopped ovulating after Orky's death and so never got the opportunity to raise a baby. The closest she came was when an Icelandic female orca attacked her, fatally breaking her own jaw. Corky adopted the Icelandic whale's baby and for a few months enjoyed mothering this little orphan, until it too was taken away.

During the meeting at OrcaLab one year, I gave a synopsis of what I'd seen in the inlets. I mentioned that I'd observed whales in every major waterway in the archipelago with the exception of Cramer Passage, the narrow waterway directly in front of my house.

While no whale captures have been allowed in British Columbia since 1976, that doesn't mean that oceanariums have stopped asking. In 1983 SeaWorld floated an outrageous proposal to capture no fewer than one hundred orcas from Alaskan waters. The marine park proposed keeping the whales for three months, during which time they'd take blood samples, perform liver biopsies, and remove a tooth from each whale. They further proposed to freeze-brand the whales, completely ignoring the advances in identification that Mike Bigg and his colleagues had made in the previous decade. (The U.S. government ultimately refused SeaWorld's application.)

With word going round about SeaWorld's looking for new ways of securing live orcas, some of the researchers at OrcaLab that year began discussing what avenues the marine parks had left. One researcher asked if it was possible that capturing a whole family might be less traumatic to the whales than taking a single member. If that proved to be the case, he argued, why not consider a less-than-intact family like the A4 pod?

This set my blood boiling.

"How can you sacrifice Kelsy and Yakat after all they've suffered?!" I said. "Their uncle died. Their mother was shot. Kelsy has lost three of her babies. They have earned the right to be left alone!"

Paul Spong stepped in to calm me down. "Alex, Alex, Alex," he said. "We're just talking hypothetically here."

Had I not spent years watching the A4 family struggle to survive, my response might have been a bit calmer. When I first arrived in the archipelago, the family had been led by an old matriarch known only as A10. In 1983 A10 and her youngest calf were shot by a boater. Researcher Dave "Eagle Eye" Briggs, the California-based researcher who perches every summer on a cliff across from Robson Bight, heard the gunshots. Dave flagged down a whale-watching boat, and they went to check on the whales. As the boat approached, the whales turned and came directly toward them. The passengers watched in awed horror.

"A10 pushed her wounded calf to my side of the boat," Dave later told me. "We could see the wound oozing blood. It really seemed that she was showing us: Look what you humans have done." Dave filed a police report, but the fellow got off. No pictures, no proof.

A10 and her baby both died that winter. The two sisters, Yakat and Kelsy, assumed the roles of clan matriarchs while still in their thirties, a young age for orca family heads.

Over the years I saw the two sisters and their brood many times in the archipelago. The sisters often bobbed several hundred meters apart, surrounded by their seven frolicking youngsters. They were the only family that frequently fished pinks, the smallest, shortest-lived salmon species up here. Because their brief life span minimizes the accumulation of planetary toxins, pinks are among the healthiest animal proteins available in the world. They travel in large, dense schools, and Yakat and Kelsy proved to be excellent herders. A number of times I watched the two sisters drive the salmon directly beneath my hull and straight into the sheer cliff faces of the archipelago's inlets. Their children, and later grandchildren, came in after them, milling slowly around the base of the cliffs, picking up the fish that were coralled or had been knocked out by hitting the rocks.

Kelsy let her babies wander more than any other mother orca I'd seen, and I suspected that the loose rein she gave them might have contributed to the loss of her offspring. She's now given birth to seven babies. Only three survived.

I grew to love this family that had suffered so many losses. I know I shouldn't project human values on them, but I couldn't help but feel tender toward a family that had experienced the shock of losing so many close companions.

Two days after the argument over family captivity at OrcaLab and my report of no whale sightings in Cramer Pass, Kelsy and Yakat initiated an extraordinary encounter behind the Burdwood Group of islands. It began as a normal day. Jarret and I followed the sisters and their family from Fife Sound into the hub waters in front of Echo Bay, where five water passages converge in one spot. I shut the motor down and drifted with the family milling in the water. The moment I restarted the motor, the two sisters corralled us. They surfaced simultaneously off port and starboard with young Sutlej broadside to the bow, all of them only inches away. Jarret thought it was fun, but it didn't look good to me. We were trapped. They buzzed around us like transients making a kill.

They repeated their blocking movements every time I tried to move. As soon as I calmed down and began to feel safe, they "released" me, turned south, and headed fast for Cramer Passage. They led us down Cramer, turned and traveled back up the passage, then turned again and traveled back down.

Sometimes I don't know what to believe with whales. This flew in the face of reason. Were the whales trying to communicate something about my defense of their family? They had clearly commanded my attention, then deliberately and in triplicate transited the passage I had told the OrcaLab group that they never entered. I know this has no place in science (or even a sound mind perhaps), but could our parameters on reality be set just a little too tight?

I often envy wildlife biologists who study terrestrial animals. They have so much to work with. They can actually see their subjects by day and (sometimes) night, follow their movements through tracks in the dirt or snow, pick through their scat to determine what's been eaten, and often study the bodies of both attackers and prey. Whales leave nothing but a thirty-second flukeprint on the water. When they die, whales most often disappear.

Finding a single killer whale body can result in a huge leap forward for the entire field of orca research. Of the 167 killer whales that have died in the twenty-nine years since Bigg and Ellis's surveys began, only 11 bodies have been recovered. So when I received a call in November 1990 from Bob Field, an artist who lives on Malcolm Island, his news filled me with both dread and excitement.

"Alex, I found a dead whale just above Donegal Head yesterday," he said. "You probably want to come over and have a look."

"Is it a killer whale?"

"Yup."

"Does it have any identifying scars?" I asked.

He described deep scoops carved in the back. My heart sank. It sure sounded like Eve.

Jim Borrowman got a call about the whale as well, and he scrambled to alert an autopsy team: Ann Pabst, from the University of British Columbia; Pam Stacey, from a whale research group at the southern end of Vancouver Island; and Graeme Ellis and his wife, Jane Watson. Some agreed to meet me the next morning in Port McNeill, take the ferry to Malcolm Island, and drive to Donegal Head, the remote beach on the far eastern tip of the island. Jim said he'd take the others in his new whale-watching boat, the *Lukwa*, and meet us there on the beach—to pull the carcass back to Telegraph Cove.

It had already been a rough autumn. Mike Bigg, who had battled leukemia for a number of years, finally succumbed to the disease in October. I was still reeling from the loss of my killer whale mentor. When we received the call about Eve, almost everybody in the whale community had the same thought: too bad Mike's not here for this.

That night I talked to Helena Symonds, who had unknowingly observed and recorded the aftermath of Eve's death. A few days before Bob Field discovered Eve's body, Helena had watched the matriarch's sons, Top Notch and Foster, circle Hanson Island, calling and calling and calling. For the first time in thirty-three years, Top Notch heard no response from his mother. For the first time in his life, he no longer heard the cavernous sigh of his mother's breath beside him as he parted the waves.

The wind blew in a southeastern fury. The weather forecasters predicted the highest tides of the century. Jarret and I piled into my International Harvester in Port McNeill, along with two aspiring filmmakers from the University of Florida, twins John and Joe Dee, and Ann Pabst. We picked our way carefully out to Donegal Head, driving over roads flooded by the high tides. Looking out the window with the ocean over the hubcaps, it felt at times as if I were driving my boat.

We found Eve cast on the beach among the driftwood. Someone had tried to cut her teeth out, but they had been too firmly embedded for the small knife used. Birds had pecked a scribbled pattern all over her white spots, leaving the black areas untouched. I felt a sense of awe creep over me as we approached. Lying fully exposed before me was a wild orca I had spent years observing. I had seen her eat, sleep, play, and greet her extended family. She had seen the last moments of my husband's life. And yet I had never seen her whole and vulnerable like this. She had witnessed plenty, too—so many changes in my own species' attitude toward hers. When she was a young whale, humans had shot her kind on sight. Now we followed orcas everywhere they went, our hostility replaced by an overbearing curiosity. I wondered which attitude she'd preferred.

We took measurements and photographs as best we could in the lashing hail. It was blowing at least 50 knots when Jim Borrowman arrived. The *Lukwa* is built like a giant speedboat, with most of the vessel above water. The wind sent the boat skidding sideways, forcing it dangerously close to the enormous breakers pounding the beach. Our plan was to tie a heavy poly line to the whale's peduncle, just forward of the flukes, so Jim could tow her off the beach and over to Telegraph Cove, where we planned to perform the autopsy and preserve the skeleton. We figured it would be easier to move the whole body by sea rather than cut it up and haul it, piece by piece, through the brush.

But Jim couldn't get the *Lukwa* through the surf to throw the line. So Jane Watson, a tall, athletic young sea otter researcher, pulled on her dive suit, took the rope in her teeth, and swam it to shore.

I quickly tied the rope around the whale, using the technique Billy Proctor had taught me to drag logs off the beach. I prayed that the knot would hold. "Ready?" Jane called. Taking the other end of the rope in her teeth once more, she swam out to the plunging *Lukwa*. Graeme secured the rope and hauled Jane out of the water. Jim put the boat in gear. Slowly the matriarch's carcass slid across the cobble beach and disappeared into the foaming breakers.

The ferry from Sointula struck a log on its way to Port McNeill and lost power. We rolled in the storm until the ship's engineers brought the big boat back on line. The entire northern Vancouver Island lost power and the roads were deeply flooded. It felt as if the gods were enraged at our transgression. We arrived at Telegraph Cove exhausted.

"Get that goddamned stinky sonofabitch blackfish off the ramp!"

"This must be the spot," I thought. The drunk local resident railed at us for a few minutes, then left to warm his couch.

The dead whale made an eerie, macabre sight. Eve lay there on the concrete ramp lit by a streetlight, her mouth slightly agape, unmoving after fifty-three years of constant motion.

The next day we explored her secrets. It felt barbarous and disrespectful to approach this lovely creature with a sharp array of knives. Graeme Ellis's Norwegian flensing knife, which looked like a large hockey stick, reminded us that whales are still regularly cut up with such instruments in other parts of the world.

I touched the gentle curve of her face, her most poignant feature. The exquisite design of her body revealed itself to us. Beneath her ¾-inch-thick skin, Eve was gloved in a white insulating layer of blubber half a foot thick. This was how she had stayed warm in water that would have killed a human in a matter of minutes. Beneath that lay a layer of rich red muscle fed by a network of blood vessels. Great ribs arched protectively over her soft inner organs.

Eve rewrote the science on orca diet. We pulled an amazing array of sea life out of her stomach. In all, there were fifty-nine individual fish from thirteen different species. In addition to nineteen individual salmon, we found fifteen lingcod, seven species of sole and flounder, and pieces of sablefish, staghorn, and great sculpin. The sculpin may have found their way into the whale in the gut of the lingcod, but we couldn't explain away all the fish like that. Who'd have guessed that these salmon eaters ate so many bottom fish? I found especially delightful the image of Eve, the aged matriarch, pursuing a flat little sole along the bottom of the strait. Did she suck them into her mouth or flip them off the bottom with her lower jaw or merely snap them up when they ventured off the seafloor?

Beneath her blowhole I found the air sacs that acted like air-filled Ping-Pong paddles bouncing Eve's ample voice—both her calls and intense echolocation—forward. Eve had changed the size and dimension of these sacs to direct her sound waves forward, preventing wasted leakage down or backward. She also used the air sacs to protect her brain from her own great voice. From there Eve's voice had entered the oil-filled acoustic lens that was her face. While the surface of her face arched outward in a pregnant curve, her skull actually curved inward, cradling a globe of fatty tissue that both amplified sound with a spiral structure of differing lipid densities and stepped its transmission smoothly from the higher-density whale into the lower-density seawater. Eve was a marvel of evolution.

It was remarkable to see Eve's fingers hidden in her paddlelike pectoral fins, little short bones laid out in perfect order. Never used, fully intact. Those fingers underscored one of the vast differences between our species. Humans use their bodies to change their environment. Whales change their bodies to adapt to their environment.

It's difficult to describe the sickening stench of decaying whale carcass; I've come across nothing like it in my life. The blubber continues to conserve the whale's body heat after death, forming truly noxious gases. The more experienced among us suited up in rain gear and rubber boots, head to toe. I made the mistake of wearing heavy leather boots, which sopped up the permeating scent like a sponge. I could throw them away, but I couldn't toss our two dogs, Kelsy and Tiger. Jarret had managed not to pick up any of the revolting odor, but the two dogs reeked. During the autopsy rubber-gloved people would occasionally stop to pet the dogs—*good girls*—which left their fur slick with whale oil. Those dogs didn't see the inside of our house for weeks.

We saved every bone. The bones were cleaned and taken to the Sidney Museum at the south end of Vancouver Island, where they were reconstructed and put on public display. Although we never determined exactly what had killed the great matriarch, by allowing us to find her body, Eve had educated my species in death as much as she had in life.

Chapter 18

~ ~ ~

After his father died, people told Jarret that he was the man of the house. I disagreed.

"You're the kid of the house," I said. "Don't listen to them."

I felt that it was important for him to feel safe. He shouldn't be worrying about money, food, or shelter. I wanted to make sure he could concentrate on the business of being a child, letting him discover the world and where his interests lay. I constantly worried that our homesteading life denied him the opportunities of town—Boy Scouts, music lessons, movies, festivals. But as I watched him grow, I realized that there were enormous benefits to be derived from a childhood at the edge of today's society. Echo Bay was too remote to receive a television signal, so Jarret and his friends never suffered the barrage of ads baiting their appetites for action figures, guns, and sugar-glazed cereal. They had the freedom to be creative. Jarret and his buddies carved swords, fashioned shields, built forts, went on expeditions in the woods, and created whatever reality they wanted. As I watched self-reliance and creativity flourish in Jarret and all the children around him, I found reason to hope that my life-style was not hurting him. Jarret managed to have a childhood, but he was always very careful with me. He never wanted to see me sad again.

It was about this time that I hitched a ride up to Wakeman Sound with Billy Proctor. I tied my boat behind Billy's—saved a ton of money on gas—and we parted ways at Steve Vessely's dock. Just as Billy jumped off his boat, he mumbled something to me.

"Y'oughta come deckhandin' with me."

"What?"

Then Steve showed up, and it was too late to discuss it further. I'm sure Billy planned it that way. He wanted me to mull over the offer. Me, a deckhand?

"I been working with a guy, and it just ain't working out," Billy later told me. "So whattaya say?"

There was more to this than Billy's needing an extra hand. Billy's father had drowned when Billy was about Jarret's age, and he knew about the financial hardships faced by a single mother and son.

"I've got two questions," I said. "Is it okay with your wife, and can Jarret come along?"

"Yep and yep," said Billy.

The commercial salmon season opened on July 1, and we headed out two days early in Billy's 38-foot wooden troller *Twilight Rock* to pick up supplies and get ourselves ready. Jarret stepped right on the boat the day after his last day of grade one. It took us five hours to get to Port Hardy, where we laid in a supply of groceries and filled the hold with ice, and another six hours to reach the fishing grounds, a broad, shallow shelf off the northeastern tip of Vancouver Island known as the Yankee Bank.

Now fifty-five, Billy had been fishing for a living since he was five, but the western coast of Vancouver Island was fairly new to him. He'd always been high boat around the archipelago, but as fewer fish returned to those inland waters, he'd been forced to travel to the open Pacific.

Billy's a troller. Instead of using nets, he runs out six steel cables with as many as twenty hooks on each line. When fish strike the hooks, the fisherman flips the gurdy lever forward and rolls the cable in. Billy brings the fish over the side of the boat by hand. Trollers are known as "swivelnecks" because they're constantly swiveling their heads from the top of one pole to the other. Billy could read exactly how many of what kind of fish had hit every one of his seventy-two hooks, how big it was, and exactly where in the spiderweb of gear it lay, by the jiggling motion of the poles.

I tied leaders, cleaned fish, and worked one side of the gear. A leader usually consisted of a snap, several feet of line, a 10-inch flasher (a chrome-plated piece of metal or plastic), more line, and then a 2-inch hook camouflaged by what's known in the trade as a hoochie, a little plastic octopus. Billy also used spoons, metal lures that wobbled to resemble a wounded herring. The length between each piece of hardware was crucial. The six cables sent out stray electrical impulses, which can attract or repel fish. Billy varied the setup daily, sometimes hourly, depending on how the fish were—or weren't—hitting.

Fishermen rarely outfished Billy. And if they did—watch out. We had to pull in every bit of gear and sharpen the hooks; fiddle with the voltage; check the action on every flasher; empty the hoochie drawer and switch to a "green alligator," an "army truck," or a "bleeding heart"; clean the jellyfish off the hooks; straighten the legs of the hoochies; polish the spoons; speed up; slow down; put on his lucky cap—try *something* new. There was no bad luck with Billy. A good fisherman made his own luck.

Our first day out, the spring salmon bit like sand fleas. I understood the meaning of swivelneck immediately. We landed fifty-four chinook in a single day, the best catch of springs he'd ever had. Unlike most skippers, Billy believed in letting his deckhand land any fish that came in on his or her side of the boat. If I jammed out, he'd gladly do it himself. But he liked me to land my own.

"Those big smileys," he'd tell me, "they'll charge your batteries!"

Billy killed and bled the fish as soon as he brought them aboard. I watched a long time before I dared clean one. It had to be done just right: any snagging the blade on the fins or nicking the ribs would crush the value of the fish. Billy always took a look in the stomach to see what they were eating, then he tailored the gear to match it.

Unfortunately the lump hit me as hard as those chinook hit Billy's line. "The lump" is what they call the ocean swell. When the Pacific's pent-up wave motion bumps into the shoals of the Yankee

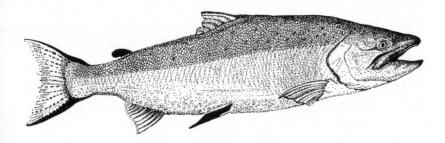

Chinook salmon

Bank, it humps up into the lump. Experienced fishermen think nothing of it, but it made me want to die. When the vent pipe burped up a whiff of diesel, I thought I'd fall unconscious. At the end of the day, Jarret and I composed a song to the tune of "Home on the Range": "Barf, barf on the Yankee Bank . . ."

"I've made a big mistake," I thought as I rocked to sleep in my bunk. "I can't take this."

Billy showed me that I could take it. He schooled me in the fine art of boating fish. If he saw a hooked fish really tugging on the line, he'd leave it on for a few minutes to let it tire itself out. "Let him soak a little longer," he'd tell me. Then he'd pull the leader in by hand, lean over the stern, whack the salmon dead with a quick, precise club strike, gaff it through its head, and lift the 30-pound fish aboard in one smooth motion. It was tricky and financially risky work. You could club the fish right off the hook, killing both the fish and your portion of the $120 it would have brought in.

The one job Billy never let anyone else do was pack the fish. He iced them himself in the hold. We had ten days from the moment we caught the first fish until we had to have them at the wholesaler's dock in Port Hardy. The early catch had to be packed with ice and set at just the right angle so that as the ice melted, it flushed out the fish's body cavity. If a fish were laid wrong, it might marinate in its own juices for more than a week. Details like that mattered: trollers were known for bringing in beautiful fish, and none were prettier than Billy's. A net-caught salmon can damage its scales or bruise itself flopping around in the net or on the deck. Billy's hand-caught and hand-packed fish commanded top dollar at the wholesaler's, and the springs ended up in the finest restaurants in New York City. I liked Billy's style for more than just its monetary value. He prepared each fish to preserve its maximum goodness. No fish that came aboard his ship was wasted.

Ten days after setting out, we pulled into Seafood Packing, in Port Hardy, our hold heavy with chinook. After unloading the fish, Billy went inside to strike a price. He came out an hour later and handed me a check for nearly $2,000.

"How do like them apples?" he said. "You earned it."

While Billy never humiliated me when I made mistakes, he never lavished praise, either. If he'd said I'd earned it, I had. The money was so good, I decided it was worth the nausea.

Fishing with Billy Proctor was like taking a ride into the soul of the British Columbia coast. I felt myself cross a boundary. I was no longer an outsider. Like so much of this coast, my life became entwined with the Pacific salmon. The waters we fished teemed with life, most of it eating or being eaten by salmon. Every settlement we ventured into—Coal Harbour, Quatsino, Kyuquot, Winter Harbour—depended on fish for survival. So did the eagles, bears, wolves, mink, kingfishers, sea lions, killer whales, Douglas firs, Sitka spruce, and cedars. The more familiar I became with salmon, the more grateful I became. What a gift. The fish leaves its birth waters, takes a few spins around the north Pacific gyre, then carries a wealth of life-giving nutrients back to the coast. Since there was no shower or bath on Billy's boat, I usually ended up wearing salmon scales in my hair. We ate fish for lunch and dinner. With the boat coated in their scent, we breathed fish. Salmon, the lifeblood of the coast, got into our blood as well.

Billy had a master fisherman's knowledge of the water and its ways. He was always checking the color of the water—too blue, bad cross tide, just the right shade of brown. He could pull up a salmon and name its home river based on nothing more than the color of its back or the shape of its face. He read the boats and the banter, too. We fished with a loose group of other trollers who kept up a constant stream of chatter on the radio. You couldn't always see the other boats, but you knew they were out there, just over the horizon. If something happened to my skipper, I knew those guys would be there. Billy watched where the highliners (boats that consistently unloaded the biggest catches) went and sussed out whether the radio reports of other catches were bona fide or bullshit.

"You gotta listen for what they're not saying as much as what they do," Billy said.

Every successful skipper was dying to brag but couldn't afford to attract the whole fleet to his hot spot. So nothing but the dinner menu came across straight.

Sockeye salmon always provided the most drama of the season. They move down the coast like a flash flood. We'd spend days waiting for the bite, and then suddenly—boom!—the socks would hit, and we'd pull them into the boat, one after another, for twelve hours straight. Boats from the federal fisheries department track the progress of each river's returning sockeye, so the commercial fishermen are receiving constant radio reports on their progress.

"They've upgraded the Horsefly," we'd hear, or "The Thompson sockeye just hit the Charlottes."

Billy constantly eyed the temperature gauge. If warm water moved in on the west coast, the sockeye would divert down the east side of Vancouver Island. If it stayed cool, the diversion went to the west side.

As August rolled around, Billy's internal sockeye radar went up. "You gotta be in the right place at the right time or you'll miss the socks," he explained.

You also had to ensure that your hold was empty so you didn't lose fishing time delivering when your ten days were up. Billy passed the time talking on the radio. I slept through the slow times. The days were long. Up at 4:30, to bed at 11:30. Jarret tied fishing line to his arrows and practiced his marksmanship on the wire rigging. One afternoon Jarret and I were so bored, we staged a contest throwing rotten grapes out the window, with one eye closed.

Bill Ford, a deckhand on a nearby troller, called over with some news to pass the time. "Hey, Alex," he said, "I just did some figuring. Based on the fish we've caught so far, we're working for four cents an hour."

Moments like that, I tried to smile and enjoy the view.

Then Billy's fishing buddy Yuki called on the VHF. "You oughta be back at that spot you tried ten days ago," he said. Billy jumped out of his seat.

"Come on," he told me. "We're gonna put our running shoes on."

When the sockeye hit, they came with a vengeance. Billy became a blur of motion. Slam the gurdy lever forward, unclip the leader, swing the fish through the air right into the fresh fish hold, then on to the next leader. While I could gaff those big springs, I never got the motion right for those twisting 8- to 9-pound sockeye, and my education would be too expensive in lost fish. I cleaned while Billy pulled.

To fish sockeye, you have to create the illusion of a school. We loaded our hooks with a dense array of "red gear," seventy-two flashers and tiny red hoochies. We hoped that it looked like a school of sockeye swimming through a cloud of shrimp, their favorite food. (That's why the flesh of a sockeye is such a deep pink.) When you tricked a school of sockeye into biting on your imitation school, *every* hook came up loaded. Free-swimming fish even followed their hooked school mates to the surface. Albatross, sooty shearwaters, and seagulls followed the boat in great squawking clouds, devouring the guts as soon as I tossed them overboard. Jarret checked each cleaned fish for any leftover bits—"Missed a spot, Mom!"—and he'd finish the job. Every now and then he popped a cookie in my mouth to keep me going. We couldn't stop to eat until the fish stopped, because at any minute the sockeye run could end completely.

In the midst of this frenzied production line, I lifted my head to relieve a cramp in my neck and two fins on the horizon caught my eye.

It was like being transported to another world: suddenly nothing existed but those fins. Who were they? Where were they going?

I looked at Billy, afraid to say anything. He looked at me, at the whales, laughed, and said, "Aw, Christ, go on, then."

I leaped out of the cockpit and waded through the deckload of salmon to get my binoculars and camera. Clutching my gear, I climbed out of the fish onto the hatch cover, which rose 3 feet from the deck. The whales were so far away that I had to time it perfectly, just at the top of a swell, to see them. Finally one fin came into focus. I laughed. It was Top Notch, out sockeye fishing with his brother Foster and Licka's family.

I made a mental note never to think of the whales as being "home" when they were in the archipelago. Here they were fishing hundreds of miles away from Echo Bay. Obviously home was a big concept to an orca.

As I scanned the whales, a sense of dread crept into my mind. Fishermen shot whales, didn't they? They talked about it on the radio. "Not sure if I'm gonna take a nap or dust a few sea lion pups," I'd heard one fisherman tell another just a few days earlier.

I swung my glasses onto the fleet. Uh-oh. I saw skippers and deckhands perched on their own cabin roofs and hatch covers, looking at the whales. This was the first day, twenty days into the season, that anyone was making money. These sockeye were like $20 bills flying aboard. Who would want to share those wages with the whales?

"I've got to do something," I thought. "I can't let these whales be shot." Before reaching for the radio, though, I looked closer through the binoculars. If I could pick out a few boat names, my broadcast would be more to the point. That's when I realized that the crews on the other boats were holding binoculars and cameras, not rifles. I felt a wave of gratitude. They *were* willing to share the sockeye with the whales. Not a single shot rang out. I said a silent greeting to my old friends and went back to cleaning fish.

My appreciation for the salmon grew with every fish I pulled over the side. In the course of their life's journey, from the mountains to the sea and back again, these fish distribute the energy of the sun to every life-form on the coast. They set the table for gatherings of orcas, put a layer of fat on a grizzly headed for hibernation, feed the eagle chicks growing their flight feathers, quiet the stomachs of seal pups leaving their mothers. Their dried meat allowed native people to build and sustain rich cultures in a challenging land. Salmon contribute to the land even after they die. As wolves and eagles drag their bodies away from the riverbank by which they expired, precious drops of their lifeblood seep down to the soil and nourish the roots of mighty cedars and firs. Big runs of salmon are recorded as broad tree rings in thousand-year-old cedars. The trees, in turn, offer salmon a life-sustaining shade, which cools their birth waters and blunts the force of torrential rains. It is a nearly perfect system, and it all depends on the continuing life, and death, of the salmon.

With my fishing money I bought myself a floathouse. I'd got tired of living next to the Echo Bay Resort generator, and a logger up in Scott Cove was looking to unload his derelict shack. By the time I handed over my $10,000, the house had deteriorated into an otter crash pad. The floor was black with dirt and otter scat, the roof offered a clear view of the sky, and its inner walls had been torn out. It had no wiring, no plumbing, and no stove.

"But," Billy said after inspecting it, "those logs will keep that house afloat for a good ten years."

It should have come as no surprise that Billy knew the place— he'd grown up in it in Freshwater Bay, where it had been the post office. The house had originally been built in 1919 to house cannery workers. Billy and his mother pulled it onto a float in 1956, when they left Freshwater Bay.

Rumor was, the house was haunted. Before putting down my money, I went over and sat in the house during the dead of night and gave it a good vibe inspection. I came away unspooked and bought it lock, stock, and barrel the next day.

Communities like Echo Bay thrive on the currency of neighborly help. Two days after I bought the shack, five neighbors showed up with hammers. We pulled off the leaking tin and nailed a tight cedar shingle roof in place. Since then I've had the pleasure of helping put up four roofs around the archipelago. It's a common form of exchange; the more you give out, the more you get in return. It's the only way we survive out here.

The best thing about a floathouse is, when you get fed up with the view, you can hitch the house up to a boat and pull it somewhere new. I started out next to Yvonne Maximchuk and her husband Al, a watercolor artist and fisherman. Over the next four years, I tried out two other bays in the archipelago. I always spun the house so that my attic office looked in the direction most likely to produce whales.

You got used to the hazards in a floathouse. Everything moved. Tub water produced wavelets, pictures lived askew, and the cats brought in fish instead of mice. Every once in a while during a low tide, one corner of the house would hang up on a rock, leaving the whole business tilted at a crazy pitch. There was nothing to do but wait for the incoming tide to right us again. When it got too bad, I'd take the dishes and glassware off the shelves and retreat to a neighbor's house. Sometimes the house slipped off the rock with a great shudder, but the house itself never looked any worse for wear.

I gardened as much as I could, raising daffodils, kale, and sugar peas. "Don't pile too much dirt on your float, Alex," friends warned me. "You'll sink those good logs."

A hose stuck in the nearest stream acted as a water line. To make hot water, Bill MacKay and Jim Borrowman helped me stick a copper tube through the woodstove.

The sounds and smells of marine life surrounded us: below our floorboards lived sea anemones, mussels, barnacles, stickleback fish, and herring. Otters often ate fish on the logs under our house, filling our nights with their chirping and grunting. The proximity of these neighbors sometimes forced us to eschew the conveniences of modern life. The same bleach that might make my sink sparkle would deal a poisonous death to the guys living downstairs. We learned to do without.

Before his death, Robin had asked Billy Proctor to consider us if he ever decided to subdivide his property. Billy's family had bought a 142-acre homestead straddling the hump of land between Echo Bay and Cramer Pass back in the 1979. Because the Canadian government is extremely stingy with its land up here, Billy qualified as one of the biggest noncommercial landholders in the archipelago.

In the early 1900s the Canadian government had encouraged homesteaders to spread out and populate the coast. But in the 1980s some federal officials decided that the coast had enough residents already. Jarret and I discovered this for ourselves when we traveled to Victoria to inquire about getting a lease to tie our floathouse to the shore.

"You want to do what now?" the man behind the desk told us. "I'm afraid not."

"People have been living in Echo Bay for a hundred years," I explained to him. "We have a school. We have a post office. We're a community. Now you're telling me we can't legally live in our own town?"

He cheerfully explained that a memorandum of understanding had been signed at the highest levels of government banning all residential-use leases.

"So nobody is allowed to live in a floathouse along the thousands of miles of British Columbia shoreline?" I asked.

"That's pretty well it."

"What about buying a piece of land?"

"Oh, you can forget about that."

As a single mother, I wanted a place of my own, a spot where I couldn't be booted out at the whim of a bureaucrat. So I went back to Billy and asked him again about subdividing his land. He thought it over and decided that the time was right. It took him seven years to wade through the paperwork, but finally Billy won approval to parcel out his property.

Selling to wealthy summer visitors would have brought Billy a hefty windfall, but he insisted that the land go only to people who lived here year-round. He wanted a community more than a fat check. "Heck," he said. "The money ain't nothing if Yvonne and I get to be the last old farts left."

I hired Billy to pull my house off its logs and onto my piece. He flattened a section of the steep hillside with his tractor, then rigged up an enormous cable system using old logging blocks and a half mile of cable. "We can put that little blue shack of yours up anywhere," he assured me. In his lifetime Billy had already moved the house three times: from land to water, back onto land, then back onto water.

The house was built of fir, which made it heavier than anybody had anticipated. And the climb up the beach was steep. Billy pulled a little, then stopped to check. Pulled a little more, then checked. Suddenly, *crack!* The logging tackle popped apart. The house shuddered back down the hill and settled at a precarious angle. One window popped. Then another. My canning jars came tumbling off the shelves. Beet and salmon juice ran out the back door.

"Should we just buck her up for firewood, Billy?" I said, as I watched my house run down the beach.

"Aw, Christ, don't panic!" he replied. "You better go get Jack Scott."

The old logger was delighted to be asked. "I'm coming, sweetie!" he called out from his floathouse. He called all the women sweetie.

The two of them tried a new plan. A splice in the cable let go. The house spent the night on the beach in the low-tide zone, partly underwater.

The next morning Billy was no longer referring to my "little blue shack."

"Today," he announced, "we're gonna move the bitch."

He and Jack tried a new, new plan. The walls of the house started to flare out, the roof buckled and humped, the floor joists hove into a rakish angle, but they eventually pulled her up the hill. Nine years later she ain't level, but she's solid.

"Not moving that house again," Billy declared. And we haven't.

Chapter 19

~ ~ ~

When the first fish farms came to the archipelago in 1987, I kind of liked the idea. The farms would create new jobs—good jobs, run by independent farmers—and their children might keep our school alive. Aquaculture also promised to take some of the pressure off of British Columbia's wild salmon stocks. I contacted a north island aquaculture association, the local industry trade group, and offered to help new fish-farming families relocate here. Little did I know that the practices introduced by those very same farms would one day halt my research, force the whales out of the archipelago, and imperil the entire life of the coast.

The Chinese have been raising herbivorous carp in freshwater ponds for thousands of years, but it wasn't until the early 1970s that a few companies in Norway began using aquaculture techniques to raise the carnivorous Atlantic salmon. From its beginnings thirty years ago along the Scandinavian coast, salmon farming has grown into a $4 billion worldwide industry. In 1997, 35 percent of all salmon consumed worldwide came from domestic fish farms. The industry's growth has been phenomenal. In 1994 more than 300,000 tons of domesticated Atlantic salmon were harvested, about 90 million fish. By 1999 that figure had more than doubled, to nearly 800,000 tons.

Farmed salmon never see a river. They're bred artificially in freshwater hatchery vats. After eighteen months they reach about

5 inches in length, at which point they're shipped to saltwater pens—nylon net cages open to the tidal waters of the British Columbia coast—and reared to market size. The fish are fed pellets of fish meal (ground anchovy, sardine, and mackerel) mixed with fish oil; slaughterhouse by-products of blood meal, ground chicken feathers, soybeans, and poultry meal; and a host of vitamins and minerals. The pellets are often infused with massive doses of antibiotics; no form of land- or water-based farming uses more antibiotics per pound of livestock than salmon farming. Wild salmon acquire their familiar pinkish hue from carotenoids that occur naturally in the zooplankton they eat. Since farmed salmon don't eat zooplankton, they're fed a small amount of pigmentation with every pellet. They're dyed pink.

Salmon farming requires protected, temperate saltwater coastline, which is why the industry has taken off in countries like Norway, Chile, the United States, Japan, Ireland, Scotland, and Australia. And it's why, when the industry underwent a rapid worldwide expansion in the late 1980s, large multinational aquaculture corporations made a land grab in the country that boasts more coastline than any other nation on Earth: Canada.

The first farmers who came to the archipelago took care to adapt their operations to local environmental concerns. John and Nadine Ebbel, who operated an early salmon farm on the north shore of Midsummer Island, consulted with Billy Proctor to find a spot where their domestic salmon wouldn't conflict with the needs of wild fish. Although salmon farming directly competed with Billy's livelihood, he freely shared his knowledge of wind, tides, and wild salmon. In his opinion there was room for five salmon farms in the archipelago. Each site he pointed out had sufficient flushing action to sustain the farm while keeping the penned fish away from wild salmon migration routes.

The Ebbels set up a cluster of eight to twenty pens, each about the size of a tennis court, connected by floating walkways. It looked like a small boat marina.

The farmers who followed the Ebbels weren't so sensitive. In the early 1990s we watched a parade of tugboats haul great trains of steel, Styrofoam, and plastic net floats through Cramer Passage. The new arrivals didn't bother to consult with the fishermen. They didn't seem to care what the locals thought at all.

"They're putting all them farms in the wrong places," warned Billy. "Those are places where wild salmon go." Billy knew where the nomadic wild salmon stopped to rest between tides and saw that the fish farmers had a knack for anchoring their pens in those exact spots. Suddenly a small dent in the coastline that might have supported hundreds of salmon for a few hours was forced to support a tightly clustered ball of 150,000 to 250,000 salmon 365 days a year. "This place wasn't designed to work that way," said Billy.

With each new operation, it became clear that this wasn't the ecofriendly industry it first appeared. Although the federal and provincial governments heralded salmon farms as the saviors of our remote coastal communities, the new farmers didn't live or socialize in the communities around their net cages. They preferred to live in bigger towns to the south, like Campbell River, and commute by boat on ten-day shifts. None of the promised benefits were bestowed on Alert Bay, Sointula, or Echo Bay, although the farms continued to pop up all around us.

We should have known better. In December 1990 a member of the Norwegian parliamentary committee on the environment testified before the Canadian Parliament about the coming industry. "We are very strict about the quality and the environment questions," she said. "Therefore, some of the fish farmers went to Canada. They said 'We want bigger fish farms, and there we can do as we like.'" Her comments were an early indication of the plans the industry had for our area.

Fish farming is to traditional commercial fishing what agribusiness conglomerates are to family farming. The corporations that dominate the industry are transforming one of the world's oldest, most honorable, and most human occupations into a faceless, environmentally destructive, profit-driven industry producing food of questionable quality. Until recently the biggest fish-farming concern in the world was Norsk Hydro, an $8 billion Scandinavian corporation with interests in everything from oil to fertilizer. In March 2000 Norsk Hydro's fish farms were bought by a Dutch corporation called Nutreco, the world's largest supplier of feed to the fish-farming industry. Nutreco now controls about one-fifth of the worldwide farm-raised Atlantic salmon market. Another Scandinavian corporation, Scanmar, brought in eight farms to British Columbia in the 1990s. Stolt Sea Farm, a subsidiary of Norwegian chemical shipping giant Stolt-Nielsen, is the major player in the archipelago, with eighteen of its twenty-two British Columbia farms operating within a few miles of Echo Bay. International Home Foods, the New Jersey corporation that produces Bumble Bee tuna and Chef Boyardee Spaghetti-Os, also has a hand in the local industry. In early 1999 International Home Foods bought the British Columbia salmon farms previously owned by B.C. Packers, the Canadian fish-processing company.

With the coming of corporate aquaculture, wild salmon became nothing more than "competition" for these ruthless conglomerates. As long as the wild pinks and sockeye remained abundant, the farmers would never control the market.

My concern about the farms grew with every fisherman I talked to. Bill Ford, who fishes for rock cod in his little dory *Thumper*, mentioned that all the best cod spots had been taken over by farms. "It's kinda spooky," he said, "because those are the fishiest places on the coast, the spots where water upwells from the deep." A prawn fisherman named Al noticed his best spot go dead after a farm moved in upcurrent. "Usually I get a lotta different life in my traps," he told me. "Not just prawns, but whelks, starfish, eels. Now they're coming up empty." More troubling than the empty traps was the black putrid sludge that now came up sticking to the netting on Al's traps.

Salmon fishermen worried about diseases that the penned stock could pass on to wild salmon. Fish farms are notorious disease amplifiers. In the wild, disease outbreaks in salmon are contained by limited contact among fish and by the natural weeding that occurs as compromised fish are eaten by predators. A diseased fish is a slow fish, and a slow fish is a seal's lunch. In a net cage, where hundreds of thousands of salmon swim fin-to-fin, disease spreads like a brush fire, the natural weeding mechanism is defeated by the net, and sick fish are kept alive and infectious with drugs.

My main concern at first was the gunfire. Sometimes while listening for whales, I'd hear rifles going off on farms on both sides of the channel. There's a reason the government enacts strict regulations about the use of firearms around water: bullets have an uncanny ability to skip over water for long distances. But fish farmers had been given predator-control permits by the Department of Fisheries and Oceans (DFO) that allowed them to kill any animals attacking, or coming near, their fish. There are no limits on the number of "predators" they can legally kill.

It's no secret that some of the archipelago's seals found the Atlantic salmon easy pickings. When a seal swam alongside a pen, the domestic salmon dove in an evasive response and collected on the bottom of the net. The seal then dove to the bottom, grabbed a fish with its teeth, and sucked the runny farm salmon flesh through the mesh. Blue herons, river otters, minks, sea lions, kingfishers, and crows also caught bullets. Jarret and I once passed a farm with seagull bodies drifting around outside the pens. We tried to save one of the wounded birds; it was still alive and floundering with holes in its head. It died the next day.

I couldn't help but worry about the whales around all these inexperienced, gun-happy young farmers. Ironically the fish-eating resident pods never saw the domestic salmon as food. For whatever reason, they simply ignored the farms.

Once the farms began attracting seals, however, transient orcas soon followed.

F1, the transient who had enticed me back onto the water after Robin's death, became a notorious fish farm inspector. On a number of occasions, I watched him cruise the perimeters of the farms, scouting for prey. I was impressed by the speed with which old F1 learned to exploit these seal feeding stations, but I knew the armed farmers would have little appreciation for the orca's savvy. They had no way of knowing that F1 would probably rather die than eat a salmon. In their eyes he was a threatening 9-ton predator casing their stock.

I spent weeks stopping in at the farms, alerting them to F1's presence. "Yeah," they said. "We've seen 'im. He comes up only a few inches out from the nets. He's got to be eyeing our fish."

Actually, I told them, this kind of orca never touched the stuff.

"In fact," I said, "he'll probably scare more seals away than your rifle." The farmers heard me out, but few believed me.

In response to the growing outcry over the spread of the salmon farms, in 1989 the provincial Ministry of the Environment sent a team of Victoria field bureaucrats up to the Broughton Archipelago to interview different "user groups" and map out a resolution to the conflict. "Tell us where you don't want salmon farms," the officials said.

They got an earful. Tugboat operators had lost their places to tie up in storms. Commercial fishermen were watching their catch dwindle and the market price plummet as Atlantics flooded the market. Pleasure cruisers were losing their favorite anchorages to net cages. Prawn fishermen couldn't drop their traps among the spiderweb of anchors radiating out from the farms.

"I don't understand what right these people have to eliminate the natural wildlife around here," said Jim O'Donnell.

I offered to show the ministry officials where the humpback whales summered, where the orcas traveled, where the seals and sea lions and kayakers hauled out. And I pleaded with local fishermen to talk with the team.

"This is your chance to set aside areas to be kept salmon farm–free," I told them.

I didn't understand their reluctance. A few finally agreed—Chris Bennett, the area's top sportfisherman, Al, and Billy Proctor, dean of the local commercial fleet. All four of us climbed aboard Billy's boat, the *Twilight Rock,* and rode a furious southeast storm to meet with the bureaucrats in Alert Bay.

I was proud of the people of Echo Bay. The sheer wealth of information that flowed from those veteran fishermen during that meeting was overwhelming. The officials took profuse notes and spent hours poring over intricate charts of the archipelago. We shared a new sense of community that night as Billy's boat crashed home through the gale.

A few months later a glossy chart arrived in the mail. The "Ministry of Environment Coastal Resource Interests Study" consisted of a map that divided the archipelago into a color-coded mosaic of red, yellow, and green zones outlining where salmon farms could and couldn't go. As I and my neighbors looked over the chart, we could see that we had won some areas and lost others. All in all, it didn't look like such a bad compromise.

Over the next few months, however, fish farms continued to move into the area. The new "zones" seemed to mean nothing to them. New farms appeared in red zones, where farming was supposedly prohibited. Sargeaunt Pass, a narrow crease of water between Viscount Island and the mainland coast and a critical spot where Knight Inlet chinook salmon school between tides, saw a 300,000-salmon farm muscle into its protected red zone. Carrie Bay, Connally Point, Eden Island, Glacier Falls—same story.

By 1994 there were more fish farms in red zones than in nonred zones. Now I knew why so many fishermen had been reluctant to talk to the government. To the fish farmers, the old-timers had done nothing but reveal all the best farming spots—put them on a map and colored them red, in fact. It had taken the fishermen a lifetime to learn the secret places where currents eddied and upwelled, delivering rich oxygen and nutrients. The fish farmers acquired that same knowledge by opening a map. And the government did nothing to stop them from turning those pieces of critical habitat into farm water. We'd been played for chumps.

I was furious and ashamed. Who were the good guys? Didn't

government serve the people, wasn't that what democracy was all about? People laughed. "Jesus, Alex, how did you get to be so naive?" I guess I'd been watching animals all my life. I hadn't paid the human race enough attention.

Hatcheries are often the last best hope for a run of wild salmon endangered by human activity. In 1979 a group of fishermen, loggers, and other local archipelago residents built the Scott Cove Hatchery to revive the runs of wild coho salmon that had once coursed up Scott Cove Creek and thirteen other creeks that drained Gilford and Broughton islands. A wooden logging dam erected in 1918 had by the early 1960s choked a run of ten thousand coho down to ten fish. In 1964 Billy Proctor happened to see those ten fish throwing themselves against the dam, desperate to get upstream. Ignoring a Department of Fisheries and Oceans order to leave the dam standing, Billy fired up his chain saw and got busy. As the last chunk fell out of the dam, the salmon swam upstream between Billy's legs.

Years later, when an American sportfisherman donated $50,000 for coho restoration, the community used the money to build the hatchery, where young coho are bred by mixing eggs and sperm from mature salmon captured in the creek. The eggs are carefully tended and the babies fed until they reach a weight of about 2 grams. Then the coho fry are released into the creeks. Since the construction of the hatchery, the numbers of wild coho have steadily increased; by the early 1990s more than seven thousand returned annually to Scott Cove Creek.

The first sign of trouble with the restored coho came in 1991.

"We're losing all our brood stock," Billy Proctor called over the radio from the Scott Cove Hatchery. "Could you help with the medication?"

The Scott Cove coho had been disease-free for ten years. Suddenly 28 percent of the adult salmon that had been collected for their eggs and sperm were dropping dead prematurely with ugly boils erupting through their skin. We sent samples of the dead fish to the Pacific Biological Station, the Department of Fisheries and Oceans' research laboratory in Nanaimo. Their diagnosis: furunculosis, a disease that affects salmon at low levels in the wild but was a notorious problem among Atlantic salmon smolts in the Scottish and Norwegian fish-farming industries.

News travels fast in Echo Bay. Within a few days we learned that a number of nearby Atlantic salmon farms at Deep Harbour, Notice Point, and Watson Cove were all suffering outbreaks of furunculosis. To get to Scott Cove, wild coho swam directly past the Deep Harbour and Notice Point farms, which were owned by the salmon-farming corporation IBEC. These farms had been stocked with diseased Atlantic salmon.

Ironically IBEC had led the successful lobbying effort to lift the government's ban on importing Atlantic salmon eggs from overseas hatcheries in the mid-1980s. Fearing the introduction of a European disease into British Columbia waters, scientists with the Department of Fisheries and Oceans and ministry of environment had argued strongly for keeping the ban. Over the protests of his own scientists, the DFO regional director approved the annual importation of 300,000 Atlantic salmon eggs.

Our captured coho could be treated with antibiotics, but I wondered what was happening out there in the rivers. Since no one had seen this disease in local waters before the outbreak on the farms, I requested the details on what strain of furunculosis was killing the Atlantics. The DFO refused to release the information. "Trade secret," it said.

In January 1993 I stopped my boat at the east end of Fife Sound and switched on the hydrophone. A painful ringing immediately pierced my ears. I ripped the headset off. What the hell was that? I turned the volume down as far as it would go and listened again. I heard what sounded like a cricket. By following the intensity of the signal, I tracked the sound to its source: a B.C. Packers salmon farm on the west end of the Burdwood Group of islands.

I asked one of the fish farmers I knew what the noise was all about.

"Oh, that's called a seal scarer. They're the latest to keep seals away from our fish. The guy who installed it said don't turn them on if a seal was too close because it would deafen the seal, and then it'd be useless in keeping him away."

"What about the whales?" I asked.

"I dunno."

I did know. With their exquisitely sensitive hearing, I knew it didn't bode well for the whales at all.

Underwater noise devices were nothing new. They'd been used to resolve conflicts between marine mammals and fisheries since the early 1980s. But never had they been used in an area with such a high concentration of whales. Noise devices come in two types. Acoustic deterrent devices (ADDs) emit low-powered noise to alert marine mammals to the presence of unnatural structures like mono-filament net. They're a relatively benign warning signal. Acoustic harassment devices (AHDs), on the other hand, are specifically de-signed to cause pain. They work on a simple theory: induce suf-ficient aural distress, and you'll drive away seals, sea lions, otters, porpoises, whales, and other potential predators. The farmers call them "seal scarers." Scientists call them "acoustic brooms."

To figure out exactly what these AHDs were doing to the acoustic environment, a group of scientists, government officials, and fish farmers went out to Retreat Pass one day and tested an Air-mar brand acoustic harassment device under calm conditions. Most people are familiar with decibels, the units used to describe the in-tensity of sound. A whisper registers 20 decibels, a home vacuum registers 80, a jet engine taking off at close range hits about 140, which is commonly accepted as the threshold of pain. The Air-mar put out a signal registering 194 decibels. Their study revealed that the diminutive harbor porpoises, year-round residents of Retreat Pass,

Harbor porpoise

fled from the noise. "Displacing" cetaceans violates the Fisheries Act. But instead of using their own research to protect the porpoise, the DFO opted not to publish the study and to grant more farms permission for AHDs. When I wrote the minister of Fisheries and Oceans to remind him to uphold the Fisheries Act, he replied nonchalantly that it was okay to displace porpoises because they would come back when the devices were turned off. I wondered how he would feel if he was kicked out of his home for a few years onto the streets of Ottawa. Would he be "okay" when allowed to return?

How well do AHDs work? Depends on whom you talk to. Some fish farmers swear by them; without the Airmar, they say, seals would slurp away every last penny of profit. Other farmers switched their AHDs off after finding that they acted more like dinner bells than deterrents. Farmers on the orca channels near Echo Bay, unfortunately, fell into the former group. Within a few months fish farmers had installed four acoustic harassment devices broadcasting continuous 194-decibel shrieks throughout the Broughton Archipelago.

Within those same months, in the same areas, the fish-eating orcas all but vanished. Salmon farms lined their fishing grounds, and these whales could not tolerate them. The mammal eaters were less affected because their prey are more widely distributed. They simply changed their travel pattern to avoid the farms using seal scarers.

At the whim of this corporate-controlled industry, eight thousand years of whale history in the archipelago came to an end. I wondered where the A5 pod would go in winter. I wondered if relatives would take them into their home inlets or if they would find other inlet territories. I wondered how long it would take the pollution of human industry to drive them from those places, too.

Later that same year the freshly stocked Atlantic salmon in a Scanmar pen at Connally Point, a "red zone" across from the exclusive Sullivan Bay Resort in Sutlej Channel, began dying of an antibiotic-resistant strain of furunculosis. Within days the disease had traveled across a wild chinook saltwater nursery area to infect B.C. Packers farms 6 miles away—farms that had been stocked with Atlantic salmon from entirely different hatcheries. This particular strain of furunculosis proved resistant to all three antibiotics that had been approved for use in fish farming. Instead of ordering the fish destroyed, the Department of Fisheries and Oceans allowed the farmers to treat the salmon with an antibiotic called erythromycin. Only a year earlier the DFO had published a warning about the use of erythromycin in its quarterly salmon enhancement newsletter, *Streamtips.* "Fish treated with erythromycin," the agency declared, "may not be used for human consumption."

Bigger problems were yet to come.

I began noticing that more and more of the fish farm nets were turning red. After making a few inquiries, I discovered that the farmers were dipping the nets in an antifoulant paint called Flexgard, which prevents the growth of mussels and barnacles. The problem with Flexgard is, it doesn't stay on the nets. Within a few months it flakes off and drifts into the current. This becomes a cause for concern when you read the warning printed on any bucket of Flexgard. *"Toxic to aquatic organisms,"* says the label. *"Do not contaminate water. Do not allow chips to enter water."* In case the message isn't clear enough, the warning is accompanied by a skull and crossbones. It was hard to fathom how salmon raised in nets dipped in toxic paint could be sold in supermarkets.

The most worrisome thing of all was the simple fact that these fish farms were raising Atlantic salmon in Pacific waters. About 20 percent of British Columbian salmon farmers raise Pacific coho or chinook, but most raise Atlantics because they come to market size faster—a well-fed Atlantic will grow to 2 to 5 kilograms within eighteen months of being transferred to a net pen. Atlantics are more docile than their Pacific counterparts, which means farmers can achieve what's known as "greater stocking density": more fish per pen.

It's likely that the Atlantics will follow the pattern set by numerous other species on earth and adapt to their surroundings. While Atlantic salmon will tolerate being crowded together, they demonstrate marked aggression toward other salmonid species. This may be why there is only one species of salmon in the Atlantic and five in the eastern Pacific. Given their aggressive nature and sheer numbers, it may be only a matter of time before the Atlantics displace the already weakened stocks of wild Pacific salmon from their native habitat.

In the early years of salmon farming, industry and government officials assured everyone that there was no way a farmed Atlantic could escape. The history of exotic species around the world belied their confidence. If there is any chance at all that an animal can escape, it will. Once free, it will adapt and survive and proliferate. And it will destroy native species to do so.

When I began contacting officials in the federal government's Department of Fisheries and Oceans, I thought, "They must not know what's going on up here." The DFO was where the good guys worked. They'd done the studies in the 1970s that resulted in strict protections for killer whales and other marine mammals. Mike Bigg had worked for the DFO at the Pacific Biological Station; Graeme Ellis still set high standards for research at the Nanaimo office. The department's mandate was the protection of all oceanic wildlife, and the people I knew who worked with the department took that mandate seriously.

I collected all the anecdotes and data I had—the farms taking over wild salmon habitat, the black ooze Al dredged up, the disappearing whales, the toxic algae blooms that arrived with the fish pens, the recurring escapes of farm salmon—and wrote letters to DFO officials.

A few weeks later I received a response from Jim Boutillier, a senior researcher at the Pacific Biological Station. No need to worry, Boutillier wrote. Everything was okay. My input, he said, would "help in the development of a strong healthy aquaculture industry growing in harmony with the environment and wild fish stocks."

Harmony? The entire ecosystem of the archipelago was under assault. Wild salmon are the lifeblood of the coast. When they disappear, everything else will wither and die. Nothing harmonious about that.

When faced with something I don't know about, whether it's childbirth or salmon farms, my research instinct kicks in. The provincial government of British Columbia and the federal Department of Fisheries and Oceans had written back to me claiming that very little was known about the impact of salmon farms. What was known, they claimed, gave them little worry.

We don't know much, but we like it anyway. That didn't sound right to me. I decided to find out what *was* known. Then we'd see if we liked it.

Chapter 20

When the acoustic harassment devices drove out the whales in 1993, I began to wonder if it wasn't time for me to leave as well.

Jarret had completed grade seven, which was as high as the Echo Bay School went, and I had grown weary of the endless chores required to survive on a remote homestead. Rebuilding our house had been a challenge, but now things were falling apart. Winter storms knocked over hundreds of 10-foot-tall pickets in the garden's deer fence. The float that had held up my house, which now served as the dock for the *Blackfish Sound,* my 22-foot dory-style speedboat, needed its chains replaced. The water line froze and got trampled by bears, interrupted by air bubbles, choked with bugs, and worn through where it chafed on the beach. Every year I had to add another layer of insulation. One year I'd chainsawed off all the siding, stuffed insulation in, then re-sided it with the help of Patty Proctor, Billy's youngest daughter. Another year I crawled under the house and stuffed insulation into the floor joists. When the raccoons ripped it all out a few weeks later, I had to do it all over again, and still water froze on the floor in winter.

I began thinking that it would be nice to have a real phone instead of my system of VHF, autotel, and cellular phone that worked only when the weather was good. It'd be nice to hop in a truck and go where I needed to, instead of braving a winter storm to reach Vancouver Island.

I found a spot on Malcolm Island that looked promising. It was a quiet clearing at the end of a logging road, up on an exposed bluff where I could use a telescope to spot whales. The land wasn't for sale, but the owner gave me permission to pull a trailer onto it.

The only drawback was the wind: I'd have to tie the trailer down to keep it from blowing over. There was no power or phone service, but I could drive Jarret to the Port McNeill school ferry in twenty minutes. I hated the thought of leaving the archipelago, but the whales were gone, I was losing steam, and loneliness crept a little more into each day.

Then I met a guy. As I was relaxing aboard my friend Kate Pinnsoneault's live-aboard barge *Sea Horse* in Echo Bay that summer, I saw the tug *Gabriola* come into the dock. I'd seen the *Gabriola* before. Her skipper, Eric Nelson, had helped me put a new outboard on my boat a few years before.

Eric was tall, lean, handsome, and incorrigibly confident. He gave the impression of being able to handle any situation. As Eric tied the *Gabriola* to the dock, I scanned the boat for signs of Eric's girlfriend. Interesting; she wasn't there.

"Kate," I said, "could you invite him for dinner?" She smiled. "Sure."

Later that night, shoehorned in around the *Sea Horse*'s galley table, I realized that I'd forgotten how to flirt. Kate cheerfully chatted Eric up and found out that he was looking for a new place to settle. His hometown of Sechelt, a Canadian coastal town about 20 miles north of Vancouver, had gone from an independent small town to a bedroom community of big-city commuters. "I walked into the hardware store last month in my gum boots and looked around," he said. "There wasn't one person I knew. They were all yuppies. I thought, 'I don't belong here anymore,' and I left."

Eric looked like someone I could rely on. I told him that I'd like to see him again sometime.

A few weeks later I got a radio call: "*Blackfish Sound*, this is *Gabriola*." My heart jumped into my throat. "Do you think I could tie a few logs to your float?"

Hmm. There were a thousand miles of coastline to tie logs to around here. Jarret laughed. "I think he likes you, Mum."

When the black-and-red tug lumbered up to the dock, my hair was uncharacteristically neat. "You know," I warned Eric, "tying your logs here will set the community talking."

He grinned. "Let them talk."

It was an awkward courtship. I'd spent the past nine years concealing my femininity. There weren't many single women living on the coast, and I didn't want any misunderstandings. I'd tried to fall in love before, but it had taken me this long to get far enough away from Robin's death.

And honestly, it was tough to find the right man. At a family reunion, my mother and sisters once asked me to describe my perfect guy.

"Well," I told them, "besides being kind and in love with me, he's got to get to Echo Bay under his own steam. He's got to know how to live out there. I don't think any relationship could survive my teaching him everything. Can you imagine? Here's the ax; here's the chain saw; this is how to tie up a boat in a storm; you gotta watch for bears; when you open a jar of salmon, check the seal or it'll kill you."

"Okay," my sisters said. "Now hold that image in your heart."

Weeks later along came Eric and filled it.

He knew what remote living was like. Over the years he'd made his living off the coast as a carpenter, a small-boat builder, and a cedar shake cutter. He also had a log-salvage license, which was why he had asked to tie logs temporarily to my float.

Logs get away from logging companies all the time. They break loose in the water, come tumbling down mountainsides. With a salvage license, you can pick up the loose timber, brand it with a government-issued stamping hammer, and tow it in to sell. Without log salvage the waterways of British Columbia would be choked with runaway logs. For Eric it was a way of getting paid for what he loved to do: wander the coast in his boat.

By winter my dock had become home port to his *Gabriola*. I

scuttled my Malcolm Island plans. Jarret was happy not to be moving to a place where the wind had once nearly torn the door off our truck. He continued his schooling by mail. It was a little dull without classmates, but his grades kept on shining.

As the whales continued to shun the archipelago, I began to worry about what might have happened. Even though I'd always dropped whatever I was doing to follow them, I'd always assumed that the whales would be here. I had taken them for granted.

Jarret and I went farther afield to find them, returning to Johnstone Strait and Queen Charlotte Strait for much of the summer. On August 1, 1993, Jarret and I were cruising across glassy water in Queen Charlotte Strait when Bud Butler, a rugged Port McNeill logger and sportfisherman, called in a dolphin sighting at Gore Rock, at the west end of Fife Sound. We never found the dolphins, but we did spy some whales. On our way back across Queen Charlotte Strait, I spotted some black fins coming right at me.

I put the hydrophone down and radioed in the sighting to the summer whale research community. "Whales inbound from Queen Charlotte Strait," I said. "I'll call again when I know who they are."

As the whales came into range, I found myself scrutinizing each fin without being able to identify a single one. Very odd. I leafed through the photoidentification book that I always kept handy in the boat. Again, I came up empty. This was embarrassing; people were waiting by their radios for my ID call. I'd been watching these pods for more than fifteen years; I'm supposed to know what they look like. I scanned the pictures of southern resident whales, orcas that almost never came this far north. Still nothing.

My embarrassment turned to wonder as more than fifty whales passed our boat. Jarret looked at me for an explanation. I pulled up the hydrophone and moved closer for a better look.

"They must be the offshores," I said. I hoped that I was right.

The offshore community of orcas had been discovered just five years earlier. In July 1988 humpback whale researcher Jim Darling came upon a large pod of orcas about 50 miles off the southwest corner of Vancouver Island. Darling didn't want to waste much time identifying the killer whales, but he knew that Mike Bigg would appreciate some photos, so Darling shot a quick roll of film and sent it down to Bigg in Nanaimo.

The pictures blew Bigg's socks off. He'd never seen these whales. After twenty years of work, he was accustomed to recognizing every whale in the photographs people sent to him. Darling's photographs suggested that there might be an entirely undiscovered community of orcas out there just offshore.

Over the next four years, Bigg documented eight more encounters with the whales. They were called "offshore" whales because Bigg and his colleagues John Ford and Graeme Ellis most often found them in the open waters of the Pacific at the edge of the continental shelf. For reasons we could only guess at, the whales began to approach the British Columbia coast in the early 1990s. In 1992 they were spotted coming into the Strait of Juan de Fuca at the southern end of Vancouver Island. My encounter with them the next August represented the first recorded instance of offshore orcas' rounding the northeastern tip of Vancouver Island.

The offshore orcas swam in formation, all abreast, until they hit the outer edge of the Broughton Archipelago. Then they turned and, still abreast, swept south toward OrcaLab on Hanson Island. I later learned that Helena Symonds was simultaneously observing Tsitika and her family backing up into Blackney Pass as the offshore whales approached.

The offshores looked slightly different from the transients and residents. Their males appeared to be smaller; none of their dorsal fins stood taller than 5 feet. An offshore's dorsal tip was rounded like a resident's but deeply torn like a transient's. They were extremely unpredictable around our small boats, although they seemed more relaxed around bigger boats like Bill MacKay's *Gikumi,* perhaps because they had encountered big boats offshore.

As the afternoon westerly rumpled the sea into a 4-foot chop, Jarret and I stopped in the lee shore of Donegal Head, at the east end of Malcolm Island, and I dropped the hydrophone in to listen.

Their calls were entirely alien. One sounded exactly like the *gong* of a raven. They put out a series of high fluty notes that cascaded down entire octaves at a time.

When the offshores turned back west, Tsitika and her family pressed forward and trailed them at a respectful distance. I wondered if she had been somewhat timidly holding her ground, indicating that this was her community's territory.

Such a move wouldn't be entirely out of character. After the first northern resident pod enters Johnstone Strait each summer, there appears to be a cooperative effort to have at least one representative pod in the area from Robson Bight to Telegraph Cove. This isn't a hard-and-fast rule, but for weeks a single pod may pace back and forth between those sites until a second pod arrives. The two pods will briefly associate, perhaps only long enough to hear each other's voices, before the first pod leaves to the north. It's essentially a changing of the guard.

The behavior of the offshore orcas had the flavor of an ex- ploratory mission: the way they'd swum all abreast until reaching land, turning south until reaching land again, continuing this ma- neuver until they ricocheted back out to sea. They had effectively covered every square inch of Queen Charlotte Strait and Blackfish Sound, scanned all the local fish populations, caught a taste of the sentinel resident pod, and perhaps laid away a map of the area in their brains for future reference.

I made no further sightings of the offshores until the next spring. On an April morning in 1994, I stopped Eric on his way to work with a tree-planting crew to ask what he wanted for his birthday dinner.

"Lemon meringue pie, please," he said.

Oh dear, I had no idea how to make a lemon meringue pie. By midafternoon I'd tracked down a recipe in an old copy of the *Fannie*

Farmer Cookbook and made good progress on a pie. Then, halfway through the meringue, I got a whale call on the VHF.

"*Blackfish Sound, Tyler Two.*" It was one of my neighbors.

"Alex, thought you'd like to know, there are a couple of your friends out here in Fife Sound."

The timing of whale calls often tests my resolve. Whaleless weeks will pass before they'll show up at exactly the same time as Jarret's school play or his baseball game. With Jarret I stuck to an unbreakable rule: Jarret came before whales. In all other circumstances, I learned to accept engagements with this promise: "I'll be there if no whales come by."

This time I was torn. I had a fantastic new relationship; I didn't want Eric thinking he mattered less than the whales. "Oh, I'll just whip out there, see who it is, and get back to the meringue," I thought.

The light had begun to fail by the time I spotted their fins near the Burdwood Group of islands. As I maneuvered in for a look, I discovered that I couldn't tell who they were—and they just kept on coming. There must have been more than seventy whales, twice the number I'd ever seen together in the archipelago. It was too dim for photographs, so I lowered the hydrophone and recorded the strange sounds of offshore orcas until long after dark.

The whales were in high spirits, surfacing in frothy bursts of white water. I followed them as they fanned out around the Burdwoods. Just before night fell, I watched a group of three dolphins streak up to a female orca with two youngsters and tuck in beside them. I was astonished. It was the first time I'd seen dolphins do anything besides flee a killer whale, resident or transient. The dolphins must have been familiar with offshore orcas and had recognized their calls.

This casual interaction between the dolphins and the offshore orcas shed light on a theory that was current among killer whale researchers at the time. Because the cuts and tears in the ragged fins of the offshore orcas looked similar to the cuts in a transient's fin, a number of researchers considered it possible that offshore killer whales were also mammal eaters. For me this encounter weakened the theory. Those dolphins were much too at ease with the offshores to ever have been attacked by them. They looked more like old acquaintances.

A few years later David Bain, a researcher from Washington State, found a group of offshore orcas that had died after becoming trapped in a lagoon. In his postmortem examination, Bain found that their teeth had been excessively worn down, even in fairly young orcas. His findings raised the possibility that offshores might eat sharks, whose sandpapery skin could have caused the tooth wear and whose ferocity might have caused the tears in the whales' fins.

I returned home slowly in the dark to the ruined meringe and a disconcerted man, my head full of questions. Had the offshores followed the dolphins, which were new to the archipelago, too, or was this a chance meeting? Had they both been lured here or driven out of somewhere else?

Those were the last whales to call me out for years.

As the whales stayed away from the archipelago, I continued to wrestle with the question of leaving. Was it important to study the *absence* of whales? Possibly. How else would we know the salmon-farming industry's effect on them? I expanded my aquaculture research, contacting scientists in Scotland, Chile, Ireland, Norway, eastern Canada, and Washington State. An Irish dentist and experienced salmon-farm critic wrote me with a bit of advice. "Dear Mrs. Morton," he said. "Your letters are far too polite. To win, you will have to slip a bit of steel beneath the velvet."

In 1994 the trouble grew. That spring wild chinook runs crashed throughout the area infected with furunculosis. The note board that traditionally tallied big chinook catches outside of Echo Bay Resort stood blank all spring, summer, and fall. Not a single chinook over 25 pounds was caught for more than six months.

Chris Bennett was outraged. "When I was a boy," he told me, "I was led to believe the government was dedicated to protecting wild salmon. I came up here and built a lodge with my own hands, only to find out they lied to me."

"Kingcome Inlet," one of the great salmon-fishing grounds, he said, "is dead. The few salmon I catch have sores on them and are crawling with sea lice," a parasitic copepod specific to salmon. These lice are generally benign except where salmon farms occur, boosting the number of lice to lethal levels.

My research told me that sea lice infestations of salmon farms had all but wiped out the wild sea trout and salmon populations in Scotland, Norway, and Ireland. With every new coast this industry exploits, its learning curve gets reset to zero.

A few months later Billy Proctor stopped by with a disturbing report.

"I was spraying down my fish hold yesterday," he said, "when Christ if my lips didn't go numb. Never seen anything like it in sixty years." We both looked down at the water around my own dock. It was red with a mosaic of cloudy suspended matter just below the surface. "Looks like tomato soup," I said.

I scooped a sample into a canning jar and put it on a seaplane to the Department of Fisheries and Oceans's research lab in Nanaimo. The report came back about ten days later: *"Heterosigma carterae."*

This particular algae proliferates in environments extremely rich in nitrogen and phosphorus—exactly what the salmon pens were dropping by the ton in the form of fish feces and uneaten food pellets. It produces a neurotoxin that kills fish and numbed Proctor's lips.

This "unusual occurrence" came loaded with irony. It was the *Heterosigma* plankton that had first brought the fish farms to the archipelago. In the mid-1980s British Columbia's nascent salmon-farming industry had settled into a number of sites around Sechelt, Eric's hometown near Vancouver. Then in 1986 a spectacular outbreak of *Heterosigma* virtually wiped out the industry. The algae killed about one-third of the domesticated fish around Sechelt, destroying $2.5 million worth of salmon. Since *Heterosigma* flourishes in warmer waters, a number of aquaculture corporations pulled out of Sechelt and relocated their pens in the cooler waters off northern Vancouver Island and the Broughton Archipelago.

The residents of Sechelt were more than happy to see them go. According to many I talked to, folks there had endured rampant gunfire and found open 150-gallon drums of maggot-riddled salmon corpses slopping up their community wharfs. Farms with all-night generators appeared overnight in front of their homes. Farmers polluted the sea with mountains of rotting feed pellets, throwing bucketfuls of pellets into empty pens to maintain the illusion of healthy stocks for investors. When the industry pulled out of Sechelt, it left behind coastal farm sites polluted with fish feces, uneaten feed, hundreds of kilometers of polypropylene lines, and even pens full of starving fish.

When I informed government officials about the toxic bloom, they shrugged it off with a vague remark about open-ocean nutrients flooding into the archipelago somehow for some unknown reason. My contact in Scotland, Alan Berry, who is a shellfish grower and marine toxicologist, reported that wherever there are salmon farms in Scottish lochs, the blooms occurred, tainting the shellfish.

The more people I talked to about fish farms, the more documents began finding their way to my mailbox. Somebody forwarded a confidential report by a young Department of Fisheries and Oceans officer that detailed instances of uncontrolled escapes, wild salmon being eaten by farm fish, and the destruction of herring spawning grounds. I began getting calls from government researchers who were concerned about the environmental damage to fish farms but couldn't talk over my cell phone for fear of losing promotions or getting fired. "If you recognize my voice," they'd say, "call me back on a landline."

A pattern began to emerge. First the salmon farmers and DFO

officials said that the Atlantic salmon wouldn't escape. When the salmon escaped, they said that the Atlantics wouldn't survive. When the salmon survived, they said that they wouldn't breed. When the salmon bred, they said not to worry because there aren't enough of them to displace native salmon. At one point DFO official Ron Ginetz asked his governmental colleagues, in a memo obtained by researcher David Ellis through an Access to Information Act search, which strategy they preferred: warn the public that Atlantic salmon would inevitably colonize the coast—"strategically plant the seed now," as Ginetz put it—or remain silent and deal with the public outrage once the Atlantic takeover was a fait accompli.

Why was this happening? Because the Canadian government encouraged it. During the 1990s the federal government decided that the future of the fisheries industry lay in farming, not in the commercial catch, because salmon in pens need no habitat outside the nets. Unlike wild salmon, farm salmon will coexist with oil wells, dams, logging, mining, freshwater sales, and other corporate endeavors. These corporations had successfully lobbied their vision of the coast as an industrial zone. The Department of Fisheries and Oceans initiated a massive buyback program that took 50 percent of commercial fishing boats out of the Canadian Pacific fleet while leaving the catch quota untouched. This policy effectively silenced the one strong political voice for wild salmon, that of commercial fishermen. At the same time the government encouraged the establishment of fish farms on British Columbia's 16,000 miles of saltwater coast. The provincial and federal governments gave fish farmers shoreline leases, interest-free loans and grants, and support for aquaculture-friendly research. As the United States runs out of drinkable water, the demand for entire Canadian rivers will grow.

Anger ran deep in my community as fish farmers got leases to the same sites that had been denied to local residents.

By the end of the decade, farmed fish dominated British Columbia's fishery. In 1999 the province produced 39,000 tons of farmed salmon valued at $300 million—more than three times the value of British Columbia's commercial salmon catch. Meanwhile, the value of the commercial catch plummeted, driven down by the abundance of cheap Atlantics. In 1989 Billy Proctor had sold his chinook salmon for $4.10 per pound. By the year 2000 that same fish brought just $1.40 per pound.

I wrote letter after letter, more than ten thousand pages. Few received an answer. Some officials told me to my face that they weren't allowed to respond to me on government stationery. I woke up in the middle of the night to pound out twenty-page missives. I developed a nervous twitch beneath my left eye. Friends worried that I was losing it. Colleagues told me that my alarm over the destruction of the archipelago was costing me my scientific credibility.

"You don't have any proof," they said.

"When the proof comes, it'll be too late," I told them. "When everything around us is destroyed, we'll be left with nothing but proof." The scientific literature that already existed indicated that wherever there are fish farms, wild fish are in a free fall toward extinction. The politicians would let that happen because farm salmon allowed them to give away the rivers, forests, and continental shelf to the highest bidder.

In the fall of 1995, Jarret decided to board with Bill and Donna MacKay in Telegraph Cove and go to high school with their son Tyson in Port McNeill. I offered to move, but he wouldn't hear of it. "You belong here, Mom. Besides, I'd like to hang out with Tyson."

I missed him terribly. To fill the holes left by Jarret and the resident orca pods, I spent every possible minute out in my boat with the dolphins.

A population of Pacific white-sided dolphins had come into the archipelago in the early 1980s and taken me by surprise. What little I knew of the species had them living in the open ocean in groups that migrated hundreds and sometimes thousands of miles. These dolphins were nothing like their local cousins, the harbor and Dall's porpoises, which maintain a low profile around the archipelago. The dolphins, by contrast, loved to bump their bodies against boats and ride the bow waves of moving vessels.

I began photoidentifying the speedy cetaceans, but they proved too quick and elusive for my whale methods. I tried a novel approach, using a remote-controlled sailboat Eric had built. The dolphins treated the toy like any other boat, aggressively escorting the tiny ship wherever I steered it (and putting themselves in perfect portrait position). In seventeen years I've identified 920 dolphins.

The dolphins' arrival set in motion a revealing chapter in the archipelago's life. The area's transient orcas observed the newcomers for nearly six years before they started snacking on the high-calorie torpedoes. The dolphins, in turn, learned to distinguish between the fish-eating residents and the deadly (to them) transients.

The dolphins actually became a nuisance to the residents, pestering them to the point where the whale-watching industry became concerned that the roving dolphin gangs might drive away the orcas and kill their business. Their playful attitude toward passing boats could sometimes get the better of them. One day, while I was following the female transient Wahkana and her son Rainy through Tribune Channel, my boat's wake attracted a rollicking crew of dolphins. I found myself leading these cheerful canaries straight to the cats. When Rainy discovered what was approaching him, he stopped and floated silently, waiting for his mother. He seemed uncertain how to deal with this mob of deliciousness coming his way.

The instant the dolphins spotted Rainy's fin, the entire group rose straight up in the air and left as if shot from a cannon. It reminded me of the Roadrunner cartoon: straight up and *bam!*—gone.

In November Eric and I tied up the *Gabriola* in Port McNeill to await the birth of our daughter.

The wait seemed interminable. I used the time in town to rent every movie I'd missed over the past fifteen years in Echo Bay and on the *Blue Fjord*.

"Hasn't that baby come yet?" people would ask at the grocery store. "You know what you oughta do? Take castor oil." Everybody had advice. Wash the floor. Eat a big meal. Play volleyball. I felt like a town project.

Finally, after thirty days in town, my little passenger decided to join the world. Clio emerged with remarkable calm, looking from her brother to her father and then her mother in turn. Two days later I lay dreamily on *Gabriola's* bunk, intoxicated by the scent of my newborn. I was happy to be home with Eric, the baby, and Jarret in time for Christmas.

Ten days after that, Clio and I went out with the whales.

As the salmon-farming industry continued to grow and wild salmon and whales declined, I kept up my letter-writing campaign. In 1993 it became clear even to the government that the problems associated with salmon farming were too big to ignore. The provincial ministries of environment and agriculture, fisheries, and food began trying to develop a salmon aquaculture "action plan." Instead of going along with another series of empty suggestions, however, a coalition of environmental groups pressured the government to mount a full-scale environmental review of the industry. Until that review was complete, the government imposed a moratorium on the development of all new farms.

As with everything in government, the salmon aquaculture review got started late (things didn't get moving until three years later, in 1996). Although he'd been once burned by the "red zone" map debacle, Billy Proctor gave the process another chance and accepted an invitation to represent our district on the review board.

For six months Billy, Clio, and I attended monthly three-day meetings held up and down the coast of British Columbia. Some meetings took ten hours of travel through snow and wind in his boat and then my truck. Billy rolled Cheerios down Clio's car seat to keep her entertained.

During those meetings I got an education in the manipulation of public concern. Fishermen, retired scientists, representatives from native communities, tour operators, grandmothers, even some salmon farmers told the government officials: Please, put the farm salmon in tanks. Keeping the fish in cages open to the wild waters is too big a threat to our native fish. And they are too important to lose.

Some people literally begged and cried.

Corporate and government researchers warped science in ways I hadn't thought possible. I listened in disbelief as one "expert" argued that the acoustic harassment devices, which had been designed to inflict pain on seals, couldn't possibly be driving away whales and porpoises, creatures whose sense of hearing is infinitely more sensitive. Another declared, with no supporting evidence, that the invasion of Atlantic salmon into the habitat of Pacific salmon would be harmless.

"We call them biostitutes," one colleague told me during a break in the meeting. "They sell their Ph.D. to the highest bidder and give scientific credibility to the corporate agenda."

Clio absorbed a lot of adrenaline in her milk that winter.

Back home, salmon farmers began dropping their pants as I passed their farms. One salmon farmer stopped by my house and told me to stop worrying.

"Mass extinction has occurred many times on this planet," he explained, "and look, everything's fine."

Another farmer came by to ask how I'd feel if he shot my dogs. I could only think that if farmers were that upset by my work, it must be doing some good.

I also got anonymous calls from people who couldn't identify themselves but wanted to cheer me on. "You're my hero"—click. A couple of salmon farmers even called because they were troubled by the impact of their farms. They called me, they said, as a last resort because they couldn't get any answers from their employers or the government. "I'm not going to tell you who or where I am, but you gotta get the Ministry of Environment to check on where the sewer pipes end on these farms. When we flushed dye down the toilet, it came up inside the pens. We're gonna make people sick. I can't get anyone to do anything, so I called you."

Through all the tough times, the people who kept me going were the members of a tribe of remarkable women and men. As we pushed against the same indomitable force, we became acquainted and aligned. Laurie MacBride, a former commercial fisher and head of the Georgia Strait Alliance, could speak remarkably fluent bureaucratese, a language that always eluded me. When I blundered in over my head, Laurie often threw me lifelines. Catherine Stewart, the local head of fisheries issues for Greenpeace, strode into every meeting like a Viking warrior, a lion's mane of blond hair framing her powerful face. In her gravelly voice, she made it clear that she knew untruths when she heard them. Karen Wristen, a lawyer who'd walked away from high wages to defend the planet with the Sierra Legal Defense Fund, guided us through the complexities of the law and the environment. Hers was the velvet-sheathed voice of steel. Lynn Hunter, a former member of Parliament from southern Vancouver Island, wore tight black and shocking red and never backed down from a fight. Teresa Ransome, a representative on our local municipal council and a worker at a Malcolm Island wild fish processing plant, voiced her penetrating questions so gently that no one guessed her point until one bureaucrat after another found himself cornered in a web of his own meaningless phrases.

My heart was bolstered by these brave people. As I got to know some of them, I learned that while they appeared to me as magnificent heroines defending the earth, each was also trying to keep together a home as women do everywhere, matching socks, tending ailing husbands and children, getting dinner on by eight. They and their male compatriots were the only hope on the horizon.

Chapter 21

On a late-summer morning in 1997, I found myself skimming over calm seas, headed west in Fife Sound. Clio was asleep in her cozy quilted bunk beside me. In the hanging mesh bags, Jarret's LEGOs had been replaced by Clio's dolls and books. The rising sun splashed the sky with a delicate palette of pinks and silver-grays. I was leaning out the window to drink in the fresh scent of sea and forest when I noticed a school of fish flash beneath me. Pink salmon? I wondered. Then another school materialized in a kaleidoscope of scattering shapes. I slowed my boat and turned back, curious.

In a patch of finely rippled water, I witnessed hundreds of fish traveling with their mouths agape, grazing at the surface. They looked about 10 inches long with a blue-green sheen. The fish scattered when I approached for a closer look. I spiraled the boat for hours, trying different strategies to reach them with a dip net. The sheer number of the fish, whatever they were, represented a significant addition to the archipelago, and I wanted to know what they were. A friend passing by saw me going in circles and thought my steering had broken.

"Do you need help?" he radioed.

"No thanks," I said. "But do you know what all these fish are, schooling around us?"

"Never seen 'em before."

I wondered if the archipelago had been invaded by the schools of mackerel that had reportedly been infiltrating British Columbia waters, riding in on warm currents and feeding on young salmon.

The next morning a neighbor, Pat Ordano, radioed to say that she'd heard me talking about the strange schools of fish in Fife Sound. Pat and her husband, Gary, worked as caretakers of the Scott Cove logging camp. Pat's one of the best sportfishers on the water.

"Gary caught one early this morning," she told me. "We can't figure out what it is either. Do you want to have a look?"

Eric and I gathered all the fish identification books we could find, bundled up little twenty-month-old Clio, and drove the *Blackfish Sound* up to Scott Cove. On the way more schools flashed beneath us. There were a lot of these fish, whatever they were.

Pat greeted us at the dock with hot coffee, cookies for Clio, and one of the most beautiful fish I've ever seen. It was about 10 inches long and had large overlapping scales. Instead of the flattened sides of a herring or salmon, the fish had a plump cylindrical shape. The color was remarkable: deep metallic blue on top with a row of black spots, lightening to silver along the belly. The side of its head was marked with a pattern like raindrops flowing down a pane of glass.

Looking through the books, I could see that this wasn't the dreaded mackerel. Neither was it any other kind of species we could find. Nothing matched the fish. After photographing it, I carefully wrapped it for preservation in my freezer.

A few days later a little boy caught a strange fish off the wharf in Port McNeill. No one recognized it until an old-timer came along and stared at it in disbelief.

"Why, that's a pilchard!" he said. "Haven't seen one of those in fifty years."

Pilchard is the local name for sardines. A relative of herring, pilchard spawn 100 to 250 miles off the coast of California. As the young fish mature, they make seasonal migrations north and south, going a little farther in each direction every year. They eat plankton, diatoms (tiny shelled algae), and copepods (microscopic crustaceans), which would explain their surface skimming when I'd come upon them in Fife Sound: they were straining their lunch.

Pilchard were an important fishery in British Columbia in the 1920s and 1930s. The local catch peaked at more than 86,000 tons in 1929. Rich in oil, the fish represented a wealth of energy and calories in a cold northern sea. A pilchard wasn't a dinner table fish. A small percentage was canned, but most of the catch was rendered into oil and meal. The oil went into soaps and shortening, and the meal became chicken feed. The local pilchard fishery began to crash in 1939, and by 1945 it was over. There hadn't been a pilchard sighting in the waters off northern Vancouver Island since 1950.

A few weeks after the Port McNeill pilchard was identified, I went out following Houdini the humpback whale. As I drifted in my boat with the engine off, trying to detect the sound of the whale's blow, a school of pilchard appeared beneath me. The fish flowed with unimaginable grace just below the water's surface. Like one living organism, the school wound a serpentine course through the water, sometimes spiraling through itself.

The pilchard avoided shadows. The school split cleanly around the stern of my boat, knitting together at the bow. Then, without warning, an explosion of brilliant pink erupted right beside me—I stared straight into the mouth of a whale no more than 5 feet away.

Water gushed in a cascading spray, hurling dozens of fish into the air. Their scales reflected brilliant flashes of the midday sun. I jumped so hard, I fell off my seat onto the floor.

It was Houdini, having dinner. I happened to be floating in the midst of the main course, looking straight into her huge distended throat. She closed her maw and forced hundreds of gallons of water through her baleen, which trapped the stomach-bound pilchard.

Houdini sank, and a moment later all was silent. From then on I moved away from the pilchard if I thought a humpback was nearby.

Other species adapted to the new arrivals as well. Harbor porpoises doggedly followed the pilchard. At first they didn't know what to do with this new delicacy, but after a few months they zoomed confidently through the schools. Harbor seals followed their own learning curve. It took them a while to devise a strategy of encircling a school of pilchard and rising beneath them. The pilchard tried to escape by jumping to the surface en masse, creating the exact *kwooooffff* sound of a whale's blow. A number of times I heard the sound of a humpback whale's long blow close to the shore and raced down to the dock only to see nothing but a little pilchard-chasing seal looking back at me.

This minor miracle of life returning to the archipelago remained a mystery until a paper on the boom-and-bust cycles of sardines crossed my desk. Examining a core sample taken from the seafloor off Santa Barbara, California, marine biologists found sardine and anchovy scales layered in an on-again, off-again pattern that repeated every fifty to seventy years for more than seventeen hundred years. These pulses of fish abundance had occurred throughout the Pacific Rim.

When you first look at an ecosystem, you don't know if a species that suddenly appears is new or returning on a cycle so big, you can't sense its rhythm. If you know where to look, however, there's often a record stored somewhere. For the pilchard it was in the seafloor. For the humpback whales, it was in the memory of long-term residents, but what about the dolphins? Had they been here before? Was their arrival related to these fish? No one alive remembered seeing them, but ten thousand people of the Kwakwaka'wakw nation had once lived here. Had they seen them? If dolphins had been here before, there might be a record of them buried in ancient village sites. Anthropologist Becky Widgon, of the Royal Victoria Museum, had the answer. "Oh, yes," she said, "dolphin teeth are well distributed through the past two thousand years of midden layers at sites in your area." Then the lights went on in my head: the dolphins were probably moving in and out of the archipelago on the boom-and-bust cycles of pilchard, anchovies, and capelin. This, it turned out, was a common scenario. When the squid moved north from Los Angeles, the pilot whales followed. Risso's dolphins took their place and later wouldn't let the pilot whales back in. As fish move in response to currents and temperature, cetacean populations bump one another up, down, in, and out along the coast. Everywhere I looked the message kept repeating: all life is interrelated, a balanced equation, the ebb and flow of energy. I was very happy that pilchard and dolphins were here on my shift!

After four years of commercial fishing, I decided to step down from the office of deckhand and find other ways to make a living. Billy Proctor's oldest daughter, Joanie, and I opened a gift shop. We sold local art, baked goods, and clothing. I began printing fish I'd caught on T-shirts and putting them up for sale. The shirts became popular, and I ended up making about a thousand a year for a couple of years before I developed an allergy from the constant exposure to the dye.

I also brought in some money from my writing. Magazines such as *Smithsonian* and *International Wildlife* sent checks for articles and photographs on killer whales, and other more unexpected means of support began coming my way. I received a letter from Patagonia, the outdoor clothing company, asking if I needed financial assistance for my environmental work. The company donated 1 percent of its sales to grassroots organizations, and someone had passed one of my notorious fish farm letters to it. Could I use a little help with expenses? You bet. Mailing out ten thousand pages of letters could get expensive. So could my phone bill; out here all we've got to work with are cell phones, and that time costs plenty.

Another organization, England's Whale and Dolphin Conservation Society, recruited me for its adopt-a-whale program, a fundraising project in which donors "adopt" a certain whale and receive updates on that whale's life. It was looking to bring the northern British Columbia orcas into the program and needed someone to write the updates. The money didn't exactly qualify as a salary, but it was enough to keep my boat running and offset the cost of photo-identification research. Several times a year I write updates on Tsitika, Top Notch, Sharky, and other A-pod celebrities, and in return

I've received joyful notes from children in Spain, families in Australia, and other whale adopters about how much they enjoyed hearing about "their" whale.

Fish farming proved to be just the first of many assaults on the archipelago. In the spring of 1998, Billy Proctor brought by a notification published in the *North Island Gazette,* the local Port Hardy newspaper, informing the community that the forestry company Interfor was about to spray a tributary of the nearby Kakweikan River with herbicides. Billy was livid.

"On May 17, 1957, they sprayed one pound of 2,4-D per acre on all the watersheds of northern Vancouver Island. I saw it dropping from the planes. Hell, they sprayed *me.* They told us it wouldn't harm salmon. A week later there were wheelbarrow loads of dead baby salmon fry lining the banks of some of those systems." He listed rivers that had stopped producing salmon after pesticide applications. "The Keogh. Nimpkish. Suquash, Nahwitti, Stranby." It was as though he were speaking of old friends who had died.

The health of a river's riparian zone—the area along the riverbank—can often make the difference between life and death for a salmon species. When baby coho hatch in a river, for instance, they swim into the tiniest reaches of the stream to find food and escape predation by trout. Often these pools become cut off from the main stream when water levels drop in heavily logged watersheds. These pools also need a rich conifer canopy to provide shade on hot summer days, keeping the water cool enough for the fish to survive. The young coho thrive when these microhabitats are maintained. After about a year they float down the river to enter the saltwater phase of their life.

If a logging company were to whack down only small portions of a forest at one time and let it grow back naturally, a number of things would happen. Leafy deciduous trees like alders would restart the succession of life. They'd be joined by bushes such as salmonberry, elderberry, and devil's club. These plants grow quickly to offer their shade to the stream, bringing temperatures back down into a coho's range of survival. Their roots also rebuild the lattice that holds the soil to the hills. In the absence of roots, rain washes the soil into the river, where it settles into the gravel and creates a pavementlike surface that can't hold and incubate salmon eggs. Young evergreens and conifers eventually appear, growing slowly with the help of the pioneering species, feeding on the organic decomposition of their deciduous leaves.

This natural cycle takes time, which is one thing that forest companies refuse to give. After clear-cutting the forest, they try to speed things up by spraying herbicides on all the pioneering species and planting uniform rows of genetically modified evergreens. It takes years before these trees grow big enough to offer shade to the riparian zone. That's just one of the coho's worries, though. Spraying herbicides near the tiny pools where coho grow can be outright lethal to the fish. And none of this has been proven to grow a vigorous forest.

As the archipelago's newly appointed representative to the Mount Waddington Community Resource Board, a council that advises mayors and provincial ministers on natural resource issues, I figured it was my duty to do something about the spraying. I made a call to Karen Wristen of the Sierra Legal Defense Fund in Vancouver. Along with a coalition of First Nations, she and I filed an appeal of the herbicide application. A few weeks later I organized a team of Sierra Legal lawyers, Echo Bay citizens, and a hydrologist to go up to look over the Kakweikan River site. While we were there, we discovered that the logging company had violated its permit by not mapping all the streams in the proposed spray areas. These unmarked watercourses would have been soused in chemicals.

The Ministry of the Environment granted us an appeal, which meant that we could present our case to an Environmental Appeal Board in Port Hardy. At that hearing members of the community came forward to speak in defense of the fish. Glen Neidrauer, a Department of Fisheries and Oceans contractor who spent most of his days counting salmon returning to local creeks, talked about all the places the salmon go to spawn. Both government and Interfor officials were stunned at how high up in the watershed Glen had seen fish.

"It all depends on the amount of rain," Glen told them. "If the conditions are right, coho will climb right up the side of a mountain in the water coming down."

Kate Pinnsoneault, my friend who was living aboard the *Sea Horse,* researched the scientific literature on pesticides. When an Interfor lawyer cited a study that "proved" the negligible impact of herbicides on young salmon, Kate pointed out that the fish exposed to the herbicide didn't start dying until the twentieth day of the study. On day 21 the study was terminated. "You don't end a study just as you start getting the very results you're testing for," Kate said. The study, to nobody's surprise, had been jointly funded by a huge herbicide manufacturer and a logging company.

We argued that it was the fish that were going extinct, not the trees. If the forestry company didn't spray its herbicide, which had been proved lethal to fish, the only thing the company stood to lose was five years in the one hundred–year growth cycle of its replanted trees.

We won some and we lost some. While not completely denying Interfor the right to spray, the Environmental Appeal Board severely reduced the overall area of coverage and denied the company's appeal to use the more lethal chemical triclopyr. In its written decision, the board characterized the Ministry of the Environment's attitude toward coho preservation as "cavalier."

Rather than reevaluating its herbicide program, Interfor laid blame for its loss elsewhere. A few days after the appeal board handed down its decision, the timber company abruptly fired the two foresters who had handled the case.

With each battle I and my new allies gained hard–won experience. Little by little, I became more adept at working the system to save our home. When the next patch of salmon habitat came up for spraying a few months later, I appealed again. This time it was the Ministry of the Environment itself that wanted to spray. It settled directly with me as soon as I appealed its proposed herbicide application. It wouldn't give up the chemicals entirely, but I ran the ministry out of a bit of salmon habitat.

By the third appeal, the Ministry of the Environment started checking with me before approving any more spraying applications.

Sometimes the things corporations try to get away with up here can make your head spin. Carmen Burrows, a young mother of two from Malcolm Island who serves on the local town council, phoned me one morning to ask if I'd heard that the Ministry of the Environment planned to approve a permit to spread the City of Vancouver's solid sewage waste on the floodplains of the Klinaklini River.

"Could this possibly be as bad as it sounds?" Carmen asked.

It could. When she faxed me a copy of the application, I wondered if the world had gone completely berserk.

The Klinaklini River runs into the head of Knight Inlet and provides spawning grounds for both salmon and eulachon, as well as essential habitat for moose, elk, and grizzlies. The eulachon, or candlefish, are still an important part of the diet and ceremonies of First Nations people.

Somebody had seen this mighty watershed and matched it with a brilliant business scheme: take away the City of Vancouver's sludge (for a hefty fee), then get paid again to apply it to a clear-cut forest floodplain as "fertilizer" for genetically modified spruce trees. Listed among the ingredients of this urban sludge were arsenic, copper, lead, and various heavy metals—enough poison to prevent the entire area from supporting life.

As soon as I read the fax, I called up Yvon Gesinghaus, general manager of the Musgamagw Tsawataineuk Tribal Council in Alert Bay. Yvon listened to what I had to say, then told me, "The world *has* gone mad. I will take this to the elders."

Yvon has the protective instincts of a mother grizzly bear. She's seen more than her share of personal tragedy and has raised two generations of children and foster children in Alert Bay. I'm not exactly sure what she did, but the next time I spoke with an official at the Ministry of the Environment, he said that the sludge-spreading application had been withdrawn. "Why?" I asked.

"Too much opposition" was all he said.

Unfortunately, there are more insidious chemicals that have found their way into the orca of British Columbia. Fat-binding molecules of polychlorinated biphenyls (PCBs) and dioxins have surpassed benign levels in most of the whales of this coast. The biopsy darting by Lance Barrett-Lennard revealed a horrifying pattern of contamination. While the transient orca are now *the* most contaminated mammals on record, the southern resident whales are threatened with extinction. Toxin loads begin at birth, coming from the mother's milk. In female babies this level rises until they give birth, at which time they pass toxins to their own offspring. The males, however, show a steady rise and are dying so rapidly now that soon there may not be any breeding males. While much of these toxins are airborne, the waters off Seattle, Vancouver, and Victoria are also contaminated. Any who believe our poisons only affect whales and other animals are missing the truth. Our bodies are collecting them too.

Chapter 22

~~ ~~ ~~

After a quarter century spent studying whales, I tend to see everything in terms of animal behavior. Whales, dolphins, and porpoises are difficult to read. Human beings, on the other hand, display their emotions and intentions like neon billboards. Sitting across from people at public meetings, watching them trying to promote herbicides and salmon farm expansion, I find that I learn more from their bodies than from their words. Eyes flutter with every half-truth. Corporate scientists glance at their benefactors, purse their lips, clench their fingers, and cross their legs in clear patterns of nervous behavior. It's always refreshing to hear someone testify honestly, with an open-faced direct stare.

Our politics are rooted in the dominance hierarchies of the animal world. What does the top dog, chimpanzee, or sea lion get? Sex and food. Our leaders aren't so different. Just replace food with power. Many species foster alliances within their societies and jostle for power. We pretend to be shocked by the behavior of our politicians, but as a species we're really not all that surprising. Not much has changed through aeons.

On the other hand, when I look at corporations, I see a dangerous aberration of our own making. The corporate animal exists only in the two dimensions of paper, yet it feeds on the wet and wild three-dimensional living world. Unlike any other user of the earth's resources, corporations have evolved untouched by the inexorable pressures that have forced each species to coexist with every other.

Their growth is cancerlike, but instead of withering on the destruction they cause, corporations escape death by lifting their heads and moving on to another unsullied energy-rich habitat.

This cannot continue.

In a not-too-distant future, the natural systems we all depend on will be crippled. They will fail to sustain life. The predatory growth of corporations has eaten gaping holes in the planet's nervous system, fragmented the essential ebb and flow of energy, and ignored the closed-loop nature of our existence.

Diversity is nature's ace in the hole. Whether it's a forest of trees, a species of salmon, or a herd of caribou, nature has made certain that the organisms are not all the same. If a certain strain of virus or bacteria develops a taste for caribou, the diversity among the species ensures that at least some caribou will survive. But corporations value uniformity—uniform species of trees, uniform pools of Atlantic salmon. This seems the height of folly. It assumes that any and all pathogens are under our control. They are not. And if the corporate world continues to defeat the world's natural systems of diversity, one day we will pay an exceedingly high price.

As the corporate footprint sinks deeper into the Broughton Archipelago, I have felt panic at its power, which sometimes seems utterly unstoppable. I believe the power that will stop that insatiable corporate drive is known as love. Fueled by an unassailable source of energy, love has a mysteriously incorruptible capacity to prevail. As I watch my neighbors, some without formal education, some on the edge of poverty, stand up to the kingpins of the corporate world, I marvel at their magnificent inner strength. I feel hope.

I am by no means the only person recording the devastating human impact on whales and their environment. On March 24, 1989, the tanker *Exxon Valdez* ran aground on Bligh Reef in Prince William Sound, Alaska. More than 11 million gallons of Prudoe Bay crude oil spilled into this pristine, island-dotted archipelago. Within a few weeks wind and tide spread the oil over 1,900 kilometers of coastline.

When oil is first spilled onto the ocean, it releases toxic vapors, some known to be carcinogens. People trying to clean the noxious, thick, black sludge off the beaches were passing out from the fumes. The cold Alaskan waters slowed this lethal gassing off, making the spill highly toxic for close to a week. Whale researchers Craig Matkin and Eva Saulitis were stricken to see five members of a genetically distinct and socially unique transient population of killer whales, AT1 pod, surfacing through the suffocating layer, trying to breathe inches above the deadly slick. Killer whales are masters of their environment, but they had no experience detecting or avoiding the silent blanket of death flowing from the ruptured boat. Only one of those five whales survived. Other pod members were probably nearby, and half of the twenty-two members of this unusual group have vanished. This transient pod never produced another living baby and is doomed to extinction.

A resident fish-eating family, known as AB pod, was also seen near the wreck of the *Exxon Valdez* a week after the spill. Fourteen of its thirty-six members have died. Some were poisoned immediately, but deaths in this pod have occurred since that day at twice the rate normal for the rest of the resident population of whales. While they have enjoyed some births, more are dying than are being born. Although the whales' bodies were never found, scientists believe that those that did not die immediately likely suffered irreversible damage to delicate mucous membranes when they sucked the toxic fumes deep into their lungs. Many of these whales likely suffered from severe, chronic respiratory ailments, which eventually ran them down to the point of death. Additionally, because killer whales are so close-knit, the death of mothers causes a domino effect, killing babies, juveniles, even adult sons. Some mothers and all their children, entire matrilineal lines, have died. Some babies were orphaned and then died. One mother took her children, left the pod, and joined another healthy group, something that has never been seen before or since in killer whales from California to the Bering Sea. Not one older matriarch was left to keep the family together.

The spill also killed three hundred harbor seals immediately, and over the next eleven years reduced this population by 35 percent. Seals were the transients' primary food source. Thousands of birds died. The *Exxon Valdez's* oil coated herring eggs freshly laid on the rocky shores of Prince William Sound, causing malformations, genetic damage, yolk sacs too small to fuel the little fish, swimming disabilities, and death, decreasing larval production in Prince William Sound herring by 99.9 percent that year. Those herring were an essential energy source for many species. Pink salmon, which typically spawn at creek mouths where the freshwater meets the ocean, were also harmed. Each high tide carried oil onto their nests just as the tiny fish were preparing to hatch. Not only was that generation deformed and killed, but a high percentage of the eggs and sperm of subsequent generations has been rendered sterile by the oil their ancestors encountered just before hatching. The effect passes from one generation to the next in myriad ways. The hydrocarbons released from that tanker twelve years ago have stained every tropic layer with a repeating cycle of death. In the summer of 2001 researchers found 10,000 gallons of the oil still buried beneath the beaches, liver damage in sea otters, and newly ingested oil in the declining harlequin ducks. Neither Prince William Sound nor the many other ecosystems polluted with oil spills will recover in our lifetimes. The true cost of oil is so immeasurably higher than what we pay at the gas pump that everyone should buy one solar panel a year in the name of life on earth.

As a new century begins, the fish-farming industry shows no signs of slowing down. Neither does the ecological destruction of the archipelago. In early 2001, 121 net cages crowded the British Columbia coastline. In the Broughton Archipelago, twenty-two sites now hold a total of about 16 million fish, and the industry is pressuring for more.

Hold is a relative term. The *fait* that the Department of Fisheries and Oceans bureaucrat warned us about years ago has become *accompli*. Since the introduction of salmon farming to the British Columbia coast in the late 1980s, more than 1 million domesticated salmon have made their way into the waters of western Canada. The Atlantics are here, and they are adapting. John Volpe, a salmon researcher from the University of Victoria, has discovered juvenile Atlantics in three rivers on the east coast of Vancouver Island—including the Tsitika River, which flows into the Robson Bight whale reserve. Volpe's find indicates that escaped adult Atlantics are spawning in the wild.

Escapes now happen every few months. In 1997, 370,000 Atlantic salmon escaped from one farm in Puget Sound's Rich Passage. In 1999 more than 49,000 Atlantic salmon escaped from farms on the British Columbia coast. As Atlantic salmon continue escaping, the DFO has stopped talking about the number of fish and slipped into terms of percentages. In 1991 almost 2.0 percent of farm fish escaped, but in 1999, it points out, only 0.2 percent escaped. This sounds like good news—an exponential decline!—until you realize that in sheer numbers of fish, twice as many escaped in 1999 as in 1991. The fish-farming industry has grown that fast.

Every summer I overhear commercial fishermen on the VHF complaining about Atlantic salmon. "The sockeye are hitting one side of my net headed south, and them slimy Atlantics are hitting the other side headed out to sea," one fisherman told another. At the end of each year, the number of escaped Atlantics reported by the DFO never seemed to match what I was hearing from the fishermen. In the summer of 2000, I decided to count the Atlantics myself.

Opening day in Johnstone Strait came on August 2. "Any vessels that have caught Atlantic salmon," I announced over the VHF, "could you please come back to the *Blackfish Sound.*"

The old fishermen were suspicious at first. "Are you a fish farmer wanting your stinking fish back?" one fisherman roared.

Once they learned I was just trying to keep track of the Atlantic infestation, boats of all sizes called the *Blackfish Sound. Outsider* reported 30 Atlantic salmon; *Dream Weaver,* 37. *Winning Edge* reported catching 60; *Surf Isle,* 28. *Brenda Mae* had caught 12 in one set along the beach in Robson Bight—"big lunkers, too," the skipper said. *Jody Lee* had 48 at Naka Creek. *Montego Bay* phoned in 4 from the north side of Malcolm Island. *Bojangle Too* radioed in: "I've got one, and I'm holding it just for you, Alex!"

During the summer of 2000, I recorded 10,256 catches of Atlantic salmon. And those were just the boats that bothered to report. I cut open more than 800 of the fish myself. My days of gutting salmon for Billy Proctor had, if nothing else, given me an education in salmon anatomy. But it didn't prepare me for the bizarre conditions I encountered inside those fish. Some had flesh so soft, I could take my finger and scoop it out like mashed potatoes. Others had lumpy spleens, orange-stained livers, vital organs completely melted together.

Despite assurances from industry leaders and the DFO that escaped farm fish would never eat wild food, I found some stomachs full of immature Pacific salmon, herring, shrimp, and other fish and crustaceans.

I took bacteria swabs from two Atlantic salmon caught by Billy Proctor in Scott Cove Creek. The fish were covered in sores. I sent half to the provincial government lab and paid for the testing of the other half at a private lab at the University of Guelph in Ontario. The lab technician called me from Ontario as soon as he got the results.

"Where the hell did you get these fish?" he said. "Every swab you took is crawling with bacteria. They're swarming the petri dish."

The bacterium was called *Serratia* and was resistant to eleven of the eighteen antibiotics tested on it, including penicillin.

The provincial government's lab returned remarkably different results. It couldn't find any bacteria in the samples I'd sent. The yellow, pus-encrusted sores, it said, must have been caused by "rubbing sticks."

I posted this on the Internet and got a response from a Scottish doctor. We found *Serratia* on salmon farms where the crew quarters' sewage had leaked into the pens. I decided I'd better wear gloves when handling farm salmon.

The lessons offered by disasters in other fish-farming regions have yet to be learned in British Columbia. In 1997 a virus, infectious salmon anemia, blazed through fish farms in New Brunswick, on Canada's northeastern seaboard. The provincial and federal governments ended up paying out about $10 million to compensate farmers for the loss of more than 1 million fish. In 2001 the virus spread to Maine, threatening the last remaining Atlantic salmon.

The news from Norway, which has the most experience with salmon farming and far stricter environmental controls, is worse. The effects of fish farming on Norwegian rivers and wild salmon have been nothing short of devastating. In Norwegian rivers farmed salmon outnumber wild salmon by as much as four to one. Up to 4 million farmed fish escape into the wild every year, and inter-breeding between escapees and wild species has been extensively documented. In the early 1990s a parasitic flatworm known as *Gyrodactylus* came over from Sweden in a truckload of salmon smolts and spread to more than thirty-five Norwegian rivers. Some rivers were so infected that officials resorted to "treating" them with rotenone, a chemical that destroys all life, infected and uninfected. After killing off the fish and the insects, officials then attempted to reestablish lo-cal stocks in the rivers. Between the parasite and the treatment, more than thirty wild salmon stocks were wiped out.

Pollution from British Columbia fish farms continues to foul the archipelago at an astonishing rate. In 1999 Lynn Hunter, of the David Suzuki Foundation, brought criminal charges under the Canadian Fisheries Act against Stolt Sea Farm, accusing the salmon-farming giant of harming fish habitat with pollution generated by its farm at Carrie Bay, about 4 miles south of Echo Bay. Lynn used the Ministry of the Environment's own study against Stolt. According to the ministry, the Carrie Bay farm, like many others, was building up a massive underwater pile of salmon excrement and uneaten antibiotic-infused pellets that spread more than 50 yards beyond the confines of Stolt's net cages. In the year 2000 British Columbia's fish-farming industry dumped the same amount of raw sewage as a city of a million people, every day of the year.

The federal government's crown counsel stayed Lynn's charges based on the fact that the government had granted Stolt its license to farm at Carrie Bay with full knowledge that such a farm would negatively affect the surrounding environment. In other words, it was okay to pollute because the government had prior knowledge that the farm was likely to pollute.

It took me eleven years to realize it was futile to try and negotiate with bureaucracy. In 2000 I learned to bypass local government and talk directly to the world community of scientists. When I observe a problem now, I get on the Internet and find an expert to partner with. This "partner" guides me through data collection on whatever the organism—from proliferating bacteria to copepods—and together we publish on its relationship to salmon farms and the environment. In this way, controversial findings can enter the scientific record without delay or prodigious amounts of funding.

In all countries where salmon are farmed a small normally benign parasite, the sea louse, has proliferated. Clouds of these lice leak out of the net pens to eat skin off wild salmonids (sea trout and salmon). In Scotland, Ireland, and Norway sea lice are considered responsible for steep declines in wild salmon near fish farms. These countries have imposed strict regulations on the number of lice allowed per farm salmon. In British Columbia, the government has taken a different approach—turn a blind eye. In 2001 I partnered with Scottish, Norwegian, and Alaskan scientists to examine 924 wild juvenile salmon in the Broughton Archipelago now overrun with salmon farms. Most of the wild fish had lice loads exceeding a lethal level. Rather than looking for a way to keep the lice from pouring out of the farms, the federal Fisheries put me under investigation. The message—don't look at this industry too closely, Alexandra Morton, or there will be consequences.

A few years ago I was granted a childhood wish: I spoke to Jane Goodall. When I heard she was scheduled to speak at the University of Victoria, I called up a friend on staff there. "Is there some post-lecture dinner I could invite myself to?"

"There's a lunch at the Batemans'," she said, "but as far as getting invited, you're on your own."

Robert Bateman is the foremost wildlife painter in Canada, and he and his wife, Birgit, are among the country's great environmentalists. Although I didn't know Mr. Bateman, I wrote perhaps the most ridiculous letter I've ever written to ask if I could join them for lunch with Ms. Goodall, including that I had good table manners. I figured it couldn't hurt to ask. A few days later Bateman's secretary called back with instructions for reaching the Batemans' house on Salt Spring Island, near Victoria.

I had met Goodall once before, when she'd given a public lecture at Hotchkiss, the prep school in my hometown of Lakeville. I was probably all of twelve at the time. After her talk I stood among the crowd of students as they asked what seemed to be terribly sophisticated questions about her research methodology. Finally all the students had drifted off but me, just a local who didn't even attend Hotchkiss. When there were only the two of us, I got so tongue-tied, I couldn't think of a thing to say. She smiled at me before turning away to collect her slides.

Twenty years later I was ready. Goodall's brilliance hadn't dimmed with the passing of the years. She radiated the grace and wisdom of the earth.

Finding my moment, I leaned over and asked her a question. "Jane, do you think there is hope?" I held my breath.

"Yes," she said. "I do have hope. Nature is enormously resilient, humans are vastly intelligent, the energy and enthusiasm that can be kindled among young people seems without limit, and the human spirit is indomitable. But if we want life, we will have to stop depending on someone else to save the world. It is up to us—you and me, all of us. Myself, I have placed my faith in the children."

As I consider my own children—a son in his third year at university and a daughter who still falls asleep in my arms—I find myself thinking there must be hope for our species, if only for their sake. Chronicling the passage of whales has led me to an understanding that we, as a species, now stand at a crossroads. We can face the possibility of our own extinction and work to avert it, or we can follow the more traditional path of earth's organisms and fall blindly over the edge. If there's one trait that characterizes human beings, it's the will to survive. This, I believe, will motivate us to work *with* the natural world rather than oppose it, which is all we need to do to give the children of earth—of all species—the opportunity to thrive.

Chapter 23

~ ~ ~

I came here to find the family of a killer whale. I stayed and have both made my own family and found new meaning in the word. After twenty-five years of studying whales, I am still at the beginning, still learning how to look. Theirs is a world so alien, it will always remain somewhat beyond our grasp, but science's methodical, cooperative assembly of truths has succeeded in revealing many of earth's mysteries. As the infancy of this field of science draws to a close, the riddle central to its existence remains intact. What is a diving mammal doing with such a large brain? Brains are greedy consumers of oxygen; they need a steady and plentiful supply. This makes even a simple brain "expensive" for an animal that spends its life holding its breath. That whales, who are in constant motion, divert so much precious oxygen away from muscles to maintain a colossal organ for thought is no oversight. Those magnificent minds in the briny deep are earning their keep, but how?

We have chipped away at the edges of this question. We know that dolphins have long, accurate memories, complex relationships, and some predisposition for our style of language, including syntax and names. They show emotion and recognize themselves in a mirror (a cognitive milestone); they even rescue us. Does that count? Dr. Denise Herzing of Florida Atlantic University, who has studied wild spotted dolphins for fifteen years, has asked us to consider granting dolphins "personhood." Based on what she has witnessed, she sees them clearly as equal members of our community. The problem, she believes, is simply that we are hopelessly biased, limited to recognizing only a terrestrial model of intelligence—based on fire, electricity, and an opposable thumb.

One of the most intriguing hypotheses on how dolphins use some of the gray matter between their ears was put forward by Dr. Peter Tyack, of the prestigious Woods Hole Oceanographic Institution in Massachusetts. With his considerable knowledge of underwater sound dynamics, Tyack feels that in addition to laser-beam echolocation, two whales may be illuminating broad swaths of ocean between them as they speak. This would require strict agreement on the timing and frequency of each call. Whales do that. As a sound sweeps through a space, holes are punched out wherever it encounters an object. By comparing what was said with what was heard, two orcas might learn that 203 pink salmon are traveling west at 4 knots between them. This would explain orca dialects, a precise set of sounds memorized by each family.

When the sisters Yakat and Kelsy enter Fife Sound, they split, each taking one shoreline. Then they call back and forth. Each call might show fish, transients, and islands in a radarlike sweep. The oil-filled antennae that are their lower jaws carry acoustic vibrations deep into direct contact with their inner ears. There translated into electrical pulses, the vibrations flash up to the auditory site of the brain on a rich weave of nerves. From there the signal is boosted on a superhighway to the neocortex—the center for higher thought. That's where the holes in each sound could be read like braille to reveal a school of salmon.

Because cetaceans are one of only three types of mammals that can mimic a sound (bats and humans are the other two), a whale might broadcast a travel-worn signal with enough fidelity to show a third whale where the mother lode of fish can be found. The possibilities multiply exponentially when you consider projection of three-dimensional images between whales.

Scientists wonder if the monotonous calling of bowhead whales in the ice-strewn Arctic seas might illuminate icebergs between the callers. It could also explain why humpback whales, which change

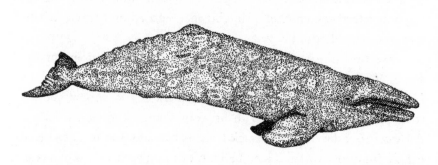

Gray whale

their songs every year, make the effort to all sing the same song each season. Their booming voices may impart information about the ocean that we cannot even imagine.

Who are these mammals who returned to the sea 15 million years ago to evolve such superb instrumentation for perception and thought? When we examine the architecture of cetacean brains, we recognize trademarks of our own brains' excellence. As we learn more, we will make increasingly better guesses as to dolphin perception and intelligence, but based on what we know now, we'd be less than truthful if we said that the cornerstones of human consciousness have not been found in this species. Have we matured to the capability of recognizing awareness in someone who does not look or act like us? Are we human enough to extend the rights of humanity to another sentient species? Are we ready to end the silence? I am.

On a breezy December afternoon, a sweet note came out of the speaker connected to my hydrophone in Cramer Pass.

Adrenaline mixed with disbelief. Must have been one of the bumpers squeaking between the *Gabriola* and the dock, I thought. Then it came again.

Oh, my God—it is a whale. It had been six years since a whale called me.

I bundled three-year-old Clio in a sweater, coat, wool socks, and boots; grabbed my coat; and fell out the door in my haste. I scrambled up and took off in the *Blackfish Sound*. By looking for whale blows and stopping to listen underwater, I eventually found the whales. The light was dim, and the warmth of my eyes fogged the cold binoculars every time I brought them to my face, but I saw a fin. And then more fins.

I couldn't see well enough to identify the whales, so I lowered the hydrophone and just listened.

As I counted the breaths of about twenty-five orcas, the calls of three clans—A, G, and R—mingled and echoed in a soul-stirring symphony of whales.

The fish farmers had turned off their acoustic harassment devices near my home in the spring of 1999. They told me later it was because of me. I am thankful for the return of the natural silence and hopeful that it may someday extend coastwide. It had taken the A clan whales six months to discover that the archipelago was habitable again, and they'd brought friends.

The whales exploded to the surface in exuberant pairs and trios, breaching and tail-slapping and sending cascades of water into the air. Tears of joy blended with drops of rain.

As the boat rocked gently in the winter storm, I heard the voices of three whale clans mingle in my head. I held Clio close to my heart and brought her to the edge of the boat where the orcas plied the waters of home.

"Look, my baby girl," I said to her. "There's one of the wonders of the world."

Born and raised in Connecticut, ALEXANDRA MORTON began her career in marine mammal research in 1976, when she moved to California to work for noted dolphin researcher Dr. John C. Lilly. Since 1984 she has lived on the isolated central British Columbia coast, where she studies and records the language and habits of the various pods of orcas that swim the waters there.